ROUTLEDGE LIBRARY EDITIONS: VICTORIAN THEATRE

Volume 2

HENRY IRVING AND THE VICTORIAN THEATRE

HENRY IRVING AND THE VICTORIAN THEATRE

MADELEINE BINGHAM

Routledge
Taylor & Francis Group
LONDON AND NEW YORK

First published in 1978

This edition first published in 2016
by Routledge
2 Park Square, Milton Park, Abingdon, Oxon OX14 4RN

and by Routledge
711 Third Avenue, New York, NY 10017

Routledge is an imprint of the Taylor & Francis Group, an informa business

British Library Cataloguing in Publication Data
A catalogue record for this book is available from the British Library

ISBN: 978-1-138-92272-3 (Set)
ISBN: 978-1-315-68102-3 (Set) (ebk)
ISBN: 978-1-138-93655-3 (Volume 2) (hbk)
ISBN: 978-1-138-93656-0 (Volume 2) (pbk)
ISBN: 978-1-315-67675-3 (Volume 2) (ebk)

Publisher's Note
The publisher has gone to great lengths to ensure the quality of this reprint but points out that some imperfections in the original copies may be apparent.

Disclaimer
The publisher has made every effort to trace copyright holders and would welcome correspondence from those they have been unable to trace.

HENRY IRVING

and
The Victorian Theatre

By

Madeleine Bingham

FOREWORD BY JOHN GIELGUD

The player's triumph is momentary, passing as the rapturous applause that attests its merit.

Macready

London
GEORGE ALLEN & UNWIN
Boston Sydney

First published in 1978

ISBN 0 04 928038 4

Printed in Great Britain
in 11 on 13 point Baskerville
by W & J Mackay Limited, Chatham

Foreword
by JOHN GIELGUD

I was still a child when Henry Irving died, but my parents and the older members of my illustrious family had all known him intimately. He used often to stay with my grandmother, Kate Terry, at her cottage in Scotland, and her four daughters always spoke of him with the deepest affection and respect. Unfortunately I only met Ellen Terry very seldom and never had the courage to ask her about Irving, much as I am sure I longed to do so. Her fascinating fairy-godmother personality was such that I became unusually tongue-tied in her presence. Later on, when I was a schoolboy at Westminster during the First World War, I used to sit in the Abbey, trying to draw the monuments, and gaze in considerable awe at the slab marking Irving's grave in Poet's Corner. Once, on the anniversary of his death, I remember begging a card from one of the wreaths from the Head Verger with 'Rosemary – for Remembrance' written on it in Ellen Terry's characteristic handwriting, and this I treasured for many years afterwards.

One has often heard some of the great courtesans and actresses of the past referred to as 'Sacred Monsters'. I have always thought the appellation might well have been applied to Henry Irving.

An entirely dedicated artist, he was evidently deeply self-centred, crafty and obstinately autocratic, possessing, as Madeleine Bingham so ably demonstrates, great authority, and personal magnetism to the highest degree. He could exercise charm and sweetness, though he was often ruthless, sardonic and shrewd. He made no claim to be an intellectual and his official speeches were concocted for him by his henchmen. He adored melodrama. His heroes and heroines were white and his villains black. He believed in the fustian which he consequently staged so well.

Most of the stories of him that have come down to us are witty but bitingly sharp. Although they may not be deliberately malicious, it is still somewhat surprising to read of him 'dreading to have to welcome some new members of his company and having to shake their greasy paws'. And there was a well-known story that on one occasion while preparing an unhappy Lyceum version of *Don Quixote*, Irving came down to view the prospective candidate for Rosinante with profound suspicion. Its owner hastened to assure him that the horse was extremely docile. 'Recently', he remarked, 'it was ridden by Mr Tree in *Richard the Second*' (in an inserted tableau of the deposed king being led back to London!). Irving surveyed the animal gingerly from behind his pince-nez, at which point the animal broke wind. 'Ah', said Sir Henry, 'bit of a critic, too, eh?'

Irving could be enchanting as a guest and delightful with children, though he was notably uncomfortable in dealing with his own sons. Well aware of his physical limitations – the dragging walk, weak voice, thin legs – one can see from the photographs the development of his noble face as he grew older and how cleverly he increased in the strength and distinction of appearance as he achieved success.

His variety of range can be guessed at from his choice of plays and parts. There were two kinds of character which gave him the best opportunities for his most inspired performances – the saintly aloof beauty of his Charles I and Becket, the craftiness of his Louis XI, Richelieu and Dubosc, the noble irony of his Shylock, and the tortured agonies of his Mathias, in *The Bells*, and Eugene Aram.

In Shakespeare he failed as Lear, and his Othello and Macbeth were evidently unequal, though striking in certain individual scenes. He succeeded however, rather surprisingly, as Benedick, made little mark as Malvolio, which one might have thought would have suited him so well, and still less as Romeo for which he must have been quite unsuited. He never played Leontes or Cassius, but Wolsey and Iachimo seemed to have been the best of his late Lyceum performances.

Both Iago and, particularly, Hamlet, must have fitted him wonderfully well, but he never played either part after his early years, and his revival of *Richard the Third* was not very greatly praised, though it had been a triumph for him when he acted it first many years before. Apart from his own remarkable talents as an actor he was of course a brilliant impresario and director, managing a loyal (but not greatly inspired) company and staff with an iron hand and a consummate skill which allowed him to show himself off to the best advantage.

A master of crowd manipulation and scenic atmosphere, he loved to fill his stage with beautiful pictures glowing with imaginative tones of light and shadow, so that his gaslit painted scenery appeared to have far more depth and magic than that used in the later grandiose productions of Herbert Tree.

By the turn of the century Irving's pride must have been very great. Pride in his own immense renown and popularity, in the princely lavishness of the way he entertained as host in his fine theatre, and the respect in which he was held both in his own profession and in private life. But the last five years of his life, as Madeleine Bingham shows, must have been very bitter, with the growing competition of a new generation of actor-managers and writers with whose work he was quite unable to find much sympathy. But he has surely left behind him a legend of extraordinary achievement, both as actor and producer, as well as a record of long and remarkable seasons on both sides of the Atlantic when, in his glorious partnership with Ellen Terry, he mounted a succession of lavish productions with such care and splendour that they will always be remembered proudly in the annals of our English Stage.

Madeleine Bingham's new biography of Irving manages to break new ground in her description of the famous partnership with Ellen Terry; she draws a skilful and convincing picture of the period and examines most perceptively their relationship both on and off the stage.

October 1977

Acknowledgements

I am greatly indebted to Mr Roger Morgan and the Library Committee of the Garrick Club who allowed me access to the twenty-two volumes of the Percy Fitzgerald Collection in their library and to two anonymous volumes of similar material. This afforded me many new angles on the contemporary reviews, gossip paragraphs, caricatures and essays about Irving's work and personality.

Miss Pamela Hansford Johnson, whose grandfather, Howson, worked as Irving's treasurer, also gave me valuable word-of-mouth accounts of Irving's attitude towards his staff and their families. I have also been helped by Miss Jennifer Aylmer and the staff of the Enthoven Collection at the Victoria and Albert Museum, as well as the London Library staff. Mr R. del Valle Grady and Mr Philip Gilbert, historian of the Bohemian Club, San Francisco, kindly sent me contemporary accounts of Irving's visit to San Francisco.

A contemporary caricature of Henry Irving in *The Bells* (1871) by APE.

Contents

Illustrations

Acknowledgements and thanks are due to the following for the use of the illustrations: The Author (*Frontispiece*); Mansell Collection (1a, 1b, 3, 5a, 5b, 5c, 6a, 7b, 8); Victoria and Albert Museum (2a, 2b, 7a); Hawkley Studio Associates (4a, 4b, 6b).

Chapter 1

A Child of the Chapel

Of all the shadows of the past, actors and their craft are the most shadowy. In spite of the bulldozer, the work of an architect may survive here and there; the work of the painter lingers on in galleries and country houses; that of the novelist may survive as a reflection of an age; and the diarist may paint a shining portrait of himself. All that remains of the actor's career is a few trumpery buckles and sword knots, yellowing cuttings, and the recollections of his contemporaries.

To walk into the splendid country houses of the eighteenth century is to walk into the past. Their owners, pictured by Reynolds or Gainsborough, still look down on their settings. But the setting of the actor is gone. His voice has gone, or only survives as a cracked reproduction. Most important of all, his audience has gone. For the audience creates the actor, and the actor creates the audience.

Henry Irving has become the archetype of the old-time actor, a cliché for a cheap laugh. Yet in his day he was regarded as a great innovator. He continued the work, started by William Macready and Samuel Phelps, of reforming the stage and restoring Shakespeare to an even more splendid setting.

Irving was born in 1838, a year after the young Queen came to the throne, and he survived her by four years. His career not only spanned the whole history of the Victorian theatre, but it *was* the Victorian theatre. It is impossible to assess the theatre of that era without considering it as a background to Irving.

Although Irving broke with tradition, he was also part of it. Audiences changed slowly in the days when entertainment had not yet become a surfeit. Macready retired in 1851, the year of the Great Exhibition, and Irving's career did not begin until 1857. Yet twenty years later he was still acting in Macready's old successes, and receiving acclaim for his performances. Fustian may have been a Victorian cloth, but it had an enduring quality.

Irving's theatre was a reflection of an age which believed in the purity of women, the sanctity of family life, and the virtues of self-help. The Victorian ethic has long been denigrated for its hypocrisy, for the split mind which accepted children in factories, listened to uplifting sermons on Sundays, and wept in the theatre over virtue betrayed while accepting open prostitution on the streets.

Before too lofty an attitude is taken towards the simplicity and double standards of Victorian society and its plays, it is perhaps salutary to reflect on the blindnesses of our own day and our own drama. It would be difficult in the present climate of opinion to depict a villainous Negro, a left-wing Maoist who was dishonest about money, or even a peer who was intelligent and public spirited. Yet Negroes are convicted of murder, arson and rape as often as white men, and not all Maoists are shining St Georges. Even the cries of Victorian children are still faintly echoed by the children of today's homes broken by divorce and disturbed by violence.

Hypocrisy is not the preserve of any single generation or any century. It is as well to be as modest and detached about the age in which one lives and its theatre as about former generations.

Henry Irving was supremely the child of his age, an age which believed firmly that will-power could accomplish all. He could have served as a prototype for Samuel Smiles, the author of *Self-Help*, for he had all the necessary qualifications. He was born of humble and poor parents, but, armed with those commended virtues of perseverance, courage in the face of adversity, and the determination to overcome immense physical and social obstacles in the pursuit of a single aim, he succeeded against all the odds.

John Henry Brodribb – later to become Henry Irving – had two strains in his nature: English yeoman stock and Cornish Celt. His father's family were Somerset farmers, and it seems as if the family had declined in fortune. They are reputed to have come from Somerton, the ancient capital of Wessex. This town still remains a peaceful collection of elegant stone buildings of different periods, with a broad eighteenth-century street, and an old stone market cross. It is built on a hill looking over the green Somerset countryside and had obviously been a walled town in its embattled past.

In Clutton, a village some miles distant, there are a number of Brodribb graves, substantial graves of a Roman coffin type with carved skulls and weathered inscriptions, some of them drawing attention to former social pretensions: 'Joseph Brodribb, died 1804 aged 78 and Elizabeth, his wife, daughter of William Purine of Havyot Manor, Wrington, aged 77, 1803' – so even in death Elizabeth's manorial origins were not forgotten. The lush grass, the feathery flowers of Queen Anne's lace and the thickening ivy make the names difficult to decipher. The social pretensions of the Brodribbs have long been forgotten and the only one of their race to have achieved lasting fame did not use their name.

The Celtic strain in John Brodribb came from his mother, Mary Behenna, a Cornishwoman of pleasant nature and narrow Methodist views who also had a yeoman farming background. But by the time Samuel Brodribb and Mary Behenna had met and married, the fortunes of both their families had declined and Samuel Brodribb was a mere travelling salesman, the Victorian equivalent of the pedlar with his pack.

Irving was born in a small, grey, dour house in the Somerset village of Keinton Mandeville. Unlike Somerton, the village is without charm or distinction, a collection of houses stretched along a main road. The house still stands, ugly and uncompromising, built straight on to the road without garden or vegetation to soften its square outline. It looks like a house drawn by a child, with square windows and a door in the centre. At the back of the house there is a hayloft and a view leading away to the distance. No doubt in Irving's day his family kept a pig and a few chickens to eke out a meagre living. Above the door a bronze plaque, grown green with age, informs the passer-by: 'Here was born Henry Irving Knight Actor 6th February 1838. This memorial was set up by his fellow countrymen and unveiled by John Martin Harvey 1925.'

Both house and village seem an unlikely and drab beginning for a man who, with lavish imagination, was to colour the lives of so many.

When Samuel Brodribb settled in the village, Keinton Mandeville supported a large store and a number of tailors making clothes from hand-woven cloth. With the rise of large-scale manufacturing, this cottage industry declined and with it the fortunes of Samuel

Brodribb. During the slump of the 1840s he decided to migrate to Bristol, a city where prosperity seemed to offer better opportunities for impoverished salesmen.

Mary Behenna, perhaps thinking of the unhealthy alleys and sanitation of Bristol, decided to send her only son to her sister in Cornwall. Sarah Behenna had married a mine manager, Isaac Penberthy, who had returned from managing tin mines in Mexico. He and his wife settled outside St Ives in Halsetown, a village built by a Mr Halse for his mine workers – a mere collection of dwellings built to provide salubrious cottages for the working poor. It remains to this day, a scattering of grey, two-storey dwellings dotted over the boulder-strewn hillside. On the summit of the hills stands the disused Ghew tin mine, a monument to an industry which became uneconomic. The machinery has long since rusted into decay, but the arched doorways and windows of the mine remain. The foundations of the chimneys could be the ruins of a medieval castle, but, as the clash of armed men retreated from the battlements of the middle ages, so the clatter of industry has retreated from the nineteenth-century mine, leaving the jackdaws, the gorse, and the weather in possession. Time covers the old sadnesses of ill-rewarded work with a gentle feeling of decay.

The mine shaft, protected by wire, remains to indicate where once men toiled and sweated. Down the road, the miners tramped to drink themselves into oblivion at the inn or to be saved at the local chapel.

There is something in the Celtic character which seems to produce dour buildings and grim villages, as if their towering imagination and the colour of their inner nature do not need the outward trappings of flowers, trees, and tile-hung cottages as an antidote to the greyness of climate or the harsh facts of life. Their character stands out rock-like and strong, like the landscape from which they spring.

Halsetown consists of a grey street of characterless houses, a shop, an inn, and a chapel. The chapel is a grim building, totally without compromise to charm or beauty. A faded '1833' above the entrance shows that it was subscribed for and built five years before John Brodribb's birth. It is approached through tall iron gates between two high blank stone walls. The school attached to the chapel is built of the same grey stone. The only spots of colour in the landscape are the summer-flowering gorse and the sparse bushes of pink escallonia.

John Brodribb, as Irving then was, arrived at Halsetown when he was about four years old. His uncle, Isaac Penberthy, was a tall, extrovert man, quick to anger and to laughter, while his aunt Penberthy shared her sister's narrow Methodism. But in spite of narrow restrictions, Irving remembered his years with his aunt and uncle with affection, and said that his ability to endure fatigue was due 'to the free, open and healthy years I lived at Halsetown and to the simple food and regular routine ordained by my aunt. We rambled much over the desolate hills, or down to the rocks and the seashore.'

His uncle he remembered as a big, bearded man, broad-shouldered and rough, with a Celtic temper:

'He was a man born to command – and to be loved. I can hardly describe how dominating was his personality, and yet how lovable. I remember that my aunt, my cousins and myself went to meet him coming home from the mine every evening, that his greeting was boisterously affectionate, and that we knew no better task than to win his approval.'

Irving remarked that his aunt was also a strong personality:

'She was a woman of severe simplicity in dress – the straight lines of her gowns are before me now, and she was deeply religious of character. It was a time of the great religious revival in Cornwall. My aunt was a teetotaller and a Methodist, and her whole life was coloured by her convictions. The stern asceticism of the daily routine imposed by my aunt may have jarred upon us youngsters, but it was tempered by strong affection.'

Until Wesley came to Cornwall in the 1740s smuggling was the honourable profession and the plundering of wrecks was legitimate commerce. Kegs of free liquor made drunkenness a cheap vice, and the strong ruthless character of the Cornish people and their physical strength gave their amusements a double fervour – cockfighting, bull-baiting, hurling, wrestling, and pitched battles on May Day and other festivals lingered on in Cornwall long after other parts of the country had turned to less savage sport. But the voice of Wesley, triumphant and minatory, spread across the country and turned men's minds to repentance. It was a slow process. The pagan legends and customs lingered on. The stories of the past which the young Brodribb heard were violent and melodramatic: tales of men's skeletons and the spars of ships washed up on the rocky shores, of servant girls who disappeared with their life savings, their bones found later under the floor of the local inn.

Methodism was a religion which also relied on histrionics to turn men's minds towards renouncing the flesh and the devil. Like many intelligent children, the young John Brodribb was seen (by his aunt) to be a suitable candidate for the ministry. As he listened to the rousing sermons in the drab chapel, perhaps he was drawn to the idea of hypnotising an audience and holding them spellbound. After all, Wesley was said to have enthralled more than two thousand people in the natural amphitheatre at Gwennap where, in a round hollow two hundred feet across, his every word was awaited by the breathless multitude.

At about the age of ten the young Brodribb was apparently overtaken by emotion during a sermon. His aunt was edified by this reaction, but children are as easily moved to religious conversion in emulation of their elders as by sincere and fervent feelings; and there is always the intense wonder that the holy child will evoke; or possibly this was they young Brodribb's first taste of an attentive audience. His imagination may have been kindled not so much by the reality of religious revelation as by its effect on the congregation – did not the preacher hold the very souls of the congregation by the notes of his voice? This could be a power to develop.

Up to the age of 10 John Brodribb was educated in the village with his three cousins, who were his constant companions. The mine manager's house was a more substantial dwelling than the cottages on the hillside. It still stands at the crossroads opposite the inn, a house of five or six rooms, facing the road to St Ives along which the pack-horses brought the coal to the mine and took back the tin to be shipped to Bristol. In early Victorian times it was a remote place, and the villagers walked to St Ives, which must have seemed to the small boy a great metropolis.

Isaac Penberthy, with his experience of foreign parts, had brought prosperity to Ghew Mine, and it seemed as if the child was destined to pass his schooldays in Cornwall. But in 1848, when John Brodribb was 10 years old, his uncle died at the age of 56. It was not only a tragedy for the widow and her family, but for the mine which he had guided to prosperity. Two thousand miners were said to have followed his coffin to the grave.

John Brodribb was sent back to his father and mother, now living in London. The Brodribbs, like the Dickens family, seemed to have lived obscurely, and how they scratched up a living is equally obscure. They lived in the heart of the City of London, at 68 Lombard Street, and their son Johnny was sent to the City Commercial School, between Lombard Street and Cornhill. Fees, £6 a year. Headmaster, Dr Pinches.

If the original thought of holding an audience was sown by hearing the preachers in the Methodist Chapel of Halsetown, the seed was nurtured by Dr Pinches, who was greatly drawn to acting and recitation. Elocution and correct speech training were his specialities, and at the end of term he was accustomed to show off his pupils' paces by holding a public recital of Latin verse, enlivened by modern recitations, all given by his most promising boys.

Johnny Brodribb had a stammer, but possibly the encouragement of Dr Pinches and the boy's drive to shine in front of an audience made this a golden moment for him. The Victorian era rejoiced in recitations from grim to gay, from farcical to tear-jerking, many of them accompanied by the tinkling of pieces specially written for amateur pianists.

Young Brodribb's choice of a poem suitable for an end-of-term entertainment was curious. Called 'The Uncle', by H. G. Bell, the published text gives the musical accompaniment as being by Sir Julius Benedict. 'The Uncle' was no tale of a dear old man dandling his nephew on his knee, for he proceeds to take the boy into his confidence: he had been in love with the boy's mother, the boy's father had strangely disappeared, and the wife, 'guessing the hand that had struck the blow', promptly went mad. And no wonder. Would the boy perhaps like to see 'what thy mother saw'? He raised the lid of an old oak chest, and there was a bare-ribbed skeleton, carefully saved up for a rainy day. The poem ended on a dark coda:

That night they laid him on his bed, in raving madness tossed:
He gnashed his teeth and with wild oaths blasphemed the Holy Ghost;
And ere the light of morning broke, a sinner's soul was lost.

Dr Pinches decided that this tale of putative adultery, madness, murder, and skeletons was hardly likely to increase the list of new pupils. 'The Uncle' was banned and young Brodribb was persuaded to recite a very long speech made by an Irish advocate called John Curran in defence of an Irish patriot – a tame substitute.

But he had been noticed. A tragedian of the day, William Creswick, a friend of the histrionically-inclined Dr Pinches, remembered Irving in his schooldays:

'The room was filled from wall to wall with the parents and friends of the pupils. I was not much entertained by the first part. But suddenly there came out a lad who struck me as being a little uncommon, and he riveted my attention. The performance was a scene from *Ion* in which he played Adrastus. I well saw that he left his schoolfellows a long way behind. Seeing that he had dramatic aptitude I gave him a word of encouragement – perhaps the first he had ever received.'

Johnny Brodribb spent nearly four years at Dr Pinches's school, and apart from the Doctor other influences were gradually pushing him towards the path he was to follow.

In 1850 his father took him to see Samuel Phelps play Hamlet at Sadler's Wells. Like the sudden view of a new landscape to a mariner approaching the shore, Samuel Brodribb had introduced his son to his chosen country. Mary Brodribb did not approve of the theatre. It was a place of evil and frivolity, anathema to a true believer. But at last she was persuaded to relent – there could be no harm in Shakespeare.

When Johnny Brodribb, at the age of 12, saw Phelps play for the first time, it was Phelps's seventh season at Sadler's Wells. The following year Macready retired from the profession he had so often heartily disliked and had come to with so much reluctance. While one actor was putting aside his princely mantle, a boy sat spellbound watching Phelps, inspired to work towards the goal of being worthy to wear it.

When he was 13, Johnny Brodribb's short schooling came to an end. Apart from the simple skills of reading and writing, he had gained little from it except encouragement for his talent for recitation, and there was no money to allow him the chance of further enlarging his mind. That he would have to do himself. Much later, he said that when he was a boy he had a habit of studying any play of Shakespeare's before going to see it, and trying to imagine how the players would re-create it. Already he had begun to see a play as something to be adapted and turned into a vehicle for actors.

But dreams were a luxury; there was first the necessity of earning his living. In 1851, the year of the Great Exhibition and the retirement of Macready, he went to work as a clerk in a firm of lawyers. Like Trollope and Dickens, he was starting at the bottom of the ladder; filling inkpots, running errands, and sharpening pens. Office boys, while dawdling from one boring assignment to another, had much leisure for dreaming, for hanging about bookstalls and picking up penny editions of old plays, and in the evenings, when sufficient money has been saved, for journeying to Sadler's Wells to pass into that enchanting world where kings died, fools capered, and the unreal was more real than the reality.

John's increasing obsession with the theatre alarmed his mother. There was no future for him on the stage; it was an evil profession given to lechery and opened the way to drunkenness and other assorted vices. Commerce – commerce overseas – was the only means of advancement that lay open to young Brodribb. He left the lawyers, Patterson and Longman, for an opening had been found for him in Thacker, Spink & Co. (East India Merchants) of Newgate Street. His future could be bright; many an impoverished lad had made a fortune in the East – and had returned to keep his aged parents in luxury.

The atmosphere of Thacker, Spink & Co. was much like that described by Trollope in *The Three Clerks* – drudgery, high jinks, and a vendetta against the chief clerk, Mr Blackwell. When he came into contact with his employers, young Brodribb began to be conscious of his country manners and of his country speech. He persuaded the other clerks, Edward Russell and Charles Ford, to begin a system of fines for bad grammar and dropped h's. It was the beginning of those self-imposed disciplines which he needed to fit himself for the high place he had decided upon. Once the grim figure of the chief clerk disappeared from the office, Johnny Brodribb would amuse his fellow inkwell fillers with dramatic recitations.

The hours of office drudgery were long, from 9.30 till 7, and yet he still found time and money to go to theatres, to buy plays, and to learn them by heart before he arrived at the theatre.

The theatre of Irving's early working days in London, from 1851 to 1856, was in a state of transition. Thanks to Bulwer Lytton's efforts, the patents which had kept it in a tight corset had been removed. But like an uncorseted figure the shape had not been improved. Some few actors like Charles Kean and Macready tried to keep the standard high, but most of the new theatres were dedicated to amusing, and not always with talent. In the days of the two patent theatres the other houses were not allowed to act straight plays, and this had encouraged the tradition of the burletta and low comedy with music which finally culminated in the music hall. The increasing number of Londoners were not looking for culture when they went to the play; they wanted coarse fun, laughter, and jolly music, with possibly a glimpse of female legs, which was not to be found in the grey streets.

It is easy to understand Mary Brodribb's objections to her son's interest in an ill-paid and raffish profession. William Macready and Samuel Phelps could be cited as models of what could be achieved, but they were isolated cases. Mrs Brodribb also objected to theatrical aspirations on religious grounds, although young Johnny had not abandoned stern chapel-going. He attended the Albion Chapel, in the West End of London where the Reverend McFarlane was minister, and, although young, was considered to be clever as well as of generally superior calibre. He had taken young Brodribb to see the principal sights of London such as the Royal Academy and the Polytechnic. The minister had married a deacon's daughter and it was said she was a very suitable wife. When imparting this news Johnny Brodribb added cautiously that he had received an invitation to visit them and would have an opportunity of judging for himself – a young man who did not even take the minister's wife sight unseen.

Mrs Brodribb's fears for her son's future had little effect on his actions; his developing will had already decided on his path. The point at issue was how to achieve his ends.

When entertainment was sparse, amateur theatricals were a growing interest, and elocution classes began to be popular. At these classes a budding Phelps or Kean could learn how to astonish supper guests with histrionic prowess. In an age when there were no drama schools, these classes also gave would-be actors an opportunity to learn their trade. One of the best known of the drama classes was the City Elocution Class which had been started by Mr and Mrs Henry

Thomas. They had begun in a small way by renting a room under a railway arch, but the increasing passion for recitation brought them success. They moved to the same Sussex Hall where Dr Pinches had given young Brodribb his first taste of a live audience. He attended the classes assiduously every week.

By good fortune the young clerk had chosen teachers who were in advance of the general low standard of the declamatory acting then admired. They disdained the old-fashioned ranting style and leaned towards the new modern technique for naturalism started by Charles Mathews, which was to culminate in the 1860s with the naturalistic comedies of Tom Robertson.

When John Brodribb joined the City Elocution Class he was much younger than most of the other young men who were drawn to inflicting their talents on invited audiences. He had already almost conquered his stammer; he appeared tall for his age, dressed in a correct black suit with a round jacket and a deep white linen collar turned over it. If his costume was that of the very junior clerk, his pale face was alive with intelligence and his mass of black hair and alert eyes gave an impression of good looks. He was said to have electrified his audience with 'an unusual display of elocutionary and dramatic intensity'. Was it possible that he had revived the formerly banned 'Uncle' for just such a debut?

One of his fellow actors, a young man called Dyall, later remembered the Thomases and their classes: 'Mr Thomas was a bright, genial mercurial and eminently lovable man and his wife was a buxom little woman brimming over with fun, but not ethereal enough for the young heroines'. The apiring actors taught one another, pointing out dropped h's, wrong accents, bad pronunciation, and awkward positions of hands and feet. Dyall recalled what a great deal of good this mutual criticism did to the class. The pieces chosen were light drawing-room entertainments, now forgotten, but no doubt *Boots at the Swan* and *Little Toddlekins* gave pleasure to the actors, and even possibly to their audiences.

When the class moved to Sussex Hall, Brodribb played Captain Absolute in Sheridan's *Rivals*. The *Theatrical Journal* commended Brodribb's Captain Absolute as displaying intelligent tact, adding that this was a compliment to Mr Thomas, his teacher – a criticism which could not have afforded the young actor that unalloyed pleasure which the artiste likes to feel when reading even the shortest notice. A recitation of 'The Last Days of Herculaneum' brought a more hopeful criticism – that he was a young Roscius. But any young actor is alluded to as a young Roscius. They are thick on the ground when they begin; it is only with staying power and real talent that one survives disappointments to become an old Roscius.

But already the young Brodribb had his eye on higher things than *Boots at the Swan*. In 1855 he decided to try Shakespeare. Amateurs could pay to act with professionals on a real stage, with real scenery, footlights and costumes. Payments for the performance varied according to the vice or virtue of the character: it was three guineas to play Romeo, while Iago came a little cheaper at two guineas.

Brodribb decided to try a performance of Romeo for three guineas. His costume consisted of a red velvet shirt, a pair of white cotton 'legs', a very tall black hat, two white feathers, and large black shoes with blue rosettes. The rest of the supporting cast were superannuated actors glad to pick up a few guineas from amateurs wishing to satisfy their vanity.

Brodribb wore a large wig and carried a dagger. During the performance he managed to lose his way in the scenery, and somehow by the fall of the curtain he had also lost not only his large wig but also his dagger. This performance, which took place at the Soho Theatre, may have lacked Italian romance but it pleased some ten or twelve of his friends, young clerks in the City; and while it may also have lacked polish, the young Roscius said, 'I went to work like a man, and a Briton.'

But he soon decided that amateur performances and the applause of friends gave no satisfaction. He had been haunting the theatre at Sadler's Wells for some time and had made friends with a man called William Hoskins, who was in Phelps's company. He was a man of education with a 'county' background, and had been educated at Oxford. Touched by the intense earnestness of Brodribb, he agreed to coach him, and, in a spirit of self-sacrifice not often found in actors given to keeping late hours, he gave these lessons at eight o'clock in the morning before young Brodribb went to his office.

The pupil made progress and was finally introduced to the great Samuel Phelps. The young actor proceeded to regale the old actor with Othello's address to the Senate. The eminent tragedian, who had started as an amateur himself, listened with patience. He then gave his advice: 'Have *nothing* to do with the theatre.'

The young Roscius looked at his idol: 'Well, sir, it seems strange that such advice should come from you, seeing that you enjoy so great a reputation as an actor.' He paused, 'I think I shall take my chance and go upon the stage.'

Now the old actor looked again at the hopeful young face: 'In that case, sir, you may come next season to Sadler's Wells, and I'll give you two pounds a week to begin with.'

John Brodribb was taken aback, stammered his thanks – and did not accept. Why he refused is difficult to understand. Perhaps he felt instinctively that he needed a tough apprenticeship. Or was he too nervous to pit his budding talents so soon against the best professionals? Or did the disapproval of his mother make him unwilling to try his frail talent so near to home? It was a most curious decision.

The next offer Brodribb received was from his friend Hoskins, who had decided to sail for Australia to try his acting luck there. He approached Mrs Brodribb. Would she allow her son to accompany him? The prospects were good, a round five pounds a week. Mrs Brodribb refused. Her son's future lay in the field of commerce where solid profits could assure a solid competence. Hoskins looked at the tall, stately, gentle Methodist lady. She was wrong, he said; one day her son would earn fifty pounds a night. She remained unconvinced. She approached young Dyall, Brodribb's acting friend, with tears in her eyes, saying she had read much of the vicissitudes of actors' lives, their hardships, and the precariousness of their employment. Could not young Dyall try to persuade her Johnny against the stage? Both mother and friend tried to dissuade him – to no avail.

But Hoskins, the actor friend and tutor, had recognised a burning ambition which had to be slaked. He gave John Brodribb a letter which, like the magic words in a fairy story, would ring up the curtain for him. The letter was to E. D. Davis, manager of a new theatre in Sunderland.

'You *will* go upon the stage,' said Hoskins. 'When you want an engagement present that letter, and you will find one.'

Chapter 2

Enter Henry Irving

In 1856 the Crimean War ended, Flaubert published *Madame Bovary*, and John Brodribb changed his name to Henry Irving, went to Sunderland, duly presented Hoskins's letter to the manager of the theatre and began his career.

His uncle, Thomas Brodribb, had given or bequeathed him £100, the proceeds of a matured insurance policy. This had been invested in a way which his careful uncle had probably not envisaged. Before setting off for the north of England Irving had laid out a good part of his capital on wigs, tights, shoes, gloves, a feathered hat, and three swords. As he proudly announced to a fellow clerk, they were 'My court sword, my fencing sword' and, of course, his sword for battle.

He had chosen the name Irving from the American writer Washington Irving, and had added his own second name Henry. It would look good on the bills, had a fine ring to it, and his mother would not be embarrassed at the Chapel by seeing 'Brodribb' connected with the stage. There was already another actor called Joseph Irving on the stage, but the new Irving with his swords, buckles, and feathered hat was aware only of the prospects stretching before him.

He arrived in Sunderland before the building of the theatre was completed and spent the first fortnight walking from his lodgings, two miles outside the town, to watch the progress, anxious and nervous in case the final touches should not be made before his first appearance. The whole world must be waiting for the début with as great an eagerness as the young actor himself. Afraid that his newly purchased properties might be stolen from the unfinished theatre, he trudged the four miles backwards and forwards from his lodging with the precious feathers, buckles, and swords clasped lovingly in a carpet bag.

At last the long-awaited first night arrived. The play chosen was *Richelieu* (*or The Conspiracy*) by Bulwer Lytton, a very suitable vehicle for the first public viewing of the hat with the feathers and one of the swords from the carpet bag. Bulwer Lytton was thought by Victorian critics to be the playwright who had lifted the romantic drama from the turgid depths of dullness into which it had fallen at the beginning of the nineteenth century. It is not an opinion shared by the modern reader.

The play begins when the Duke of Orleans, brother to Louis XIII, is discovered reclining on a large fauteuil while his mistress Marion de Lorme (in the pay of Richelieu) offers him a jewelled goblet. It is questionable whether a youth fresh from chapel, city office, and elocution class could blossom forth thus early, fully equipped with mistress, dark sins, and even darker conspiracies, to give a convincing performance – notwithstanding the feathered hat.

He spoke his first words on the professional stage: 'Here's to our enterprise.' Irving himself said he was not able to speak these opening words properly. They stuck in his throat.

A local critic advised him to take the first steamer back to London, sea travel being the cheapest form of transport at the time. But he did not give up, and said that the kindness of Mr Davis, the manager, gave him the courage to endure the first months until the audience began to warm to him.

Davis remembered the first engagement differently. Although he was busy as manager, producer, and actor, he could not have failed to notice the minute care which the young actor had given to his costume. This was particularly appreciated as managers had to provide a costume, but the props were supplied by the actors themselves. Irving was remembered for the splendour of his white hat and feathers, a perfect picture from head to toe. He had obviously studied an engraving of the Louis XIII period. It is not often that an impecunious manager acquires such assets, and, for the sake of splendid props and dedication, the manager was prepared to be lenient.

Irving's next appearance was even less lucky. A youth of Sabbatarian leanings, he was unwilling to study his part on a Sunday and relied on his good memory to learn the role of Cleomenes in *The Winter's Tale* on the Monday. He was over-sanguine.

This was too much for the local critic, who remarked that Mr Irving had utterly ruined the last scene, coming on to the stage without knowing a single word of his part, and added: 'Although he had his cue pitched at him by the prompter in a tone loud enough to be heard in most parts of the house, he was unable to follow it, and was compelled to walk off the stage amid a shower of hisses.'

But he endured. He did not take the steamer back to London, and stayed in Sunderland for five months to redeem his reputation and gain the valuable experience of acting with such leading players as Charlotte Cushman, Sims Reeves, and Ira Aldridge, the coloured tragedian.

The system which prevailed up to Irving's day was that the local resident company supplied the background characters to the play and the leading actors would arrive to give a performance. The anecdote which best illustrates this system is one told of Kean, who on arriving at a local town went straight to his hotel, where the theatre manager arrived, hat in hand, to ask when the great actor was going to rehearse.

'Rehearse, rehearse!' Kean retorted. 'I'm not going to rehearse, I'm going to bed. Tell the actors to keep out of my way, and do their damned worst!'

With all its disadvantages, this system did mean that young actors could perform with the leaders of their profession, and those who showed promise might be encouraged by the bright travelling stars. Even in his first months of professional work, Irving had been praised when he played with Charlotte Cushman.

For the first month of his acting career, Irving received no salary, but after the month was over he received the munificent salary of twenty-five shillings. After his preliminary months of apprenticeship he was offered an engagement in Edinburgh. It was here that he laid the hard foundations of his subsequent career with two and a half years of unremitting work, during which, it has been estimated, he played between 350 and 400 parts.

Audiences in the 1850s expected plenty of entertainment for a small outlay – a long play, a ballet or burletta, and then an afterpiece. Good value for the sixpenny galleryites and the gentry in the stalls at half a crown. Sometimes these entertainments lasted more than four hours, the curtain rising at 6.30 p.m., and none of the actors would expect to be in bed until long after midnight.

Irving was nineteen; he enjoyed superb health and burning ambition. While not strictly good-looking, he had a pleasant appearance, but with his neat suit and long hair he still gave the impression of a bank clerk with poetic leanings. He had, as he afterwards admitted, all the disadvantages – a bad gait, a voice which retained traces of its Cornish origin, and a face which did not fit in with the contemporary ideas of a young man to be cast in the heroic mould. The Victorians liked beautiful young men, and he did not fall into that category.

But as Irving said, 'An actor's luck is really *work*.' In Edinburgh this was not lacking. During the two and a half years he worked in Scotland he never played in less than three pieces in a night and no part was too small or too undignified for him to tackle. He played in pantomime as Scruncher, the Captain of the Wolves; he played the villainous fairy Venoma and was commended for his make-up – 'astonishingly correct even to the minutest detail'. Whether the theatre critics were accustomed to equate wicked fairies with ladies they picked up in bars, or by what fairy-tale standard they judged Irving's make-up, is hard to know. Perhaps he had used some contemporary fairy-tale illustration as a basis for his impersonation. He was always, throughout his career, apt to use books on which to build the mirrored details of face and costume.

He played many parts in nautical dramas in which a solitary British tar had only to turn his noble gaze on a number of Frenchmen for the whole pusillanimous horde of 'frogs' to flee immediately. Simple patriotic dramas were still immensely popular, and many of them were turned into subjects for the toy theatre. Those penny plain and twopence coloured dramas give an authentic picture of the style of acting of the time and the simplicity of the plays, for much of the scenery for the toy theatres was drawn at actual performances. Nearly twenty plays in which Irving is known to have acted were printed for the toy theatre, and in many of them, during his long provincial apprenticeship, he played several of the parts.

Nautical dramas in which Irving played included *The Pilot*, a piece which hymned the fact that the British Navy ruled the waves, and concluded – to cheers from the gallery – with a general combat and the triumph of the British flag. Occasionally the audience took such a piece too much to heart. Edward Stirling, playing Tom, a noble British tar in *El Hyder* (*Chief of the Gaunt Mountains*) by W. Barrymore, was trapped by the enemy in a rocky defile. During the mêlée a real sailor, half-seas over, slid down the gallery and box pillars on to the stage and throwing off his jacket called out: 'Messmate, I'll stand by you – seven to one ain't fair – pour a broadside into the blackamoor lubbers!' So saying, he knocked down two of the supers and put the rest to flight.

In Jerrold's famous *Black-eyed Susan* Irving played Seaweed, one of the seamen – 'Avast there messmate! Don't rake the cockboat fore and aft.' He also played Captain Crosstree, intent on seducing the noble Susan – 'Mischief on that little rogue's black eyes!' And finally Lieutenant Pike – 'Smugglers surrender, or you have not a moment's life!'

The iron discipline of these early years in the theatre earned Irving a reputation not only for hard work but also for the meticulous care with which he attacked his make-up and costumes. Less dedicated actors in the company regarded this industrious apprentice with a jaundiced eye. He was held up to the young actors as the model of how a budding performer should behave, the manager also remarking that Irving would have given a whole week's salary in order to get his costume and make-up right – a sentiment calculated to have more appeal to a manager than to fellow actors.

It might be thought that with these heavy programmes many of the characters which Irving played could have been hardly more than revue sketches, rather than properly developed stage characters. But the actors of the time were accustomed to learn by heart many stock pieces, and Irving had done this long before he became a professional. Actors were expected to know a good number of plays so that should a visiting star suddenly decide on *Black Eyed Susan* or *Othello* the local company could fill in the necessary background, if not with finish, at least adequately.

Irving looked back on the old Theatre Royal, and the Queen's Theatre, Edinburgh, where the company afterwards transferred, as his university: 'There I studied for two and a half years my beautiful art, and there I learned the lesson that

> Deep the Oak
> Must sink, in stubborn earth its roots obscure,
> That hopes to lift its branches to the sky.

This was a lesson he did not need to learn, for it was part of his inner self, something which could always be relied upon – the will to endure and the will to succeed.

The visiting actors and actresses who came to Edinburgh at this time included Helen Faucit, who had acted with Macready and Phelps and had created Bulwer Lytton's heroines, including that beloved of the Victorian theatre, *The Lady of Lyons*.

With Helen Faucit as Imogen in *Cymbeline*, he played Pisanio. An eye-witness of this performance, watching from the gallery, remembered a tall, thin, angular, nervous-looking young man making his entrance. The check-taker said to the galleryite, 'That's a young man lately joined the company – he's on his mettle, and will give a good account of himself tonight.' When it came to the scene where Imogen draws Pisanio's sword and forces it into his hand, urging him to do her husband's bidding and strike, suddenly the actor's pent-up feelings broke through the carapace of his experience:

> Hence, vile instrument;
> Thou shalt not damn my hand!

The flung sword left the stage, and the electrified audience burst into a round of applause.

One of the many charms of the Victorian theatre was the enthusiasm of the audience. A well executed duel, a rousing speech, an unfair number of villains against a British tar, and they were totally involved. Tears and laughter came to them easily, and across the years the enthusiasm of their applause for good acting still echoes with the pleasure of their clapping hands.

But Irving was still earning only thirty shillings a week. While the manager, Wyndham, was quite prepared to encourage his acting, there was no sense in letting young actors get above themselves by rewarding them too well in cash.

In Edinburgh he also gave a good account of himself in many Scottish dramas or comedies: *Cramond Brig*, *The Flowers of the Forest*, Scott's *Bride of Lammermoor*, and *Douglas*. Yet even when he played Scottish parts he seems to have pleased his critical local audience. In *Hamilton of Bothwellhaugh* Irving played Cyril Baliol, an Iago-like priest, a Popish character carefully tailored to Lowland taste. This part, the plotting priest, was the beginning of his success in

Edinburgh; he was called for at the end of the third act, and a reporter remarked that 'by his excellent acting Mr Irving fairly won the honour'. But other critics remarked that he walked too quickly, emphasising his obvious nervousness, and that he lacked essential subtlety. His walk was constantly criticised from the beginning of his career: 'We notice in this gentleman's acting, a tendency to mannerism, particularly in his walk and gesture. We pray him to avoid that, and to walk as nature dictates, and not as actors strut. Mr Irving is sure to rise in his profession and he can quite afford to take our hints in the spirit in which they are meant.'

The audience was not easily to be won over. They still preferred noble-looking heroes. One newspaper defending him said: 'We noticed with regret a disposition on the part of a certain class amongst the audience to receive Mr Irving with marked disapprobation. Mr Irving is a young actor of greater promise and intelligence than any who have appeared in the ranks of the Edinburgh company for a long time.'

From the outset Irving learned, like Coriolanus, the fickleness of the mob; he never despised them, but he treated them with a certain detached caution.

It was in Edinburgh that Irving met a lifelong friend, the comedian J. L. Toole. J. L. Toole, like Irving, had begun his career as a clerk. He had been encouraged by Dickens to leave his lowly post in a wine merchant's office and become a comedian. A naturally ebullient man, it was his cheerful enjoyment of life which he managed to give to his audience. His acting ability ranged wider than comedy, and when he played Bob Cratchit in *The Christmas Carol* he was said to draw tender tears from his audience by virtue of his pathos. But he was seldom allowed by his admirers to leave the farce at which he excelled. His humour, like that of his audiences, seems to have been drawn on the broadest lines. Clement Scott, who was afterwards to record many of Irving's triumphs, said that Toole was one of the kindest and most genial men, and no one acted with more spirit, or so thoroughly enjoyed the mere pleasure of acting.

It was an attribute which he shared with the young Irving. The two men seem to have been immediately drawn to one another. They shared many things – a humble origin, difficult beginnings, and a dedication to their chosen profession. In this last they were single-minded; the theatre was their whole horizon.

The first play in which they appeared together was *The Winter's Tale*. Toole played Autolycus, the pedlar of gloves as sweet as damask roses. With his broad humour, he descended in direct line from the clown invented by Shakespeare himself to keep the groundlings happy. Life was a simpler matter before the profession discovered the psychological significance of custard pies.

Toole encouraged Irving and recognised his merit. He needed appreciation in spite of his progress, for he was still nervous. But when he played the villain Beauséant, in *The Lady of Lyons*, the audience hissed his discomforture at losing the hand of the heroine, and this was after all 'no mean testimony to the ability evinced in the part'.

Beyond the flickering gaslight, in the dark auditorium there was a beast to be appeased, or to be wooed, but never to be despised. Gradually he was winning their approbation. When he played Charles Courtly in Dion Boucicault's *London Assurance*, the audience, though appreciating the bowing stars, yet called out for Irving to come before the curtain.

Among the plays in which Irving acted at this time was the successful Charles Reade and Tom Taylor piece, *Masks and Faces*. Originally produced at the Haymarket Theatre, London, in 1852, it is a pastiche of eighteenth-century comedy, with strong overtones of the Victorian tear-jerking tragi-comedy. Peg Woffington is the courtesan with the heart of gold, a part naturally graced by Mrs Wyndham (the manager's wife). The manager, Mr Wyndham, played Triplet, the Ben Webster part. For the part of the poor playwright none of the heart-stirring trimmings were omitted. The writers had tricked him out with starving children, a sick wife, and a cold attic devoid of furniture. Into this underprivileged setting walks Miss Woffington bearing baskets of food and nourishing wine. Irving played Soaper. Woffington introduces him with his friend: 'Mr Soaper, Mr Snarl – gentlemen who could butter and cut up their own fathers!' Mabel, the noble and long-suffering wife exclaims: 'Bless me, cannibals!' Woffington, with a sweet smile puts her right: 'No – critics.'

Most of the parts in the play are pale shadows of eighteenth-century characters, yet some of Triplet's speeches must have echoed in the mind of the young actor: 'Madam, you have inspired a son of Thespis with dreams of eloquence – I felt fame must come, soon or late. How was it possible I should go on perpetually starving?'

The play ended with an epilogue spoken by Miss Woffington:

> Yes, sure those kind eyes and bright smiles one traces
> Are not deceptive *masks* – but honest *faces*
> I'd swear it – but if your hands make it certain
> Then all is right on both sides of the curtain.

A sentiment which no doubt sent both actors and audience home to their suppers in a warm glow, feeling that all was for the best in the best possible of worlds.

Irving joined the Edinburgh company on 9 January 1857 and left on 13 September 1859. The hundreds of plays, good, bad and indifferent, and the extraordinarily varied range of parts he played in them, make the mind reel. It seems almost incomprehensible that one actor, however dedicated, thin and wiry, could have encompassed such a vast amount of sheer physical and mental work.

In Shakespeare he played Cleomenes and Florizel in *The Winter's Tale*, Cassio in *Othello*, the Earl of Surrey in *Henry VIII*, four different parts in *Macbeth* culminating in Macduff, Paris and Tybalt in *Romeo and Juliet*, and two different parts in Garrick's *Katherine and Petruchio*, a truncated version of *The Taming of the Shrew*. He acted in stage versions of five or six of Scott's novels, playing the name part in *Rob Roy*. In Dickens he played David Copperfield, Dombey, Nicholas and Mantalini in *Nicholas Nickleby*, Sparkler in *Little Dorrit*, and Monks in *Oliver Twist*.

Although eighteenth-century plays, except in their acceptably bowdlerised pastiches, were not in vogue in Irving's day, his theatre being given to the lachrymose or the robust, he did play in *The Rivals*, *She Stoops to Conquer*, and *Jane Shore*. Pantomime time gave him a chance to shine, not only as the much-praised bad fairy Venoma, but also as an ogre, and a demon in *Puss in Boots*. He played in tear jerkers like *A Poor Girl's Temptation*, and in the blood and thunder of the toy theatre's *Sixteen String Jack* and the *Spectre Bridegroom*.

In June 1859 Wyndham moved to the Queen's Theatre, Edinburgh, which he opened under royal letters patent, which meant that he could stage any kind of play there, for it had become a fully licensed playhouse. At the new theatre, Irving made a hit in burlesque. This is not to be confused with modern burlesque of the American variety; there were no topless, free-stripping ladies to be seen. It seems to have been a version of what would now be called intimate revue or satire. Very often contemporary plays and actors were mocked, so the pieces seem to have been simple skits, interspersed with song and dance, which the eighteenth century might have called burlettas. The burlesque in which Irving made his greatest success at the new theatre was called *The Maid and the Magpie*. The local paper commented that the most cleverly enacted part was undoubtedly the Fernando Villabella of Mr Irving. His make-up was most original, and his whole conception no less so.

His progress towards success at this time was rapid; King James in *Cramond Brig*, that perennial favourite with Scottish audiences, Dazzle in Boucicault's *London Assurance*, and the King in *Hamlet*.

In the autumn of 1859, the year when Samuel Smiles published his *Self-Help*, Irving took his farewell benefit in Edinburgh. The vehicle in which he had chosen to shine for the last time on the Edinburgh stage was *The Lady of Lyons*, and he played the hero, Claude Melnotte.

The local paper remarked:

'We observe from our advertising columns that Mr Irving, a member of the dramatic company at the Queen's Theatre, is about to take a farewell benefit. Mr Irving is one of the most rising actors among us; and it is with regret that we part with him. Always gentlemanly in deportment, his conception of the parts he undertook was just and accurate; while his acting was marked by a taste and an ability that give promise of the highest excellence.'

Victorian critics always laid much stress on gentlemanly deportment and correct speech. The rising manufacturing classes liked to be shown good patterns for behaviour on their stage. They could laugh at low-class characters as being part of a stratum of society which they had long left behind, and the more exaggerated these were the better, but when it came to ladies and gentleman, amongst whom they placed themselves, they expected to see neat models for their children to follow on their upward climb.

The paper deplored Irving's leaving his faithful audience in Edinburgh, and hoped that the public would make his benefit the financial success it deserved to be. It was later reported that Mr Irving's numerous admirers did their duty, and there was a bumper house. At the conclusion of the play the hero of the night came forward and addressed a few words to his friends.

Irving was only 21, and this was to be the first of a lifetime of curtain speeches, but that was hidden in the veil of the future. Combining modesty with self-possession, he said that he had undertaken a difficult task, he risked being charged either with ingratitude— or presumption. But he did not want to go away without saying goodbye to old friends. It had been a long time before he had succeeded in giving satisfaction (cries of No! and applause) – 'I was sometimes hissed in this theatre, and I can assure you that thousands of plaudits do not give half so much pleasure as one hiss gives pain – especially to a young actor.'

The young actor concluded his speech and retired amidst applause and encouraging adieux.

With the plaudits of his Scottish friends still echoing in his ears, he set out to conquer London. He had been offered an engagement at the Princess's Theatre by Augustus Harris, father of that celebrated Augustus Harris II who produced dramas and pantomimes at Drury Lane. The play in which he was to appear was *Ivy Hall*, from the novel *Le Roman d'un Jeune Pauvre* by *The Times* dramatic critic, John Oxenford. It all sounded most promising – until Irving read the play.

He had only six lines to speak, and those right at the beginning of the piece.

He had signed a three-year contract with Harris, but in spite of the modest security which this offered he now showed a steely determination not to appear at a disadvantage. His first appearance in London was important to him, and his absolute confidence in his powers led him to reject this shabby beginning. He persuaded Harris, against the manager's judgement, to release him from his contract.

He had come in triumph, thinking to speed along the broad London highway to success, only to find it a dead end. He resolved to accept no further engagement in London until his merit was recognised and he achieved a chance to shine in a part commensurate with his talents.

Twenty-one years old and without employment, to Irving his Edinburgh successes seemed a long way away. But his nerve did not fail. Undeterred, he decided to give a reading at Crosby Hall on 19 December 1859. This was a courageous decision because, when he was in Edinburgh, during the unpaid holidays which actors had to suffer, he had tried to do this with dismal results.

With another actor he decided to hire the Town Hall at Linlithgow. The play he had chosen to read was the hardy annual, *The Lady of Lyons*. Sitting near Arthur's Seat, he worked himself into a romantic fever over the play. The posters were printed and paid for; his name figured large: 'At eight o'clock precisely Mr Irving will read *The Lady of Lyons*.' The doors were opened, the gas lighted and Irving's friend Saker was poised to take the money. No one came. It was 'Preaching Week', and a hell-fire sermon could offer more thrills than a reading by a young actor.

In spite of this rueful memory, Irving again decided to read *The Lady of Lyons* at Crosby Hall. This time, the part which he knew so well became a way to display his talents to the London critics. They came and they were congratulatory. The *Daily Telegraph* said the performance was characterised by considerable ability and showed a correct appreciation of the spirit of the dramatist. Mr Irving possessed a good voice, and combined it with dramatic power of no mean order. He was likely to make a name for himself in the profession of his choice. The *Standard* was equally praising, and another critic who turned up expecting to be profoundly bored by yet another piece of elocution remarked that the actor showed a quality not often found in so young a man, and proved that the fire of genius is present in the artist.

Praise, that incense to the nostrils of the actor, encouraged Irving to give another recital on 8 February, two days after his twenty-second birthday. The play he chose was *Virginius* by Sheridan Knowles, a prolific writer of classical tragedy, cousin of the great Sheridan. *Virginius* had been written for Kean, who refused to act in it, but it had become one of Macready's greatest triumphs.

Virginius, with its turgid pentameters, makes hard reading. Its stodgy pseudo-classicism wends its heavy way through five acts – from Virginius's introduction of his daughter to her suitor, with the strong recommendation that she is 'a virgin from whose lips a soul as pure exhales as e'er responded to the blessing breathed in a parent's kiss', until eventually he remarks, 'There is only one way to save thine honour – This, this!'. Whereupon he stabs the daughter, and ends up in gaol with the girl's ashes in an urn. Not an enlivening evening, it might be thought.

Irving went to work 'like a man and a Briton' and undertook the five acts single-handed, reading every part from Virginius the centurion, and Virginia his daughter, to the old nurse, Servia. The play was hardly news in London. It had been produced at Covent Garden in 1820, but even this old and well-tried vehicle proved a good venture. Some dozen or more critics praised the young actor. His sharp delineation of characters was praised, he had intelligence and ability, scholarly feeling, and correct taste: 'There is a gentlemanly ease and grace in his manners which is exceedingly pleasing.' Exceedingly pleasing to Irving was the fact that he was beginning to get the measure of his Victorian audience, and to calculate its taste to a nicety.

Thanks to the sparkling readings and the good notices, Henry Webb, manager of the Queen's Theatre, Dublin, offered him a four weeks' engagement. It seemed a lucky outcome, and encouraged by the London notices Irving took the boat to Ireland.

What he did not know was that a favourite actor of the Dublin audience, George Vincent, had been dismissed by the manager. The Dublin audience, at that time renowned for its rowdy behaviour and partisanship of all kinds, was lying in wait for the unsuspecting young actor.

On 5 March 1860 he went on to the Dublin stage for the first time playing Cassio to the Othello of T. C. King. From the very first moment of his appearance a storm of hisses filled the theatre. He stood aghast. He had not uttered a word and yet in front of him was a raging sea of angry faces, shouting, gesticulating and swearing. The disturbance was not temporary, night after night he had to fight his way through his part in the teeth of a house concentrated in personal antipathy to himself. He endured this six nights a week for three weeks.

The Dubliners were convinced that in some way the Englishman had schemed to supplant their favourite. Eventually the manager was stirred into action. He told the audience the truth, and reproved 'the boys', who then warmly applauded Irving during his final week. It was an experience which he never forgot.

Having braved the hissing, Irving left Dublin for a more friendly Scotland, where he joined the company at the Theatre Royal,

Glasgow. He was received kindly, but had dropped back into playing small parts. His career had gone backwards since his last triumphant months in Edinburgh.

'A Glasgow journalist, Hodgson, remembered Irving vividly at this time. Journalists about to start work and actors who had finished their evening performance often joined together for convivial suppers at a hotel in Wilson Street. Good talk, laughter, and an evening drink made the hotel into an unofficial club. Hodgson and Irving were the two youngest men in the room and their pleasure was to listen quietly. He remembered the young actor with long, glossy black hair, liquid eyes of subdued fire, and a great richness of features. He talked little, and if he spoke at all it was usually in monosyllables.

At the Glasgow Theatre he had made no mark. It was a moment of intense discouragement. He had spent all his capital, and instead of a brilliant three-year engagement in London as a net against poverty he was faced with a blank future.

But one Thomas Chambers had noticed the young actor, and also an actress called Henrietta Hodson. He engaged both of them for the Theatre Royal, Manchester, then being run by the actor-manager Charles Calvert.

It may have seemed that he was getting nearer to London and eventual recognition, but he still had a long apprenticeship to serve, and a chilly apprenticeship too, for actors playing small parts in the provinces were on the poverty line. They often had to mimic rich, grand heroes on stage, but off stage they were much more likely to feel the pangs of hunger and cold suffered by the playwright Triplet in *Masks and Faces*.

The men and women of Irving's age were prone to delight in the sentimentalities of family Christmases, lighted puddings, and hearts aglow with love for all the world. Irving was once asked for his memories of Christmas, and they were not comfortable. Though he told the story in the third person, it was a recollection of his days in Manchester:

'A poor actor went to dine one Christmas Day at the house of a comrade. The invitation was a godsend for a guest who had no prospects of a good meal, or even a fire. The day was icy and the actor's salary left no margin for winter garments, and he shivered on the way to his friend's house. Once arrived, he gave an excellent imitation of a young man who had enjoyed a brisk walk. His host gazed at him, fidgeted a little, seemed unable to speak, and finally said that as it was nearly dinner time the young actor might like to wash. He led the way to the bedroom where some warm underclothing was hanging over a chair. The host glanced at the underclothes and then made for the door, and, as if he had had a sudden thought, he then put his head round the door, and said, "Those clothes on the chair, old man – upon my word, I think you had better put 'em on."'

Irving, looking back on his poverty-stricken beginnings, added that the gift, which the old actor could ill afford, still warmed his heart, although it was many years since he had been that young actor.

The only part of any significance which he played at Manchester with any success was the villain Hardress Cregan in Dion Boucicault's *The Colleen Bawn – or the Brides of Garryowen.* This drama, written in the deepest Irish, concerned itself with Hardress's secret marriage to the pure and lovely Colleen Bawn, a girl of modest wants – 'I'll work for the smile ye'll give me in passing, and I'll be happy if ye'll only let me stand outside and hear your voice.' Hardress installs her on Muckross Head, and, growing tired of being rowed over there to achieve his marital rights, he gives the lovely Colleen short shrift: 'You're a fool, I told you that I was betrothed to the richest heiress in Kerry; her fortune alone can save us from ruin. Tonight my mother discovered my visits here, and I told her who you were. It broke her heart.'

Fortunately, in the way of secret marriages, the priest who had performed the ceremony had gone to his rest and the sole remaining witness was Gregan's hunchbacked boatman, Danny. Eily's only hope was her marriage lines, to which, at the outset of the play, she is clinging, with the strong backing of the local priest, Father Tom: 'Be the hush and spake after me – by my mother that's in heaven, this proof of my truth shall never leave my breast.'

The hunchbacked Danny bodes no good for the girl, for while she is still going on about the first day Hardress met her, 'when there was dew on the young day's eye, and a smile on the lips of the lake', he has been plotting with old mother Cregan. He rows the girl out to a handy cave with an equally handy precipitous rock and demands the marriage lines. She refuses, having as she said sworn on her mother's grave never to give up the blessed paper. 'While I live, I'm his wife.' Seeing how the land lies, Danny promptly pushes her into the now unsmiling lake, telling her to take her marriage lines with her to the bottom. But surprisingly the play ends quite happily, with Hardress reconciled to the resuscitated Colleen Bawn, and his rich intended, not wishing to waste her wedding dress, marrying his best friend. The Colleen closes the play by remarking, 'If I could hope that I had established myself in a little corner of their hearts, there wouldn't be a happier girl alive than the Colleen Bawn.' An astonishing sentiment in view of what the girl had gone through, including being pushed off rocks, and rescued dripping to be restored to her unwilling spouse.

The Colleen Bawn had been first produced at the Royal Adelphi Theatre, London, in September 1860, with the author himself as Myles-na-Coppaleen, the Colleen's faithful peasant suitor. When the playwright saw this new Manchester production, he dismissed the acting as being unworthy of his delicate dramatic piece. Only one performer was commended as being worthy to pass through his critical net. That actor was not Henry Irving. Later, Boucicault claimed to have been the sole discoverer of the latent talents of the young actor, an honour hotly contested by several other claimants.

Reading the history of his early career, it is hard not to come to the conclusion that Irving, after long years of neglect, apprenticeship, struggle, and disappointment, had discovered himself.

Laurel wreaths are bestowed by many hands once the laurels have been hard won.

Chapter 3

The Black Cloak of Hamlet

While the young actor was at Manchester, the 300th anniversary of Shakespeare's birth was celebrated with a series of readings and tableaux. The manager of the theatre, Charles Calvert, gave the readings. In the tableaux Mrs Calvert appeared as Sarah Siddons in the 'grand fiendish part', and Irving was chosen to represent Mrs Siddons's brother, John Philip Kemble, as painted by Thomas Lawrence.

On 23 April 1864 he stood for the first time in the black cloak, wearing the tragedy plumes of Kemble's period and holding the skull in his hand. It was a glimpse into the mirror of the future which lasted for no more than a few fleeting seconds.

It was to be many years before the part carried him to the pinnacle of his profession in London. But even this silent representation of the part had inspired him to re-study it. He had spent the last years playing small parts, and the progress he had made in Scotland had been eroded. It was time to break out from his menial apprenticeship. Feeling the power within him, and with a determination to succeed, when it came to the moment for him to take his Manchester benefit he decided to play Hamlet — not in the dusty plumes of the past, but according to the light of his own feelings.

On 20 June 1864 he played Hamlet for the first time, with Mr Calvert playing the Ghost and Mrs Calvert as Ophelia. She was an adequate Ophelia, and highly professional, having been on the stage since she was a child of six. The critics praised her performance, but were less happy about Irving's attempt at a classical part.

The *Manchester Guardian*, in spite of its Liberal politics, was less liberal with its praise. When a man aims high, the paper said, it does not always happen that he strikes high, and this actor's achievement was not equal to his intention. A more robust body was needed for playing Hamlet, and the actor's voice did not seem to be equal to the demands the part made upon it. But even this critic was forced to add a rider: the applause showed that the *Guardian*'s opinion was not shared by the public.

When Irving looked back on his youthful self he was amused at his temerity. When he was little more than a walking gentleman he had attempted the part of Hamlet the Dane. 'I was looked upon as a sort of madman, who ought to be taken to an asylum and shut up,' he said. But he found that the audience warmed to him, and before the play was half done he had been received with fervour and kindness. This gave him hope. In the far-distant future he might benefit from that kindness. It was a beginning.

During the summer holiday, when they were not paid, some of the company moved to Oxford where they attempted to make a living from the beginning of August until the middle of September. Here Irving played Hamlet again. He wore a fair wig, as Fechter did, and this time he achieved even greater success.

During the six weeks at Oxford, Irving played Orlando, Macduff, and the old romantic lead Claude Melnotte in *The Lady of Lyons*. But he was also acting in popular contemporary melodramas like Tom Taylor's *Ticket-of-Leave Man*, which had been playing to great acclaim in London the previous year. In this tear-jerker he was Bob Brierley, the ticket-of-leave man himself, 'a Lancashire lad, an only son, the old folks spoiled him, left him a few hundreds, and now he is kicking 'em down, seeing life'. His tempter lays the plot down clearly. 'I'm putting him up to a thing or two, skittles, billiards, sporting houses, night houses, every short cut to the devil and the bottom of a flat's purse. He's as green as a leek, soft as new cheese, but steady to ride or drive, and runs in a snaffle.'

When Bob makes his first appearance, he is trembling on the edge of what his evil companions describe as 'Del. trem.' They prescribe a devilled biscuit: 'Waiter, a plate of biscuits toasted hot, butter and cayenne.'

The Lancashire lad is speedily tricked by Dalton (alias the Tiger) into passing a false £20 note, and is immediately caught by Hawkshaw 'the Great Detective'. The *vox humana* is supplied by May Edwards, who has been singing, rather badly, for her supper in the Bellevue

Tea Gardens, and as a consequence starving. May represents the semi-prostitute character of many contemporary dramas. Like Dickens's Nancy, the exact nature of her profession is glossed over. She is represented as a pure young girl singing around cafés. Before Bob is arrested he manages to slip her two golden sovereigns to save her from a fate worse than death.

May keeps up a correspondence with the unlucky Bob while he is in gaol, and the second act opens with May having a long conversation with her canary in order to let the audience know what has happened to Bob and how he has redeemed himself.

The piece has everything from kindly old ladies and gentlemen befriending both May and Bob to the last minute reappearance of the crook trying to prevent the union of the innocents. But in spite of its crudities, many of the characters still spring to life, both on the page and on the stage. The opening scene in the café, the hurrying waiters dashing backwards and forwards with tea, muffins, shrimps, 'four brandies for number 3 and a cobbler for the lady', paints a quick impressionistic picture of the period.

Irving played the falsely accused Bob Brierley on several subsequent occasions during the next two or three years. It was obviously one of the more successful of his 'personations', and the vivid sketch of innocence in the wicked city which it presented had a strong contemporary appeal.

He was to spend four years under Calvert's management, but his progress was slow. Mrs Calvert, in an interview many years later, remembered bringing him back to a much-needed supper. When the fire went out in the sitting-room, they all three went into the kitchen where the fire in the stove still glowed. With their feet on the fender, they discussed plays and playing until nearly daybreak. Mrs Calvert was asked whether Irving showed either in his looks or his talk those strange powers which were to sway people so forcibly. No, he did not; he seemed a pleasant intellectual young man, that's all.

The audience in Manchester was slow to accept Irving, as audiences had been in Edinburgh and Dublin. He had to work hard and long to earn the smallest praise. His mind was filled with battles lost and battles won, with pleasure and with pain, youthful hopes dashed and aspirations unfulfilled.

Calvert inspired his affections. He gave Irving encouragement and great kindness. They fought and worked together, and endlessly discussed how to bring their beautiful art to its dreamed-of fruition. They patted one another on the back, and Calvert would say to Irving, 'Well, old fellow, perhaps the day will come when you may have a little more than sixpence in your pocket.'

It was not an exaggeration. The young actor was earning at the rate of £75 a year, and this was only for some thirty-five weeks out of the fifty-two. The enforced vacations had to be filled with readings, or acting in another town. Even 'benefits' sometimes ended in failure, and left the actor they were supposed to reimburse some twenty or thirty pounds worse off, an immense slice from meagre earnings. In Manchester he was not making much headway with the audience because he was too raw, too unacceptable. He had not yet learned the way to use his powers fully.

In the autumn of 1864, Charles Calvert left the Theatre Royal. Backed by some admirers, he took over the newly-built Prince's Theatre and began a series of Shakespearean productions. Why he did not take Irving with him is hard to understand. Possibly Irving's lack of progress with the audience was the reason. Or perhaps Irving felt that he might stand a chance of better parts once the competition from the manager and his wife was removed. The decisions of actors about their careers are often made on so many flimsy grounds, and with such sudden bursts of feeling, that it is difficult for outsiders to understand them. They are the children of fashion, of audiences, and of their age.

Like other actors before and since, Irving was the reflection of his age. Beloved as an intellectual actor at the height of his fame, he always – right up to the end of his career – interspersed great Shakespearean parts with melodramas and farce. It is hard to baulk at the idea that he must have had sympathy and understanding with innocent boys led astray, and even colleens betrayed by villains, and noble-hearted fellows dying for friends or country. Had he not had sympathy and understanding in creating these parts, he would not have been able to convince his audience of their truth.

There is also the desire of the actor to please, and the taste of an audience is not always on a high intellectual plane. Laughter and tears are seldom manifestations of deep philosophical feelings.

When Irving remembered his years in Manchester, he cast a clear eye on the theatre of that time. Theatrical management was not a very complicated business. There was little competition. The audiences were dull, but the actors were a 'merry family'. Their wants were few, and what they did not earn they borrowed from one another. But Charles Calvert with his revivals of Shakespeare had advanced the stage as an art.

Perhaps those long sessions with the Calverts in front of the kitchen fire had given Irving the feeling that the stage need not necessarily be the fit-up business which it was when he joined the profession. Possibly one day actors would not have to supply their own feathers and buckles, or play eighteenth-century drawing-room fops in sets representing kitchens.

Calvert left the Theatre Royal, but Irving's long apprenticeship continued. He was reduced to playing humbler parts, and even to appearing in small curtain-raising farces which 'played in' the audience to the main attraction of the evening, the pantomime.

It was, as so often, one step forward and two steps back. When Irving spoke of Kean, he spoke out of his own deep feelings for his young self:

'His life was one of continual hardship. With that unsubdued conviction of his own powers, which is often the sole consolation of genius, he toiled on and bravely struggled, through the sordid miseries of a strolling player's life. The road to success lies through many a thorny course, across many a dreary stretch of desert land, over many an obstacle from which the fainting heart is often tempted to turn back. But hope – and the sense of power within which no discouragements can subdue inspired the struggling artist still to continue the conflict, till at last courage and perseverance meet with their just reward – and success comes.'

For a few moments Irving pulled aside the curtain of his mind, and gave a glimpse into the bitterness which he had felt during those long years of struggle. But even in this moment of self-revelation he had to don the mask of Kean, and to project his own sentiments back into the past of Kean's early life, not his own.

Playing in pantomime was hardly a glittering reward for the slogging devotion and thought which Irving had given to his art. Edward Stirling, that prolific adapter for the stage of Dickens and Scott, described pantomime as 'jigs, dances, knocking down and picking up red-hot pokers and sausages'. All was action. Nor was Stirling more impressed with contemporary melodrama. Tragedy actresses generally had 'a plentiful display of black hair', he remarked. Heroines like May Edwards and her darling little canary were usually blondes. These recognition signals gave the audience the right idea when the curtain went up.

Dark ladies, being either wicked, wronged, or led astray, ended up dead or despised, while blondes could be calculated to be rewarded with being rescued and presented with a plain gold band.

It was a long way from the sense of power within the young actor's mind. There were glimpses of light and they came – as his first successes were to come – from playing villains. In a curtain-raiser called *The Dark Cloud* he played what was called 'a bold shameless ruffian' – Philip Austin. His reading of the part was hailed as showing careful preparation and study, and the *Examiner* newspaper was happy to add that this was a testimony to that versatility of talent which increases with years.

One thing which did not then increase with his years was his salary, which still stood at thirty shillings a week.

Robert Macaire was the next villain he played, a showy part originally played by Frederick Lemaître. Lemaître had disembowelled the tragedy by Antier, Saint-Armand, and Polyanthe, and turned it into a comedy which included such subtle touches as scaling the boxes and dress circle at the end of the play. The *Manchester Guardian* did not like Irving's ruffianly dandy, and felt that he was too refined and lacked that dash and vigour which constituted an important part of the genuine villain. It is to be doubted whether the drama critic of the *Guardian* was more acquainted with French villains than Irving himself, but the writers of the day liked pontificating. They had their *idées fixes* on the exact nature of all the plays and characters they wrote about.

In the days of stock plays they had seen them over and over again with many different actors. It is difficult, even for a professional critic, to blot out the first viewing of a play. It tends to imprint itself on the mind. The viewer was perhaps younger and more impressionable when the play was first seen, and provincial actors of the period were up against the fact that most of the famous touring actors had trod the boards before them in the parts they played. This was the great cross which Irving had to bear in his early 'personations'.

At the beginning of 1865 a chance of bringing himself to the attention of the public and earning a little money came to Irving's notice.

In mid-Victorian days there was a great interest in spiritualism and the occult. This was perhaps a reflection of the morbid attachment to the trappings of death and sorrow. Once an attachment to the other world and to the angel voices which have gone before is well established, a belief in the occult is there ready to be exploited. In Manchester there were two men calling themselves the Davenport Brothers who specialised in spiritualist seances. Their agent, in an uninspired moment, offered £100 to any person 'who could perform their feats'.

This nice round sum had some appeal to Irving and two of his fellow needy actors, Philip Day and Frederick Maccabe. They decided to reproduce the Davenport seance and its marvels at the Library Hall of the Manchester Athenaeum on 25 February 1865. Five hundred ladies and gentlemen filled the hall. Irving, putting on a wig and a beard and with what was called a 'few adroit facial touches and a lightly-buttoned surtout', quickly turned himself into a carbon copy of the Dr Ferguson who had introduced the real brothers Davenport.

His speech, considered at the time to be a witty skit, was received with loud applause, cheers and laughter. It now hangs a little heavy in the hand. But that criticism could apply to much Victorian humour. They were a simpler people, and if they were more easily gulled by charlatans they were also simpler in their reactions to their exposure. There was a fundamental honesty in their quick response, and it was to this that Irving appealed.

The newspapers were ecstatic in their praise of Irving's exposé and admired the way that he had addressed the audience with all the serious demeanour of the original doctor, reproducing the exact tone, accent, and expression so accurately as to be irresistibly ludicrous in their likeness to nature. He ended his long peroration in the character of the doctor:

'If scientific men will subject these phenomena to analysis, they will find why darkness is essential to our manifestations – (laughter), . . . we want them to be blinded by our puzzle, and to believe with implicit faith in the greatest humbug of the nineteenth century – (loud applause and laughter).'

After his opening address he and his fellow actors were able to reproduce all the tricks and phenomena of the Davenport Brothers. Audience and press were again ecstatic in their praise of Irving, and even the *Manchester Guardian* could scarce forbear to cheer, and commended the readiness of the actor's repartee and the 'smartness' of his art.

Great excitement was roused by this performance when it was repeated at the Free Trade Hall, which was thronged by crowds of the 'most highly respectable and influential persons in the city of Manchester'.

The management, sensing a financial coup, tried to get Irving to carry on the performances in the Theatre Royal but he refused. Already he was conscious of the necessity of upholding the dignity of a theatre. It was not a place for comical representations and ephemeral skits. He cherished the thought of his beautiful art, as he had called it. The management, piqued at his refusal to make them some easy money, dispensed with his services.

He was given some work by his old friend Calvert: Claudio in *Much Ado* and Edmund in *King Lear*. Charles Calvert also produced that perennial favourite *Louis XI*, a popularised version of a play by the prolific Boucicault from a play of Casimir Delavigne. Boucicault had toned down the original and added a few little touches of his own, though not to the play's advantage. The author of *The Colleen Bawn* could hardly be said to wield a subtle pen.

Calvert played Louis XI and Irving played the hero, the Duc de Nemours. But Irving was watching Calvert in the part originally played by Charles Kean and when his own time came he knew he could put more into the part of the dying king than Calvert. He was watching the play with his own future in mind. But would there be a future? There seemed to be no continuity in his career.

He took his benefit in April 1865. This time he decided to play for popularity and selected characters which would be more likely to fill his empty purse. He chose the farce *Raising the Wind*, playing Jeremy Diddler, the confidence trickster with refined manners and holes in his gloves. To fill out the evening, he repeated with his actor friends his success as the doctor in his skit on the Davenport Brothers.

But he was not to leave Manchester for a brilliant future in London; he was now without a permanent job and went back to touring. In Edinburgh he played some five parts in a couple of weeks, including his two villains, Robert Macaire and Philip Austin. He was already making a small reputation for his playing of villainous roles.

He was well received, the *North Briton* warmly congratulating itself that Mr Irving had taken to heart some of the tips which it had kindly given him five years before. The hundred and fifty parts, and the ups and downs of those five years, were details which escaped the paper's notice. But – *sursum corda* – the critic now risked his reputation by predicting that Mr Irving *would have* a career.

From Edinburgh, encouraged by this far from heady praise, Irving went to Bury in Lancashire, where he played Hamlet, this time with a mixed bag of professional and amateur actors, Polonius being acted by a local architect. Hamlet was not considered to be a full evening's entertainment, and the programme was rounded out with a farce called *My Wife's Dentist*.

From Lancashire he journeyed to Oxford, where he played Macduff. Although his tenderness when learning of the murder of his wife and children was commended, the main applause of the evening was given for the fighting. 'During the long and fierce struggle' between Macbeth and Macduff there was incessant cheering. There was nothing that the audience of the day liked better than a duel to the death. Perhaps with the banning of duelling and the rise of the calm, middle-class ethic such scenes gave contemporary spectators a vicarious thrill and a nostalgic whiff of the good old days. In our present age, when violence has become a cliché, the audience is impossible to shock either with physical or sexual spectacle, and the only shock would be to hear actors evincing unfashionably 'respectable' sentiments.

Then from Oxford to Birmingham for a few weeks, to act in *East Lynne*, playing Archibald Carlyle, the wronged husband.

Mrs Henry Wood's famous melodramatic novel was adapted several times for the stage. One of its first adapters was John Oxenford, dramatic critic of *The Times* and a prolific writer for the nineteenth-century theatre. He churned out adaptations of all kinds – mostly from the French. In spite of having translated classical authors like Goethe, Molière, and Calderón, he was drawn to the idea of popular successes. He had adapted *Ivy Hall*, the first play in which Irving had appeared in London, but his greatest success was *East Lynne*. When Irving first appeared in it in 1865 it had not yet achieved the pinnacle of its success.

East Lynne has become a symbol of Victorian melodrama at its worst. Even people who have never read the play can quote the famous line, 'Dead, dead, and never called me mother', which was not in Oxenford's version, but added by a later adapter, T. A. Palmer.

Careful study of *East Lynne* stuns the mind with the complexities of its plotting. The first scene is as thick with plot as a plum pudding with sultanas. Jealous wives, brothers falsely accused of murder, wicked adulterers masquerading under false names, and a loving girl, Barbara, wrongfully cheated of her suitor by the high-born but impecunious Lady Isabel. This lady is tempted into jealousy by the evil Captain Levison. He lets her have a glimpse of Archibald, her husband, and Barbara walking in the garden. Leaping immediately to the conclusion that she is betrayed, an insult to her noble blood, she jumps the gun and elopes with Levison in a chaise.

As with all errant heroines, punishment must pursue her. By the end of Act IV she has been deserted by her seducer Levison, is involved in a railway accident, learns of the fatal illness of her only son, and arrives back at East Lynne disguised as Madame Vine, a governess, only to discover her husband married to Barbara. She tends her dying son, but even this is not enough punishment for a wife who chose to leave her husband's bed and board: the noble husband Archibald can hardly be left on stage at the end of Act IV with a wife surplus to his requirements. So the errant Lady Isabel promptly, and conveniently, decides to die herself, remarking to Archibald, 'Our little William awaits us now. Keep a little corner of your heart for your poor, lost Isabel.'

Isabel was played for the first time in London with great success by Avonia Jones. Her portrayal of the wild burst of agony with which the unfortunate mother threw herself upon the lifeless body of her child was especially commended. The pathos of this piece of acting made a profound impression on the audience. For good measure the play also included a short scene or two in which Archibald Carlyle and the wicked Levison ran as rival candidates for Parliament.

When the piece was first given in London, the critics, wishing it well, added the information that the pantomime of *King Chess* (or *Tom the Piper's Son and See-Saw Margery Daw*) concluded the evening's entertainment. While the audience sobbed with Lady Isabel, they also wanted a good measure of sausages and red-hot pokers to cheer them up at the end.

Irving's portrayal of the betrayed husband was commended as being 'quiet and gentlemanly'. A gentlemanly performance was much appreciated, possibly because there was a great discrepancy between the high-born heroes in the plays and the low-born raffish actors who represented them. The theatre had not shaken free from the trappings of the rogues and vagabonds of the past. Even fifty years later trains were said to carry 'Fish and Actors' – in that order.

The lowly character of the actor was something which occupied the mind of Irving. His beautiful art deserved both a better status and a better background. One day he would change it all. Instead of farmhouse kitchens doing service for every play, he would cause cloud-capped towers and gorgeous palaces to rise which would reflect the vision in his mind and astonish the world.

Endurance was needed – but 'how long a time lies in one little word!'

Chapter 4

Some Heroines and a Villain Unknown

When Irving left Manchester he was twenty-seven years old and had been nearly nine years on the stage. But still the touring went on, fish and actors being shunted with the scenery from town to town – Liverpool, the Isle of Man, Edinburgh, back to Manchester – and although the parts were varied Irving was still little more than a walking gentleman.

Despite the numerous parts he had played, and despite certain successes, his real status had not changed, and the reviews did little to encourage him.

Liverpool boasted two weekly journals, called *Tomahawk* and *Porcupine*, and they did their best to live up to their names. *Tomahawk* said that Irving was a sterling actor, but had many disagreeable peculiarities: licking his lips, wrinkling his forehead, and speaking through his nose. The tone of his voice was not liked either; it had a certain disagreeable drowsiness. He would do better if he were more himself and stopped falling into a monotony of attitude which was far from pleasing.

But there were some consolations. At Liverpool he met the famous comedian Charles Mathews again, and from him he received much encouragement. Mathews produced a play called *The Silver Lining*, and in this Irving won some praise as Arthur Merivale, another villain. Even *Porcupine* retracted its prickles and offered praise. There was something handsomely diabolic in the fixed sneer on Irving's appropriately pale face; and the almost snarling tone in which he gave some of his most disagreeable speeches added immensely to his portrayal. Suddenly *Porcupine* seemed to feel Irving's power – it added that another actor might have made the part ridiculous but with Mr Irving manner, bearing, facial expression and voice become full of alarming suggestiveness. It should be recalled that suggestive, a word often used about Irving's acting, has changed its meaning. In Victorian days it simply meant an ability to suggest, or to raise ideas in the mind of the audience.

In Liverpool, in the role of Arthur Merivale, Irving was stretching out to touch the future. He was said, at the height of his powers, to have a mesmeric quality, an ability to coerce the audience into believing in terror, and it was a real terror which he knew how to communicate. This was the first time he had touched that power at the centre of his art.

In another small part, his make-up was said to have been much above the smallness of the part he played. The wily hypocrite was noticeable in every lineament of face, form, and voice. The thin, black moustache gave a ghastly grimness to his smile that might freeze the blood in the veins of anyone over whom the wretch had power.

Another critic described his make-up as being like Mephistopheles in reduced circumstances, with a cross of German philosopher and a dash of Wilkie Collins's Count Fosco. This description gives a vivid picture of that quality of strangeness in Irving which had been his greatest disability and was to prove his most shining asset.

He later remembered his days in Liverpool as days of apprenticeship and struggle. 'Perhaps I was not quite so buoyant as to anticipate the course that events were to take. What I did in Lime Street I have forgotten, but what other people did, or failed to do, had the effect of leaving me to walk that thoroughfare with a total lack of anything tangible to cling to.' Hardships are forgotten by others when a man attains his goal. The man himself does not forget; the scars they leave are permanent.

His employment in Liverpool ended, and at Christmas 1865 he was again forced to take an engagement in the Isle of Man for three days, playing farces and pantomimes with amateurs.

It was as low a point in his career as the moment when he had been glad to accept warm underclothes from a fellow actor. But his sense of power within, as always, held him on course, and, in 1866, he was at last given the chance to create an original part.

Dion Boucicault, busy as always, was seeking a man to play the villain in his new piece *The Two Lives of Mary Leigh* – afterwards to be called *Hunted Down*. Unable to find the right man, he suddenly thought of Irving, who had played the villain Hardress Cregan in his touching piece *The Colleen Bawn*. When this play had been produced in Manchester, Boucicault had thought little of Irving's acting as Cregan, but now, presumably when he was having some difficulty in casting his new masterpiece, he recalled Irving. He was a stop-gap villain who could fill the bill – at least in Manchester.

The programme of *Hunted Down* reads like a trailer for an old-fashioned film, but unlike a film trailer it gives away the plot.

FIRST ACT	The Home of Mary Leigh. A picture by John Leigh R.A. 'Shut in with flowers and spanned by a cloudless sky' – a Dark Shadow is flung across the painting.	
SECOND ACT	Scene 1.	Scudamore's lodgings – The Gambler's Home.
	Scene 2.	The Bowling Green at Mount Audley The Pursuit John's picture becomes faded and the colours fly.
	Scene 3.	The Shrubbery – Mary is Hunted Down.
THIRD ACT	The Dark Shadow is dissolved and John Leigh's picture is restored.	

When Boucicault asked Irving to play Scudamore, the young actor had been long enough on the stage to know that if the word of princes is not to be relied on, the word of authors and theatrical managers is even less stable. He agreed to play the part of Scudamore with the proviso that should the play succeed with the public and be brought to London he should remain in the part. He was beginning to feel the extent of his power.

On 30 July 1866, *The Two Lives of Mary Leigh* opened in Manchester. It was soundly trounced by the local critics as having a trashy plot; even the dialogue was condemned. Ironically enough, in view of

Boucicault's previously tepid attitude towards the actor, Irving was held to have saved the play from total disaster. Even the *Manchester Guardian* abandoned its customary leery approach to his acting. His Scudamore showed progress. He had begun to realise and reflect the subtle traits which in inferior hands are overlooked: 'Mr Irving never neglects the little things which go far to sustain the unity of a character, nor does he deal with them with any seeming art.'

At last his capacity to use art to conceal art was beginning to be recognised. The ten years of touring and trials were nearly at an end. He had played 588 parts up to that July of 1866. It was a formidable apprenticeship.

On the strength of his polished and villainous performance as Scudamore, he received no less than three offers of work – from Boucicault himself, from Charles Reade, and from Tom Taylor. They were an impressive trio of men, writers of crude melodramas and farces. Everything and anything was grist to their theatrical mill. They were prolific plagiarisers of French plays, but that was a cross-Channel traffic which had been going on since the time of Vanbrugh. These men did not improve on the originals; they bowdlerised them and hacked them to pieces to suit the taste of their audiences.

Looking at the faces of those solemn bearded men, Taylor and Reade, it is difficult to realise that in their time they were regarded as raffish bohemians of fiery temperament and artistic feeling. Even Boucicault with his thin whiskers and watch-chain was of a respectable man-about-Pall-Mall appearance. Yet he was, in origin, that joke of the music hall, the son of his mother's lodger. Born in Dublin, even the year of his birth carries a question mark. In spite of his English education, he had a thick Dublin accent which precluded him from playing the fine gentleman in the plays of the period. At the end of his career he departed under a small financial cloud to America where he prudently remained. The Victorians did not always live up to their outward appearance.

Charles Reade remarked that Irving was an eccentric, serious actor. He was afterwards to play an even greater part in shaping the course of Irving's career, for it was he who tempted Ellen Terry back to the stage. But that was years ahead. He was essentially a novelist, but had written *Masks and Faces* in which Irving had played in Edinburgh. The best playwright of the three was Tom Taylor, whose plays and people still keep their feeling for life in spite of their old-fashioned dialogue. The worst was Dion Boucicault, whose first play, *London Assurance*, was his best.

But, like many bad writers, Boucicault was complacent and undeterred by the scathing comments about *The Two Lives of Mary Leigh*. He had accepted an offer to transfer it to London from Miss Louisa Herbert, then in management at the St James's Theatre. Miss Herbert was a beauty who had supplied many of the pre-Raphaelites with angelic faces for their canvases. She was anxious to suffer beautifully as Mary Leigh, and was prepared to take on Irving as part of her business arrangement. But in the prudent, if unangelic, way of managers, she only agreed provided that he on his side agreed to become stage manager as well as acting his original part.

To act as stage manager at the time was the equivalent of helping to produce the play, and this was an added burden to an actor about to seize his first opportunity to shine in a part which he knew suited him and to which he could give the full value of his strange personality.

But even this first chance eluded him. For some reason the production of *Hunted Down* was delayed. The first production in which he appeared on his return to London was *The Belle's Stratagem*, an old comedy by Mrs Hannah Cowley, dating from the late eighteenth century. Written in imitation Sheridanesque dialogue, it was said to have been 'much admired by Queen Charlotte and performed for George III and his family once every season'.

The hero, a grand eighteenth-century gentleman, was new to Irving, and he thought it did not suit him. 'I felt that this was the opinion of the audience soon after the play began. The house appeared to be indifferent.' This was not perhaps surprising, as the whole production was haphazard. One critic said 'it was execrably put on the stage. In four or five different scenes intended to represent interiors of various rooms in *gentlemen's* houses, we had a wing on which was painted a rickety old cupboard surmounted by jam-pots and pickle jars. On the other side was a bit of a cottage; over the jam-pots hung a portrait.'

One possible reason why this comedy had endured into Irving's age was the touches of patriotic chauvinism which occur here and there in the dialogue. Doricourt remarks: 'I never found any man who I could cordially take to my heart, and call friend, who was not born beneath a British sky,' and he invokes 'Curses on the house in which British ladies shall sacrifice to foreign ways the grace of modesty.'

In spite of the pickle jars, and the fact that Miss Herbert, who played Letitia Hardy, received all the notices, Irving managed to take the audience with him in the mad scene, and during the play's short run was called for every night in the middle of the Act. This was considered a remarkable compliment and it was carefully pointed out in the public prints that Irving was not connected with the management, and, what was more, had no friends in the front of the house.

At last, on 5 November 1866, he opened in *Hunted Down*, to immediate recognition:

'Of Mr Irving's Rawdon Scudamore I find difficulty in speaking too highly. His make-up and general tone indicate precisely the sort of scamp intended by Mr Boucicault. When he is seedy, his seediness is not indicated by preposterous rags or by new trousers with a hole in them; his clothes are well, but not too well-worn. In the second act which shows him under more prosperous circumstances his prosperity does not take the form of flashy coats, white hats, and patent leather boots; he is dressed as a roué of some taste would dress himself. The cool, quiet insolence with which he treats his devoted wife, the insolence of a man who is certain of her love, and wishes he was not – is the finest piece of undemonstrative acting that I have witnessed.'

The critics were unanimously laudatory. There were two eminent people in a box for this first night, distinguished in letters and good judges of the art of the player. These were George Eliot and her acknowledged lover, George Henry Lewes. Lewes was a leading critic and connoisseur of acting. Learned in French, German and Spanish, he had travelled and done theatrical criticism in many different countries. The couple were completely absorbed by *Hunted Down*, and even more by the appearance of Henry Irving in the role of the villain. To the inquiry of the lady: 'What do you think of him?' George Lewes said, 'In twenty years he will be at the head of the English stage.' She replied: 'He is there, I think, already.'

George Henry Lewes was under no illusions about the drama in nineteenth-century England, which he considered to be in a deplorable state of decline. He also remarked on the gradual cessation of all attempts at serious dramatic literature. He was not deceived by bombastic pseudo-poetry or heart-warming domestic scenes. But, however low an opinion he had of the drama of his time, he had the honesty to salute Irving the actor, in spite of the poverty of his material.

From October 1866 to November 1867 Irving played fourteen parts, including Joseph Surface in *The School for Scandal*, and Count Falcon, one of Ouida's more unlikely characters, in an adaptation of her book *Idalia*.

In December 1867 he moved to the Queen's Theatre, where he acted in *Katherine and Petruchio*, Garrick's version of *The Taming of the Shrew*.

There he acted with Ellen Terry for the first time. She later said that she had met him on a very foggy night in December 1867, possibly Boxing Day. Acting with Henry Irving ought to have been, she said, a great event in her life, but 'at the time it passed me by and left no wrack behind'.

She dismissed all the imaginary accounts of their first meeting as fairy tales:

'Until I went to the Lyceum Theatre, Henry Irving was nothing to me, and I was nothing to him. I never consciously thought he would become a great actor. He had no high opinion of *my* acting! He has said since that he thought me at the Queen's Theatre charming and individual as a woman, but as an actress *hoydenish*! I believe that he hardly spared me even so much definite thought as this.'

Ellen's view of Irving at the turning point in his career shows an insight and feeling which cuts across many of the romantic legends which were to cling around him:

'His soul was not more surely in his body than in the theatre, and I, a woman who was at this time caring more about love and life than the theatre, must have been to him more or less unsympathetic. He thought of nothing else, cared for nothing else; worked day and night; went without his dinner to buy a book that might be helpful in studying, or a stage jewel that might be helpful to wear. I remember his telling me that he once bought a sword with a jewelled hilt and hung it at the foot of his bed. All night he kept getting up and lighting matches to see it, shifting its position, rapt in admiration of it.'

Ellen, remembering her first impressions of his acting, said he could express very little. She had been on the stage as a child. It was her home, but he was stiff with self-consciousness – his eyes dull, and his face heavy. Both of them played very badly.

He had been toiling away in the provinces for eleven years, and until he played Rawdon Scudamore he had no substantial success. Even this small triumph was wiped out by the bad notices he collected for his Petruchio. Henry Irving's power was imprisoned, and it was only after long and weary years that he succeeded in setting it free.

Apart from the advantage of having been a child actress, Ellen, being truly professional, was getting £15 a week to Irving's £8, which added to her feeling that he could hardly be a good actor.

Irving's early biographers, after recording Ellen's first appearance, then remark that after playing Katherine to his Petruchio, 'Miss Terry retired into private life'. This short sentence was an attempt to bring down the curtain on her complicated love-life. She had been married to the painter G. F. Watts, who spent a good deal of time painting her but in other respects does not appear to have relished the role of husband and lover. He had lived for some time under the innocent protection of a Mrs Prinsep, being kept by her, living in her house, allowing her to foster his talent, and suffering gently from ill health. When he married Ellen, she was a bouncy, healthy sixteen and he was well on into his forties. After their divorce some years later, the Signore, as he was called in artistic circles, drew a hazy picture of their relationship. 'Very soon after his marriage', according to the Signore, 'he had found how great an error he had made. Linked to a most *restless and impetuous* nature, accustomed from earliest childhood to the stage, and forming her ideas of life from the exaggerated romance of sensational plays . . . demands were made upon him which he could not meet without giving up all the professional aims his life had been devoted to.' Her recollections of this ten-month marriage, in the refined atmosphere of Little Holland House on Campden Hill, are equally sketchy, and mostly concerned with the people she met and the silk dresses she wore.

Mrs Prinsep had arranged the marriage, and now she brought it to an end. Ellen was as quickly discarded as she had been taken up and went back to live with her family. She had achieved nothing except an allowance of £300 a year. She was not yet divorced, merely *declassée*, an embarrassment to her family who, she said, 'practically drove her back to the stage'.

This was the moment when she met Irving for the first time. The renewal of her stage career was not to last. Back in her home, with her broken marriage and a hatred of the theatre which had bounded her whole life from early childhood, she was unhappy and dissatisfied.

At this point she 'bolted', as the current saying went, with Edward Godwin, an architect given to designing Gothic fantasies. Godwin was also in his forties, and does not appear to have been in love with Ellen. From the veiled references in her 'Story of my Life' she seems to have gone to Paris with him before they settled down in Hertfordshire. The idyllic picture she paints of her rural existence has more *rapport* with a play of the period than with real life. As far as her family was concerned she had simply disappeared from their lives. When a lovely woman stooped to folly in the 1860s she was prepared to be dead in all but name to her family.

The situation was not improved by Ellen's sister Kate, a rising star in the theatre, and considered by some, including her father, to be one of the best young actresses on the stage. She appears to have been perfect for playing the pure young heroines of the time. In 1867 she met and married Arthur Lewis in the teeth of his family's opposition, and was wafted from the background of theatrical digs to the heights of Campden Hill were she lived in great grandeur with relays of servants.

The play *Trelawny of the Wells* is supposed to have been based on Kate's romance. But the real life Kate had a much greater inner toughness than 'Rose', and on Campden Hill she lorded it over her household and servants as to the manner born. She had not played aristocratic heroines for nothing. Nor was she prepared to jeopardise her new-found grandeur by association with a sister with a sullied reputation.

Ellen may have been dead in all but name, but now melodrama flowed from the stage into real life.

A body was fished out of the Thames – a young, slim, blonde body, which Ellen's father identified as his daughter Ellen. ('One more unfortunate gone to her death.') Mrs Terry, more practical, refused to believe it was Ellen and stoutly maintained that her daughter Ellen had a birthmark on her left arm, though here the old actress had made a mistake in the script because the birthmark was on Ellen's hip.

Possibly Mrs Terry knew better than to believe that Ellen, with her basically practical nature, was likely to plunge to a watery grave – whatever had happened to her. Ben Terry, however, continued to believe the story, and his two daughters Floss and Marion, away at boarding school, were duly put into deep mourning.

When Ellen heard the grisly story she reappeared from her rural solitude – to be forgiven by her family, if not reconciled with them. There was little question of her being received on Campden Hill by Kate in her glittering respectability, and the rest of the Terrys had to be careful too if they wanted to profit by Kate's elevation in the social sphere.

So Ellen 'retired into private life', and there she remained for six years. Her mode of life could not be condoned by her family and she accepted that. But her glowing accounts of washing babies, rising at six, feeding two hundred ducks and chickens, walking across the common to fetch the milk, and going to church in a blue cotton frock draw a pink-and-blue veil over any reality which may have crept in. Did she realise from the first that Godwin was as useless a provider as Watts, or was her delight in her two children so overwhelming as to obscure reality? Her gushing accounts give no clue.

While this alleged idyll was being performed in Hertfordshire, Irving toiled on with his eyes on the tinselled crown which he had set himself to gain. He was back in London, and it seemed as if at last the driving force of his ambition was about to open the door to success.

He began to think of marriage. When in Manchester he had met a young actress called Nelly Moore. She had already appeared in London when she met Irving, and seems, like Kate Terry, to have typified the heroine so acceptable to the Victorian stage. She was fair, with vast quantities of golden hair. The stiff photograph which remains of her gives the impression of a round-faced girl with dark shadows under her large eyes, who could easily be typecast as a wronged heroine.

The tangled tale of Nelly and young Irving is full of inconsistencies and question marks. He is supposed to have fallen in love with her when they were in Manchester together, and to have been a constant caller at the lodgings she shared with her mother. The whole Moore family, like the Terrys, were on the stage. Nelly was the rising star in a family of actors. Shortly after her spell in Manchester, she was asked to join Buckstone's company at the Haymarket, London, where she was hailed as a shining asset to the company.

While she was succeeding in London Irving had stayed in the provinces, and during that low point of his career at the end of 1865 and the beginning of 1866, when he was accepting any hand-to-mouth engagement he could get, she was delighting the stalls and circle in the capital. He had written to her with gloomy accounts of his failures. It would not have been surprising if Nelly had failed to be as sympathetic towards Irving as perhaps he felt he deserved. The professional tensions between ambitious actors and actresses can cut across their personal feelings, and very often succeed in destroying them.

The story goes that when Irving fell in love with the sweet and charming Nelly he cherished in his heart the thought that one day when fame came to him, as he knew it would, they would marry. His success as Rawdon Scudamore had put him on a level with her; they were both acting in London, and there was no longer a professional gap between them.

At this point the tentative love story becomes less clear. Irving was asked to a party by the critic Clement Scott. This was to take place in the leafy suburb of Kensington. The reception was in Linden Gardens, and Irving went to the wrong house. It was while he was engaged in complicated explanations with the servant that Miss Florence O'Callaghan, tall, statuesque daughter of Surgeon-General O'Callaghan (of her Majesty's Indian Army) appeared in the hall to clarify the situation. Florence was already dressed for the same party, and she and Irving went together.

Florence instantly fell in love with the young actor. He was a breath of another and more interesting world, and at the age of 30 his looks had not hardened and he still retained a romantic poetical air. To a strictly brought up girl of the period, he must have seemed like one of the heroes of a drama who had suddenly stepped from the stage into her life.

Irving does not seem to have fallen in love with Miss Florence, but in the context of the sharp social differences of the age it would be surprising if he had not been impressed by the cool assurance and aristocratic bearing of the girl. If she saw him as a figure of poetry and romance, he may have seen her as one of the haughty aristocratic heroines he had, up to that moment, encountered only on the stage. The attraction of opposites, added to the fascination of a door opening to another world, is not to be discounted when it comes to the relations between men and women.

When Irving first met Miss Florence through that eminent if lenient critic, Clement Scott, he is supposed to have been still happily in love with Nelly Moore. They are said to have met again on the same loving terms as when they were in Manchester, and Irving was visiting her in the lodgings she shared with her mother in Soho Square. It is a touching picture, and may be the truth. But Irving's driving will was ever set towards his goal. Nothing was to frustrate his achieving it. He had written to his parents that whatever rumours they may have heard about his marrying were untrue. Sentimental passages with Miss Moore were irrelevant to his purpose. Or so it seemed.

Yet in the event the skeins of their two destinies were never disentangled completely either in life or even in death, for an enigma remains, tantalising and impossible either to solve or to dismiss permanently from the mind. It is possible that the cold words of Henry had come back to Nelly by devious routes and may have lost nothing in the repetition. She may have suspected that Irving's ambitions came before his affection for her. His eyes were ever fixed on the future, and his hands ready to grasp the glittering sword-hilt of fame.

Possibly Nelly had heard of his meetings with the General's daughter. In the context of the pretensions and social background of the 1860s, she was no match for the lady from Linden Gardens. Women do not care to be treated as mere appendages to a career, and it is easy for other more insinuating men who are not so devoured by the future to take the place of ambitious rivals. Whatever the reason for the rift, Nelly Moore and Irving were no longer on the same terms when they were engaged to play together at the Queen's Theatre, London, in 1868.

One of the plays in which they acted was *Oliver Twist*, with Irving playing Sikes to Nelly's Nancy. This play was dramatised by John Oxenford from Dickens's novel. The critics damned the play, they damned Toole's Artful Dodger, but they praised Nelly as Nancy and Henry Irving as Bill Sikes.

'Nancy has always, in spite of her cotton gown, cheap shawl, curl-papers and her street door key, been a real favourite with the readers of the story and Miss Moore equally retains the sympathies of those who see the play. Her acting is full of gentleness, force, pathos and ready – when the need is – to brighten into humour. As for Mr. Irving, in the grim brutality of Sikes's face there lives a rooted bitterness of loathing for himself, his life, his luck, his surroundings, which exhibits to us a probable source of all his callous and unmitigated ruffianism.'

Irving was once asked how he had managed to portray a cockney ruffian so well. He said that he had watched such people carefully in the markets, on street corners, and outside public houses. Almost unaware, he used his memory for people as a painter would use a sketch-book.

In the same season at the Queen's Theatre Irving played Joseph Surface to Nelly's Lady Teazle, and in *London Assurance*, Cool to Nelly's Grace Harkaway.

During this theatre engagement Miss O'Callaghan became extremely jealous of Nelly, and wrote cattily to Irving reporting gossip and denigratory opinions about the actress. Irving wrote back to say how much he disliked the retailing of gossip, and the condescending opinions of others: 'These I cannot endure. They tingle through my veins and cause my blood to circulate.' Florence had made the female mistake of being cruel about her rival, and had roused Irving's pride not only in his former affection for the girl, but in his profession. Condescension was something he was not prepared to accept.

Most of Irving's early biographers skate carefully over his relations with women and concentrate on burning incense to his theatrical reputation. It may have been true that Nelly Moore was the one love of his life, and could have been the perfect complement to his career. But it is hard not to suspect that there were misunderstandings and clashes of career on both sides.

Early in 1869, while Irving was still acting at the Queen's Theatre, Nelly was taken ill and left the company. Her mother and sister were in America touring, and she was alone in her lodgings in Soho Square. Irving called round and was told that she had been struck down by scarlet fever and that her life was in danger. Again this may have been true, but subsequent events seem to raise a slight but permissible doubt about the 'scarlet fever'.

Unable according to the customs of the time, to visit her in person, Irving asked a woman friend of his to go and see if she could help to nurse the sick girl. So on 22 January Laura Friswell went to call on the ailing actress. The sun was shining, and as the girl went towards the house she met Irving rushing away. She looked up at the windows. The blinds were drawn. Irving halted for a second in the street and told her briefly that Nelly Moore was dead, and then he pushed the bunch of violets he carried into her hands. She muttered some inadequate words, regretting that so beautiful and talented a girl should die so young.

His reply was curious: 'It is not always a misfortune to die young'.

The rest of the story is shrouded in one of those impenetrable fogs which drifted up from the river in novels of the period. It was said that a man with whom Nelly had fallen in love had done her a 'grave injury' and that Irving had come face to face with the villain after Nelly's death and had told him that 'his guilt may have been buried with his victim, but the suspicions remained'. It was a line from one of Irving's favourite melodramas, and it is difficult not to suspect that 'scarlet fever' may have been a polite euphemism for a miscarriage, or possibly an abortion.

Whatever the reasons for the girl's death, their misunderstandings and tentative love passages were over. When Irving himself died many years later, a picture of Nelly was found stuck on to the back of one of himself taken at the time of her death. Those who die young are not forgotten and the charm of their personalities and the flower of their beauty can remain forever unsullied and untainted by life's shifts and evasions. They have many advantages over the living, as Henry Irving implied to Laura Friswell in the street in the sunshine outside the house where the blinds were drawn.

It is a curious, sad little story, as if the errant heroines and evil villains which the two actors had played had suddenly come to life and the youthful dying heroine of so many of the dramas they had simulated had suddenly become the truth.

The blinds were drawn in Soho Square and the violets soon faded, but in Linden Gardens the lamps were lit and Miss Florence O'Callaghan was waiting.

Chapter 5

Wedding Bells and Sleigh Bells

Florence O'Callaghan, having fallen in love with Irving, conducted her campaign to marry him with neat military precision and determination.

Her family's pretensions, and their opposition to her infatuation, pushed the couple nearer to the whirlpool of marriage. Irving's iron will to succeed in everything he did was in fact spurred on by the family's disapproval, and his grief at the death of Nelly Moore demanded the solace which the devotion of Florence seemed to hold out.

In India, her father, the Surgeon-General, had come to a quick choleric boil and had forbidden all communication between the lovers. Had the General consulted literature he might have realised that there is nothing like a clandestine romance to push a modest flirtation over the border into a grand passion.

An actor! It was not to be thought of – not for the daughter of a man who had been Master-at-Arms to William IV. Good-looking daughters were to be bartered and not to be let go at knock-down prices to actors with an uncertain future. Actually, Florence's own brother-in-law was a mere phrenologist at Ludgate Circus, but that connection was brushed aside and forgotten.

Florence may have sensed the power in Irving and felt that he was going to become one of the great figures of his age. Although the petty pretensions of her mother and family still clung round her, like Elizabeth Barrett she was driven and she was drawn.

When Irving's London season came to an end in the spring of 1869, Florence's family finally if reluctantly agreed to an engagement. Irving went off happily on a lucrative tour with his friend J. L. Toole.

Florence wanted to get married as soon as possible, but Irving wrote counselling caution and delay; he did not want her to start married life tumbling about from one town to another. Eventually Florence agreed they should wait until the end of the tour. There had been many doubts on both sides; reproaches from Florence and misunderstandings on Irving's side. He upbraided her for her coldness even as late as July, the month they were to be married. Finally he wrote and asked her point blank *if* she still loved him as she had, and added '*answer this*', underlining the words.

The very different society of the genial J. L. Toole and the cheerful suppers after the show with his friends must have given Irving many a pang and pause for thought. But the assurances of love, from a good-looking, high-born girl seemed to outweigh momentary doubts. The people of Irving's day, despite their strict moral code, were apt to veer between mistaking physical attraction for true love and marrying for self-interest, regarding passion as an irrelevance. Both Florence and Irving seem to have been caught in the former trap, while their heads were urging them to a different course of conduct.

By July, Irving had paid off his debts with the proceeds of his tour, all legal matters had been settled and only one thing was missing – a secure background and a safe career. This Irving could not supply.

Florence's family, having agreed to the delayed engagement, were finally forced to agree to the marriage. On 15 July 1869 the General's daughter was married to Henry Irving, who, to please her family and make the union absolutely legal, had taken out the licence in the name of Brodribb. They were married in the parish church of St Marylebone, in London, and Mr Morgan, Florence's brother-in-law, gave her away. As is so often the case in marriages when sharp social differences divide the consenting parties, Irving's family did not choose to brave the upper-crust stares of the bride's family.

Irving's father, Samuel Brodribb, was still alive, but his mother seems to have died some time during this part of his career. She had always disapproved of her son's choice of a career, and until his outstanding success should shine out it would have been difficult for him to prove to her that the struggle had availed. Yet all through his life he constantly referred in speeches to the fact that the theatre could do good, and stand for good, and that it was not against the teaching of church or churchmen. This was a recurrent theme, as if he were forever answering his Methodist mother's objections to his profession, even after her death.

Irving chose as his best man an elegant actor called H. J. Montague. Samuel Brodribb, who did not appear at the wedding, is described in the register as 'gentleman', a somewhat inaccurate description in that day and age of a failed commercial traveller.

The reception was held at the house in Linden Gardens, Kensington, a house which remains, a lone survivor of a past age, still surrounded by a garden with romantic roses, statues of cupids, and creepers veiling the garden walls. It gives the impression of a house in the country. In the late sixties, when Irving was married, it was still remote from the offices and theatres of the City and the West End.

Three days after the wedding, reality brought Florence face to face with the facts of being an actor's wife. He was playing in *All for Money*, a piece which unfortunately did not live up to its name and quickly failed. Many years afterwards when the author died – she was called by the unlikely names of Roma Guillon Le Thière – it was said that she had produced this play. Irving, whose memory for the facts of his failures was sharp, wrote: 'No she did not, she *wrote* the comedy. Miss Amy Sedgwick produced it – and forgot to pay the actors' salaries for the last week – *I* was one of 'em.'

It was not a good beginning for the high-born Florence. The situation was mitigated by the fact that by the beginning of August Irving was chosen to play another of Dion Boucicault's villains in *Formosa, or the Railroad to Ruin*.

The *Sunday Times*, while congratulating itself on its broadminded attitude to life, went on to get muddled in its metaphors. It would leave the artist's finger, it said, free to roam at will over the gamut of life, choosing whatever notes produce the fullest harmony. But when it came to *Formosa*, the critic, and the finger, seem to have become less free to roam, for the critic whipped out his sharpest moral knife: 'To vindicate the production on the stage of such scenes as those exhibited in Mr. Boucicault's second act, on the ground that they are common, would justify a good many things dramatists are not likely to attempt.'

Then the *Sunday Times* had a final slash at the play: 'For God's sake, let us leave to the French the exhibition of the sickly splendour and sentiment of the life of the courtesan. To exhibit at length, with however moral a purpose, the nastiness of life in the demi-monde is an innovation we see with regret.'

Manon or *La Dame Aux Camélias* might, like frogs, be food for the French, but good British appetites should be supplied with something healthier.

In spite of or perhaps because of such reviews, the piece ran for 117 nights, a very long run in the sixties. Boucicault seemed to have the knack of providing titillation without offence.

When the run was finished, Irving and his best man, H. J. Montague, resorted to the Victorian actor's stand-by, the dramatic reading. They could not even afford muscians to help the entertainment, but gave a mixed selection of pieces of uneven range: selections from *Othello*, Talfourd's *Ion*, the death of Joe the crossing sweeper from *Bleak House*, the Waterloo episode from Byron's *Childe Harold*. Irving also popped in his favourite, *The Uncle*, bones and all. The selection concluded with scenes from Sheridan's *The Rivals*. The performance was given at the Westbourne Hall, Westbourne Grove, not far from Florence's home. History does not relate whether Florence and her high-born family and friends attended.

During the winter and summer of the first year of his marriage Irving was gradually making his presence felt on the London stage. Montague and two friends had taken a lease of the Vaudeville Theatre, and here on 4 June Irving opened in *The Two Roses* by James Albery and won his first really outstanding success in the part of Digby Grant.

James Albery, who had escaped from his family's rope-making business and become a full-time playwright, had been commissioned by Montague to write the play. Not because he was considered to be a brilliant writer, but because his previous play *Coquettes* had not been produced. Mr Albery, perhaps because he was more used to dealing with rope-makers' contracts than contracts for plays, had stipulated that he was either paid compensation for *Coquettes* or commissioned to write another play.

Irving was summoned to a secret meeting with the playwright, who was impressed with his acting and had written the part of Digby Grant especially for him. The result of all these complications was a showy part in which Irving could shine for the first time in a character which was different and of his own creation. For Albery had written a success which was produced and reproduced all over the world. In the United States it was especially successful; it was produced at Wallack's Theatre in October 1870 and toured from coast to coast. It was still being played in 1883, and the last production was in May of that year at the Bijou Theatre in New York. The tough rope-maker had struck gold.

In *The Two Roses*, Lottie and Ida were played by Amy Fawsitt and Miss Ada Newton. The dapper Mr Montague played the hero, Jack. But for the first time it was Irving who merited all the notices and got them. As a character actor he was said to have no rival on the English stage. His delineation of the hollow-hearted meanness, the contemptible presumption, and the disgusting hypocrisy of Digby Grant was extraordinary. The whole impersonation was at once a work of art and a triumph of genius. Another critic took particular pleasure in the fact that he spoke the English language like an English gentleman.

The plot of *The Two Roses* was the simple one of the pretentious pseudo-gentleman who comes into a name and fortune and drops his erstwhile friends – the benevolent commercial traveller, the blind piano tuner and the lady publican – and insultingly pays them off with 'a little cheque'. His subsequent humiliation and the discovery that the real heir to the fortune is the blind piano tuner provided a neat if unlikely plot.

But the Victorians liked a good, well constructed piece, with an authentic background, in front of which moved a collection of contemporary characters like Jenkins, the commercial traveller, forced into religiosity by his wife, and Digby Grant himself, who typified the parvenu of the period. Jack Wyatt, a writer and suitor to one of the 'Two Roses', goes in for some fine speeches. He has some romantic views on the role of women which, in his opinion, is to stitch up the souls of men which have been sadly torn and frayed in their scramble through the world. The sweet office of woman is, he alleges, to come with her love as with a needle and thread and sew up the rents which the thoughtless make in a loving life.

The lawyer Furnival takes a less rosy view: 'Women are like boots, very useful and desirable, but a torment if you get a misfit' – a sentiment which has a nice hard-wearing quality.

All ends on a financially happy note, with Ida about to marry the newly enriched blind Caleb, Digby Grant's bacon saved, and Jack, secure in the possession of Lottie, reciting:

One like the rose when June and July kiss,
One like the leaf-housed bud young May discloses,
Sweetly unlike, and yet alike in this –
They are – Two Roses.

The published piece concludes with a neat map showing where all the characters should stand at the final curtain. Digby Grant is placed behind Lottie, the fair rose, but no doubt the audience soon made sure that he was the nearest to the footlights, where he was to stay for over thirty years.

Irving, after twelve years of struggle, could at last see the future opening before him with well-founded confidence.

Later he admitted that, like his portrait of Bill Sikes, Digby Grant had been drawn from life. He had based Digby Grant on the Chevalier Wykoff, an old buck from the court of Napoleon III to whom he had been introduced at the house of James McHenry, an Anglo-American financier whom he had met in London. The Chevalier was one of those international social characters who exist in every age. He had been born in Philadelphia, and was supposed to have acted as an agent of Napoleon III and, after the débâcle of the Franco-Prussian war, to have smuggled the last remaining treasures of the Bonaparte family into England.

From Wykoff, Irving borrowed mannerisms and ways of dressing in the outmoded D'Orsay manner. When Wykoff was old, ill, and no longer a social asset, Irving sent him grapes, and the old man smiled, saying that he knew Irving had 'taken him off' in *The Two Roses*. Although the superficial shell may have been borrowed from Wykoff, the character was Irving's own creation. He said: 'If you do not pass a character through your own mind, it can never be sincere'. The Chevalier, once seen, had passed through the actor's mind and reappeared as Digby Grant.

While it may have been *The Two Roses* all the way on stage, off stage with Miss Florence the path of true love had taken a wrong turning. Florence's capricious temper and social pretensions had grown rather than diminished once she had married Irving. She was determined to oppose and disapprove of everything connected with his profession.

His habit of relaxing with friends over a drink or two after coming home from the theatre she exaggerated into debauchery. A few jokes with Toole were looked at askance as vulgarity beyond the bourgeois pale of Linden Gardens. No doubt visits home to mother revived maternal disapproval and stoked the fires of revolt against Irving in Florence's mind.

Even during the rehearsals for *The Two Roses*, an anxious time for any actor, Florence continued to nag and to disapprove. Irving put it down to the fact that she was in the last stages of her pregnancy, and pandering to her caprices he hired himself lodgings near Drury Lane, where he could concentrate on bringing Digby Grant to life in peace, away from Florence's anger.

Little Henry Brodribb Irving was born on 5 August 1870 in London, and Florence took herself and the baby off to the seaside to recuperate. Irving went back to his old bachelor days, writing cheerfully to James Albery, asking him to come back so that 'we can have long chats', and adding in quotation marks a line from *The Two Roses*: 'Why did I marry?'

Florence, now even more ennobled by motherhood, returned from Southend. For a few weeks all was sweetness and light, but soon the atmosphere created by her trenchant remarks and general air of disapproval hung like a pall over any passing success which Irving achieved. Financially, Irving was disappointed. With a wife and child, and an old father who needed support in the form of constant and regular postal orders, the future again did not look bright. He asked the management for an increase in salary to bridge the gaps, but was refused.

By December 1870 he was separated from Florence and living with a friend, co-actor and former best man, H. J. Montague, in Mount Street.

He wrote very coldly to his father about his marriage, never referring to his wife except to say that he was allowing her four pounds a week when he was in work, to cease when he was 'resting'. There was, he said, no question of a legal separation, and he added that mother and daughter were together, very cosy with Mama's five hundred and Florence's two hundred.

After a month or two with Mama, Florence became tired of the situation, and went round to see Irving to ask him to take her back. He was prepared to start married life again – but not in the house of his mother-in-law, from whom he would even refuse to accept two weeks' rent. The tone of his letter hardly breathes the impatient air of disconsolate love, but rather suggests someone putting a business proposition down on paper before agreeing terms. Florence had chosen a man of a more inflexible purpose than she had imagined.

Irving, having stated his terms, wrote gladly to his father that his married life was about to recommence on a firm and happy footing. He had good reason for optimism. At the end of March 1871 he took his benefit. After the performance of *The Two Roses*, he came in front of the curtain and announced that he was going to recite Hood's poem *Eugene Aram*.

This poem, which was later turned into a play, had always had an obsessional appeal for Irving. His acting, particularly with regard to his more sensational portraits, was constantly described as mesmeric. But an actor is only great insofar as he is able to tap the deep well-springs of unconscious feelings in his audience. Irving was able to understand and reflect the deep sense of romanticism, sentimentality, gruesomeness, self-deception, self-discipline, and sheer guts which lay at the root of the Victorian soul. On the night of his benefit, when he recited *Eugene Aram*, he demonstrated this ability.

Among the audience was 'Colonel' Hezekiah Bateman, an American who after a varied career had married Sidney Frances Cowell, sister of a comic vocalist, Sam Cowell. Mrs Bateman has been described as resembling Dickens's Mrs Crummles. She certainly produced a collection of children, and put four daughters on the stage.

At the time when Bateman saw Irving for the first time Kate Bateman was already launched, but Bateman had two other fledgelings on his hands, and also the lease of the derelict Lyceum Theatre. He may have believed in the shining talents of his female brood, but he was showman enough to know that he needed some good professional backing. He saw Irving and offered him a three-year contract to play the leading man – £15 a week rising to £19 for the third year. Before signing, Irving made one stipulation: Bateman must agree to produce a play called *The Bells*, which had recently been translated from the French. It had played with great success in Paris with Tallien, and Irving held the rights. Bateman agreed. He would have agreed to anything to save his theatre and get another daughter, Isabel, launched in a suitable manner on the London stage.

Irving went off happily on tour with *The Two Roses*, to Leeds, Bradford and Bristol. From Bristol the company crossed to Dublin, the scene of his great humiliations. This time he opened to triumphant notices and full houses. He enjoyed Dublin, the countryside around it, and staying at the Gresham Hotel. The picture of her husband drinking tumblers of punch at literary dinners and staying in luxury at one of Dublin's leading hotels incensed Florence.

Scarcely two years of marriage, one separation and a second pregnancy had shortened her temper. Irving's letters alternated between arranging for their future (credit at Maples for decent furniture) and recording that, as he was driven through County Wicklow, his soul was filled with soft, religious calm, and his eyes were full of tears. Neither the tears nor the religious calm seem to have crossed the Irish Channel or to have touched the heart of Flo.

Irving was in the highest of spirits on this tour, and when in good spirits there was nothing better than a hearty practical joke. Once, when on tour with Toole in England just before his marriage, they had hidden all the silver from an inn dining-room, jumped out of the window, and, when the alarm had been raised, promptly jumped back again, replaced the silver, and rung the bell for pudding as if nothing had happened.

In Ireland the joke was more grimly realistic. Montague and Irving, out on a picnic, were seen to be on bad terms and were heard quarrelling in loud voices. Montague insulted Irving in front of the party. Both actors disappeared and the rest of the picnickers went out on to the rocks to look for them. They found Irving with a bloody knife in his hand muttering, 'I've done it! I told him I would. He provok'd me.' When one of the party tried to come near him Irving raised the knife crying, 'Back!'

'Where is Montague?'

'There he is – the false friend!'

Irving pointed dramatically to the foot of the rocks where Montague lay prone – with his face down amongst some bushes. He was laughing so much that he had to put a handkerchief into his mouth to keep up the joke. Irving had carried the practical joke to the end and cut one of his wrists so that his menacing knife could be stained with genuine blood. His passion for realism extended even into practical joking. No doubt Florence was little amused by these actors' japes. The cost of Irving putting up at the the Gresham Hotel touched her more closely.

While in Dublin, Irving was seen by two men who were later to influence his life for good and ill. Among the audience was George

Bernard Shaw, who afterwards said that the success of *The Two Roses* was entirely due to one actor, who played in a way which Shaw had never seen before. It was 'modern'. Shaw said later that he felt instinctively that a new drama inhered in this man, though 'I had then no conscious notion that I was destined to write it.'

The other young man in the house was Bram Stoker, now only remembered as the author of *Dracula*, who was later to become Irving's friend, business manager, adviser, protector and publicity agent. Bram Stoker makes the point that he was only fourteen when he saw Irving for the first time, acting in Dublin in 1867. He had remembered him particularly because in those days performances were absolutely stereotyped. The broad lines of the play were established by more than a hundred years of usage. At the beginning of his career, Irving could only improve on the traditional method of acting and was forced to remain within the established lines of movement. Stoker remembered Irving as Captain Absolute in Sheridan's *The Rivals*, and although the play was set in its straitjacket Irving shone out as the young soldier – 'handsome, distinguished, self-dependent, with dash, a fine irony and buoyant with life and well-bred insolence'.

But with *The Two Roses* Irving had broken through the mould of tradition, and two people at least in the audience were aware of it and remembered him for the feat.

He returned to London full of hope, with his contract in his pocket, the reconciliation with his wife in his heart, and with every prospect of a glittering career and a happy family life before him.

The play in which 'Colonel' Bateman proposed to launch his daughter Isabel offered a less glittering prospect. From a story by George Sand, *La Petite Fadette*, the play had been translated from French into German, and then finally crossed the Channel where it had fallen into Mrs Bateman's hands. Mrs Bateman was much given to cobbling together her daughters' dresses for reasons of family economy. She also cobbled together plays, presumably to save paying royalties to people outside the family.

'La Petite Fadette' herself became Fanchette, a charming, capricious coquette. This was an unfortunate piece of casting because Isabel was a grave, serious-minded, religious girl who was later to become the Reverend Mother of an Anglican convent. As she skipped about the stage in peasant clothes or listened to Irving as the lovesick peasant boy, Landry Barbeau, mouthing his sentimental speeches, it was not surprising that the play lacked conviction. But Bateman had engaged Hawes Craven to paint idyllic country scenes, and jolly peasant music had been written especially for the play. All these splendours made him oblivious to the badness of the play.

Bateman, feeling the sudden chill of failure, backed up these peasant caperings with a farce by John Oxenford of *The Times*. The criticisms were lukewarm; both the play and actress narrowly missed getting their just desserts. Fanchette quickly capered off the stage, being replaced by an equally cobbled-together version of *Pickwick* by James Albery. The critics did not like this either, calling it 'pickings from Pickwick', and found one of the actors extremely offensive to good taste in the bedroom scene.

Irving's Jingle saved the play. Even the Liverpool *Porcupine* stayed to cheer, and to paint a quick vignette of his comedy method: 'He turned minor stage accidents and shortcomings to account as though they were part of the personation. The facile hands were never quiet, the plotting eyes were always glinting, and the ready tongue was never at a loss. All the other characters were completely thrown into the shade by Jingle.'

His imperturbable impudence, shabby-genteel appearance, and the dignified serenity with which he pursued his ulterior aims were all praised. The audience applauded his every scene, and at the end a 'tumultous recall brought him before the footlights'. The six hundred parts Irving had played had served him well.

At Irving's house in West Brompton, furnished on credit by courtesy of Messrs Maple, things were going better. Irving wrote to his father that everything was very comfortable at the theatre, and they were settled in their new home 'which Flo and I like very much'.

Surgeon-General O'Callaghan had returned from the hot plains of India and had retired on a comfortable pension. Far from breathing fire and brimstone against the acting profession, he had now taken a great liking to his new son-in-law who obviously had the actor's capacity to amuse. This made a change from pig-sticking and Poona. The General and the actor had tastes in common, such as sitting up late, drinking punch, and chatting. This unexpected *rapport* seems to have been a sharp disappointment to Florence and her mother. They had expected better things from the General.

Owing to lack of support for Fanchette's caperings, it became obvious even to the optimistic Bateman that the lease of the Lyceum was hardly a current asset. Money was short. Kate Bateman, touring in *Leah*, was subsidising the Lyceum to the tune of three or four hundred pounds a week. Even a dutiful daughter could not be expected to carry daughterly devotion to financial lengths beyond the call of duty. Something would have to be done.

Irving's moment had arrived. Now was the time to bring forward *The Bells*. The rights were Irving's. He had bought them from Lee Lewis, who had adapted the piece from the original French *Le Juif Polonais* by Emile Erckmann and Alexandre Chatrian. It was later alleged that this 'simple étude dramatique' had never been intended for the stage, but French theatre managers saw its possibilities as a melodrama, as did Irving.

The part of the Alsatian burgomaster had been played by Tallien, by Coquelin *père*, and by Gôt. French actors had seen the burgomaster Mathias as an easy-going Alsatian who had killed the Jew for pure gain, whose fears were based on the imminent collapse of his image of bourgeois respectability, and whose death, according to the original authors, was due to hallucinations brought on by drinking too much white wine. Mathias, in this view, was a character from Balzac's *Comédie Humaine*, and could possibly still be brought to life in this manner.

This was not Irving's reading. His strange Celtic mind had seized upon the idea and re-imagined a man who could fit in with the images he had conjured up: a conscience-haunted wretch whose naked fears would take the audience by the throat.

But there were obstacles between dream and reality. Bateman was against it, and was even amused by the thought of Irving as a middle-aged burgomaster. He was only 33 and slim – everyone knew that burgomasters were fat, red and comfortable-looking. Further chill intelligence discouraged the manager. Just before the play went into rehearsal another version, called *Paul Zegers*, had been tried at the Alfred Theatre. It opened on 13 November and closed shortly afterwards, which was not surprising as the hack author F. C. Burnand had given it a happy ending.

The failure spurred Irving on to even greater efforts to win over the sceptical Bateman. In Bateman's defence it must be said that an anonymous critic wrote: '*The Bells* is not a good play, it is poorly Englished and poorly built. One is a good deal less interested in the remorse of Mathias than in the devices of the man who plays him.' A view which it is difficult to fault.

Even Bateman was at last convinced by the fervour of Irving's belief in the play. Once convinced, he went into the production with American optimism and salesmanship. He crossed to Paris and brought back a Monsieur Singla, who had composed the original music for the French production. Music was considered to be an essential part of a melodrama. It was used to emphasise the mood as it is in films or television plays today. The 'hurry music' of *The Bells* was later much commended as lending added terror to the piece.

Bateman also decided not to penny-pinch on the scenery and costumes. Finance was provided by another American, the financier James McHenry, a man with a liking for the theatre, who had made a fortune from the Lake Erie – New York railway and could afford to indulge his tastes. Hawes Craven painted effective scenery and the play went into rehearsal.

In West Brompton, Florence was within a few weeks of the birth of her second child. She was in no mood to be sympathetic to an actor's nerves. Nor did the haunted conscience of imaginary burgomasters have the least appeal for her. Once again Irving left Florence with her mother in the fussy comfort of Linden Gardens, nursing her grievances and her pregnancy. When he came back late from rehearsals, it was not to his wife that he turned for comfort and relaxation, but to the untidy raffish atmosphere of the Bateman family. They understood his nerves, his problems, and his hopes. He could sit up late, allowing nervous tensions to be soothed with congenial companions.

During these vital rehearsals he did not see his wife at all. He was afraid that her nagging and recriminations might upset him when he needed all his powers for the task in hand. He had not only to drive himself on, but to drive and convince his fellow actors. Once the play had succeeded he felt that his wife's view of himself and his profession would suffer a sea-change. Success could be the remaking of his marriage, an optimistic view not confined to Irving.

A couple of days before the play opened, he asked Laura Friswell, the girl who had tried to call on Nelly Moore on the day of her death, and Hain Friswell, the essayist, Laura's father, if they would take Florence to the first night, sharing the stage box which had been put at Florence's disposal. This took place less than a month before the birth of Irving's second son, Laurence. Florence agreed to go; she even graciously agreed to attend a supper party which the Friswells were giving in honour of Irving after the play.

Laura Friswell saw Irving coming out of her father's study a day or two before the opening of the play. She described the actor's uncertainty at this turning point of his career:

'As he turned I saw his face – it was melancholy; then I put my head over the balusters and said "Well, so you are to act *The Bells* – are you not glad?" "It may not be a success," he said with a sigh.'

Laura replied with the assured optimism of youth that of course it would be a success, Irving was a rattling good actor, her father said so and now 'You will be a great success and I shall be the first to congratulate you.' Irving said he took the girl's words as a good omen and ran down the stairs smiling. Laura's father called out, wanting to know if she were shouting at Irving. 'Yes,' she replied. 'They are putting on *The Bells* and he don't seem at all glad.' Hain Friswell replied slowly: '*I* can understand – people are often nervous when they attain their desire.'

It was fifteen years since Irving had started out with the cheerful words: 'Here's to our enterprise', and now much had to be risked again on one play. Financial failure would ruin not only Bateman and the theatre but himself. In a frail world like that of the theatre, the cobwebs of failure cling about an actor long after the reasons for that failure are forgotten.

On that cold night on 25 November *The Bells* opened to an equally cold house. It was only one part of a triple bill, the first piece being *My Turn Next*, with the comedian George Belmore, and *Pickwick* concluding the evening, with Belmore as Sam Weller taking top billing over Irving as Jingle.

Once the initial comedy was over, Irving with his long experience of failure was only too conscious of the indifference of the house. A spirit of boredom hung over the auditorium. Now by the sheer terror and grip of his own imagination he must sweep into his cold audience and carry it on with him into horror and belief.

Gordon Craig said that he had seen *The Bells* thirty times, and he describes the beginning of the play, everything leading up to the entrance of Mathias – the storm raging outside; the sudden blowing open of a window, which smashed crockery; the looking at the clock; and, above all, the queer 'hurry music', which proved astonishingly dramatic:

'The thing Irving set out to do was to show us the sorrow which slowly and remorselessly beat him down. As no matter who the human being may be, and what his crime, the sorrow which he suffers must appeal to our hearts, so Irving set out to wring our hearts, not to give us an exhibition of antics such as a murderer would be likely to go through.'

It is hard for a modern reader to re-imagine the impact which Irving made. If the pity and terror of his performance have disappeared into the dusty wings of time, the play itself remains a curiosity. Set in the parlour of a village inn in Alsace, it is tricked out with plenty of local colour, heavy peasant furniture, stove, clock (for ticking and striking at dramatic pauses), and a large window through which snow can be seen falling:

'I do not remember to have seen so much snow since what is called the Polish Jew's winter.'

The arrival of the Jew is then described, how he had greeted them – 'Peace be with you' – opened his cloak and threw down his heavy money-belt, so that the ringing of the gold it contained could be heard. Then we learn how the Jew had disappeared and how everything had gone well for the Burgomaster since that time.

To the sound of Singla's sinister 'hurry music', Mathias the Burgomaster passes the window and enters wearing a long cloak covered with snow, an otter-skin cap, gaiters, and spurs, and carrying a large riding-whip. (Chord. Tableau.)

'It is I! It is I!'

Mathias had been to a demonstration of mesmerism at which a Parisian had sent people to sleep and made them tell him everything that weighed upon their consciences. Mesmerism was, as Irving knew from his Manchester experiences, a topical and intriguing subject for his audience and it was an intrinsic part of the play.

Once the friends and relations of Mathias are safely off stage, the play falls into the chief actor's hands. He is alone.

'Bells! No one on the road. What is this jangling in my ears? What is tonight? Ah, it is the very night – the very hour.'

The clock conveniently strikes ten, on cue.

'I feel a darkness coming over me. A sensation of giddiness seizes me. Shall I call for help?'

He answers himself promptly: 'No, no, Mathias. Have courage! The Jew is dead!'

The sound of bells draws ever nearer, and the lights fade to disclose the Bridge of Vechem, the snow-covered country and the frozen rivulet, and a lime kiln burning in the distance. The Jew is seen seated in the sledge, and there is a vision of a man dressed in a brown blouse with a hood over his head carrying an axe. The Jew in the tableau turns his ashen face towards Mathias, fixes him with his burning eyes, and the Burgomaster falls senseless to the ground.

The third act opens with merriment and drinking to celebrate the fiançailles of Annette, Mathias's daughter, and Christian, her gendarme fiancé. When the company have gone off (revelling), the curtain rises to disclose another tableau, this time a court of justice. In his dream, Mathias is accused, evidence is given against him, and he is finally put in the power of the mesmerist, who, putting him to sleep, forces the confession from him.

'To the lime kiln – how heavy he was! Go into the fire, Jew! Look, look, look – those eyes, those eyes! How he glares at me!'

The Judge pronounces sentence: 'Mathias to be hanged by the neck until he is dead.' The death knell tolls, the scene fades, and the wedding guests dance in.

'Hurry music' is heard and Mathias staggers in from his sleeping place. 'Take the rope from my neck – take the rope from my neck!' He chokes and keels over, and Catherine, his wife, removes all doubt by placing her hand on his heart and saying, 'Dead!' And the sound of sleigh bells takes over.

The Times gave the best account of the effect of this piece on the audience:

Mr H. Irving has thrown the whole force of his mind into the character, and works out bit by bit, the concluding hours of a life passed in a constant effort to preserve a cheerful exterior, with a conscience tortured 'til it has become a monomania. He is at once in two worlds between which there is no link – an outer world which is ever smiling, an inner world which is a purgatory. The struggles of the miserable culprit fighting against hope are depicted by Mr Irving with a degree of energy which seems to hold the audience in suspense. On Saturday, it was not 'til the curtain fell, and they summoned the actor before the curtain with a storm of acclamation, that they seemed to recover their self-possession.'

From this simple report the audience reaction comes alive again across the years. The stillness born of terror and belief, and the sudden pistol shots of acclamation which started the storm of applause. As the curtain fell, Irving knew that he had London in the hollow of his hand.

He went backstage to his dressing-room, convinced at last that his long struggle had been worthwhile. The tide had turned. His dressing-room was crowded with critics and friends. He took off his make-up and at last, as the theatre emptied, made his way to the carriage where Florence was waiting to go with him to the first-night supper party at the Hain Friswells.

The actor and his friends drank champagne and went over the evening's successes, speech by speech and move by move. It was a happy and triumphant occasion. At the end of the table Florence was ominously quiet, and inclined to suggest that the triumphant actor was being a bore. She was tired and anxious to get back to West Brompton. Eventually she managed to get Irving away from his friends, cutting short the moment of his greatest triumph.

Once in the carriage he still mused on the beauty of his art which was, at last, to give him the rewards he had so patiently worked for. Later Irving remembered Kean at a similar moment:

'He was in a state of too great ecstasy at first to speak, but his face told his wife that he had realised his dream and that his great powers had been instantly acknowledged. With not a shadow of doubt as to his future, he exclaimed, "Mary, you shall ride in your carriage", and taking his baby boy from the cradle, said, "and Charley, my boy, you shall go to Eton", and he did.'

Irving turned to his wife with the self-same feelings and the self-same ecstasy of achievement, and said that she would soon have her own carriage and pair.

Florence spat out her reply: 'Are you going on making a fool of yourself like this all your life?'

Irving did not reply. He spoke to the driver, who stopped the carriage. He got out. He left Florence to go back to West Brompton alone.

He walked across Kensington Gardens in the cold and darkness to the warmth and friendliness of the Batemans' house in Kensington Gore.

He neither saw nor spoke to Florence again.

With the cheers of the audience still ringing in his ears, he left his wife. She had spoiled his moment of triumph and sullied his beautiful art. A wife was perhaps surplus to an actor's requirements. He went out of her life, without an exit line, to a new beginning.

Chapter 6

Easy Tears and Hard Settlements

The Bells had opened on Saturday, 25 November and the first night audience had been rapturous, but the critics had a day to brood before taking up their pens to condemn or praise, away from the heady fervour of the playhouse. Bateman and Irving waited.

Yet even when the terror and pity of the first night was over the critics were still unanimous in their praise. Irving, like Byron, woke to find himself famous.

The *Athenaeum* spoke of the actor's ghastly power, not easy to surpass, adding that he had histrionic ability of the rarest kind. Other critics brought out their best and brightest adjectives – nothing finer had been seen for years, it was a masterly performance, and a tragic impersonation. There was hardly a dissenting voice.

Irving's own account of the sudden turn in his fortune is characteristically simple: 'Much against the wish of my friends I took an engagement at the Lyceum under the management of Mr Bateman. I had successfully acted in many plays besides *The Two Roses*, which ran three hundred nights.'

His friends felt that he should identify himself with character acting, but he did not understand the phrase. Every part was a character. His yearning was towards the 'higher drama', and even when he had been at the Vaudeville Theatre he had recited the poem 'Eugene Aram' simply to test his power over the audience when handling a tragic theme. He had succeeded. For a modern reader 'Eugene Aram' might fall into the category of the 'horrid' rather than the tragic.

When Bateman engaged the actor he told him that he would be given an opportunity to play various parts. It was in the manager's interest as well as the actor's to discover what he thought would be successful. Here the actor's idea contrasted with the manager's. Irving's thoughts ran on Hamlet and Richard III, while Bateman envisaged providing charming little roles for his daughter Isabel.

'Well, the Lyceum opened', Irving recorded, 'but did not succeed. Mr Bateman lost a lot of money and intended giving it up. He proposed to me to go to America with him. By my advice – and against his wish – *The Bells* was rehearsed, but he did not believe in it much. It was produced to a very poor house, although a most enthusiastic one. From that time the theatre prospered.'

Irving was thirty-four. He had suffered cold, hunger, disappointments, and hisses. He had been estranged from his mother and his wife. He had been cheated of his two sons. Now, at last, the curtain went up on a glittering future. He was successful, and alone.

Irving's early biographers are coy about the break-up of his marriage. 'For reasons which do not concern the public, the husband left his domicile and took up his abode with the Bateman family,' wrote one. In fact, the Batemans had some trouble in keeping Irving from drinking heavily when he came home after the evening performance. It was a Victorian failing. He remembered his uncle's bouts of drinking when he was a child. The Bateman ladies tried to compensate for his domestic disappointments with home comforts. Beef tea and sympathy were freely dispensed after the show. They realised how hard he was working and that he needed support. Every evening, besides acting in *The Bells*, he played Jingle in *Pickwick*. Even the *Observer* critic wrote that unless Mr Bateman wanted to lose the services of a valuable actor, he ought to make some arrangement to avoid his playing Mathias and Jingle on the same night. It is a pity to over-drive a willing horse.

Irving went on playing both parts until the end of the run. But the success of *The Bells* had changed the balance of relationships at the theatre. Isabel Bateman, who was to have been supported by Irving, became the supporting actress. Even Bateman, convinced though he was – by the time he read the notices – that it was his own judgement and shrewdness which had brought the golden sounds from *The Bells*, had become eager to defer to Irving's judgement.

To his credit it must be said that as soon as Bateman realised the gold-mine which the play had become he used his American enthusiasm to promote it. He placed advertisements which printed in double columns the names of the forty-one London newspapers which had praised the play, beginning with the *Athenaeum* and the *Army and Navy Gazette* and proceeding through most letters of the alphabet to *Vanity Fair*, the *Weekly Dispatch*, and the *Westminster Gazette*. Occasionally his advertising methods were considered vulgar. When the Prince of Wales was making some pompous official journey to the City, Bateman strung a garland of papier-mâché bells right across the Strand near the theatre. Officials were scandalised, but Bertie, unlike his mother, was amused.

Between the opening and end of this first season, Irving played Mathias 151 times. *Pickwick* was still running as an after-piece until March 1872, when it was replaced by *Raising the Wind*. This old farce by James Kenney, with the principal part of Jeremy Diddler much resembling that of Jingle, gave Irving similar opportunities for comic eccentricity. Both play and part had a link with theatrical history, for the first Jeremy Diddler had been 'Gentleman' Lewis, the original Faulkland in Sheridan's *The Rivals*.

When the run finished in the spring of 1872, the company went on tour. Already the pattern of touring was changing. No longer did the leading actors arrive from London to grace the local stock company and put it in the shade with a dazzling display of expert acting. Now the whole company went off to the provinces, complete with leading actors, supporting cast, and scenery.

Percy Fitzgerald described such a company *en voyage*:

'A huge theatrical train containing one of the travelling companies with all their baggage, comes up and thunders through. Here is the Pullman car in which the performers are seen playing cards, chatting, or lunching. They have their pets with them, parrots, dogs, etc. It suggests luxury and prosperity, but this ease is dearly purchased.'

So too Irving's success had been. Although his situation may have given the appearance of success and luxury, the reality was less glittering. Out of Irving's £15 a week his offending, if offended, wife was taking £8 and his ageing father another £2, which left him £5 a week on which to keep up appearances as London's leading actor. But he had won the right to choose his own plays and to see that they were done in the right way.

His goal was Shakespeare, but Bateman had well in mind the saying 'Shakespeare spells ruin, and Byron bankruptcy', and having just escaped the latter fate he was not prepared to fall into the former. Bateman had on his payroll a hack playwright, William Gorman Wills. He was one of those men who are universally acknowledged to have talent from their beginnings at university, but cannot quite make up their minds in which direction their genius lies. At first he practised as a painter, and reached the dizzy heights of depicting the royal children at Osborne in idealised crayon. But when his father died, taking his allowance into that bourne from which no interest is drawn, the Bohemian life Wills lived, as well as the number of failed geniuses who sponged on him, made it necessary for him to earn some sort of living. Like Sheridan, he turned to writing plays as a quick way of keeping afloat.

Wills had a mother, and two clubs, the Arundel and the Garrick, to support. Bateman took him up, and although two of his early plays failed he commissioned Wills to rewrite Euripides's *Medea* for Kate Bateman. She had a modest success in it.

Irving and Wills were attracted to one another's ideas. They both had an excess of optimism, an essential quality in a profession given to sudden squalls and shipwrecks. Wills put up the idea that he should write a very poetic play about the life and death of Charles I. Bateman, as an American, had few tears to shed for the Royal Martyr. But when it was intimated that Isabel Bateman would have a good chance of suffering nobly as Queen Henrietta Maria he agreed.

When Wills suggested this idea, an engraving by F. Goodall, 'The Happy Days of Charles I', was a popular adornment for drawing-rooms. It was on this contrast between death and execution and the happy children frolicking with their father at Hampton Court that the play was based.

The author, unfortunately, became inspired with his idea. The masses of poetry of inordinate length which he produced brought both Bateman and Irving to despair. There must be some human interest. The manager thoroughly disliked the ending. 'Oh, bother politics,' he said; 'we must wind up with another domestic act.' One evening in Kensington, when all possible endings had been put forward and rejected, Bateman suddenly woke from a half doze. He had found the solution – in the penny plain twopence coloured world of the toy theatre: 'I've got it! Look at the last act of *Black-eyed Susan* with its prayer book, chain and all.'

There the unjustly condemned sailor William parts with tears from his sweetheart Susan: 'Come Susan shake off your tears. There, now smile a bit we'll not talk again of graves . . . if you love your husband do not send him on the deck a white-faced coward.'

Irving, who in his time had played Seaweed, Captain Crosstree, and Lieutenant Pyke in the melodrama, intuitively understood the old showman's ideas. He persuaded the shocked poet-playwright to throw his poetry overboard and to write in a pathetic scene to bring the play to a lachrymose conclusion.

A successfully lachrymose conclusion, as it turned out. *Charles I* opened on 28 September 1872, with Isabel Bateman playing the Queen and George Belmore as Oliver Cromwell. Irving as the King was showered with praise. He looked as if he had stepped from the canvases of Rubens and Van Dyck, a magnanimous, gallant, chivalrous, right royal King, loving to his people, faithful to his friends, passionately devoted to his wife and children. The effect of the King's entrance with the royal children, dressed as Van Dyck's family group, was considered perfect.

History had been interpreted in the light of the current sentimental steel-engraving. It was still possible in Irving's day to regard civil strife and civil war as old unhappy far-off things and battles long ago, and to concentrate on the pictures conjured up by shattered domestic bliss which could bring the easy romantic tear from stalls and gallery. The *Standard* confessed shamefacedly to a very awkward lump in its throat. Another critic advised those who love a good cry to hurry to the Lyceum with a supply of pocket handkerchiefs.

Irving's interpretation of a sympathetic and noble role surprised the critics. He had unquestionably asserted his right to take the foremost place among the tragedians of the day. To Mr Irving's playing alone went up such shouts as only English throats can send forth, wrote one critic.

The author was less cheered by his notices. He was berated for historical inaccuracy. Cromwell was a travesty. There was no basis for showing him as ready to desert his cause for a mere earldom. The part was not improved by being played by George Belmore, the erstwhile Sam Weller, for Cromwell is hardly the part for a low comedian. Liberal opinion was incensed by the reading and acting of this part, which kept the pot of controversy nicely on the boil and provided endless opportunities for publicity – for the audience now declared for Cromwell, and now for the King.

Bateman was enchanted with his success, and even more gratified that his daughter had a part which suited her. She was able to drift about the stage nobly suffering with a French accent, and was even, for a change, commended for her acting.

George Belmore beat a strategic retreat from the part of Cromwell and was replaced by Henry Forrester, who was playing the part when the Prince and Princess of Wales saw the play. Everyone waited breathlessly to see what the royal reaction would be. But the audience made it an occasion for a demonstration of loyalty. When Queen Henrietta burst in at the head of the loyal gentlemen of Lincoln's Inn to the cry of 'God Save the King!', the audience took up the cry to cheer the Prince and his Princess in their flower-decked box. It was all very heartwarming.

The purists might decry Wills's travesty of history, but Irving's Charles I suffered triumphantly in his black satin suit, adorned with the rich ruffles of Spanish lace. He wrung all hearts and his parting with his children 'always made the handkerchiefs busy'.

Backstage there were no tears. All was good humour and good business.

'Lyceum – 5th Month. *Charles I.* Mr Henry Irving in his great historical impersonation. Seats can be secured one month in Advance. Additional stalls have been provided to meet the unprecedented demand.'

It was all richness and golden harvests in theatre and box office; in Irving's private life, it was haggling rather than roses all the way. His father had saved a little money from a legacy and this he was prepared to lend his famous son, in return for an insurance policy guaranteeing the loan and an agreement to pay the old man thirty-shillings a week, rain or shine, whether employed or resting.

Florence was refusing to make any settlement at all until she had been paid her arrears. She was also keeping the furniture. Irving had taken nothing except his books and pictures. Women scorned are not only disagreeable, but expensive.

Eventually the Batemans found Irving suitable rooms at the corner of Bond Street and Grafton Street, and here he was to stay for almost thirty years. He enjoyed furnishing and decorating with no interference from Florence. Friends gave him presents towards his comfort. The sight of the lonely and suffering male evokes a great deal of sympathy and virtue in the female population. To a Mrs James, who had offered him a set of rich shirt studs, he wrote back asking if she would mind giving him either an easy chair or a 'lounge' (settee).

By Christmas 1872 he was able to send extra money to his father, suggesting that he bought himself a turkey and a bottle of port, but specifying that the port should not be cheap. He spent Christmas with the Batemans, although he had seen his sons and taken the elder one to dinner at his club. Bateman had given Irving a watch and chain inscribed as an 'outward visible sign of the inward spiritual affection and esteem for his Friend H. L. Bateman'. The cup of theatrical happiness overflowed in the Bateman household.

But after a brilliant success like *Charles I*, the question was what to choose for Irving's next offering. The captive playwright Wills had been busy. He seems to have been a man of such haphazard methods of writing and absent-minded habits that it was surprising that any play was finished. He is supposed once to have boiled his watch instead of an egg. While his Bohemian life and his impassioned characters and hasty way of writing gave him the look of a genius, it was said to be a misleading look.

But he and Irving had in common a fierce romanticism, and somehow, with Irving's drive behind him, Wills finished a play, *Eugene Aram*, based on Irving's favourite dramatic poem. The real Aram, aged 55, with three sons and three daughters, had murdered a man for money, and had been duly hanged.

This would not do. Wills began all over again, giving Aram a charming fiancée, Ruth (daughter of a vicar), and turning Aram into a much-wronged man. Audiences liked pure girls and wronged men, and that was what Wills and Irving intended to give them.

The play begins with Jowell, the gardener, and his son Joey making garlands and nosegays for the wedding. There enters the stock stranger who promptly borrows a spade, letting slip the fact that he is using a false name. The stage is left clear for Aram who, to show that he is a serious character, speaks in a kind of verse:

How long ago it seems! Again I'm here
To part with her once more – and only once –
First I shall see her at the church's porch . . .

As he broods by the old sundial, Ruth trips in. He still seems broody, but admits that the green shelter of her love surrounds him. Not to be outdone with garden similes, Ruth confesses that she saw in him 'a life as gentle, blameless and pure as blows the wind o'er beds of lavender'. He wrings a confession from her that she would love him even if he had lost honour and good report, and immediately a choir of boys (off stage) sing a hymn, specially composed by Robert Stoepel.

By Act II the sinister stranger has reappeared and upset Ruth with hints about other women, which Ruth takes badly, as well she might. In the last act Aram admits to killing the man, but in mitigation explains that he had only killed to avenge wrongs done to himself, including the disgrace of his affianced bride: 'Her honour, like a diamond, burnt to charcoal.' Having confessed all, he promptly dies to the sound of soft music:

RUTH. Oh God! His smile is fading!

ARAM. I would find
My burial in your arms – upon your lips
My only epitaph; and in your eyes,
My first faint glimpse of Heaven!

Slow curtain

Shouts of acclaim greeted Irving's performance. The play might be horrible, but what variety the actor managed to wring from such unrelieved gloom. Clement Scott described the last moments of Aram: 'Now writhing against the tree, now prostrate upon the turf, the actor brings into play an amount of study little less than astonishing.'

Although the final scene was a long soliloquy, interrupted only occasionally by remarks from the long-suffering Ruth, Isabel Bateman managed to reap a small harvest of praise.

One critic dissented, taking exception to the fact that the playwright had dispensed with the trial and execution of his criminal hero and 'permitted him to escape almost unpunished and undisgraced'. But the high merits of Miss Isabel Bateman, 'in a part that depends on the exhibition of a gentle nature, placed amid untoward circumstances, must not be overlooked'.

Even at home Miss Isabel's circumstances were untoward. She did not receive a salary. Her reward was merely pocket money – and the clothes her mother made. Deprived of a rich return for the playing of leading parts, it was hardly surprising that she took the veil at last.

Irving was luckier. Bateman, ever conscious that his family's prosperity depended upon Irving, doubled his salary to £30 a week.

Eugene Aram opened on 17 April 1873, and on that day Irving was blackballed by the Garrick Club members. He took this badly, being always over-aware of slights and hisses. The Garrick had been established in 1830 with the alleged aim that it should be a club 'in which actors and men of education and refinement might meet on equal terms'. The men of refinement clubbed together to keep the actor out.

The outcome was more soothing to Irving's sensibilities. He received a consoling letter from the chairman of the club's committee: he had been astonished at the result, and hoped that Irving would very kindly allow him to put Irving's name forward again. Anthony Trollope also wrote: 'I think that the caprice of one or two men should not give you personal offence.' Frederick Sandys, one of the pre-Raphaelite painters, wrote: 'I think your pilling on Saturday was a disgrace to the Club.' He hoped that when Irving was accepted he would either resign to show his contempt, or remain – whichever he wished.

The storm of support was highly gratifying to the actor. His portrait by Millais now dominates the upstairs drawing-room; painted as a man of distinction, he looks down on new members as an old member who was blackballed and afterwards became a cornerstone of the club.

The season ended in July and Irving went off touring. This time his tour took him back to the West Country. He was able to see the settings of his childhood and remember the stirrings of ambition and imagination in his young mind. It had been nearly a quarter of a century since he left Halsetown – the journey upwards had taken longer than he had once hoped. Even now every play was a new test, but also another step towards his goal of producing Shakespeare in his own theatre.

He was still under the tutelage of Bateman and restricted by the necessity for Bateman to provide roles for his family. The next play proposed was *Richelieu,* the first play Irving had attempted on the professional stage. He knew its pitfalls well, for it had been one of the great roles of Macready and of Phelps. Macready himself died in the year when Irving acted Richelieu, and he felt that many who had seen the old actors in the role must now be waiting for him to undertake a part above his capacities.

The play had first been produced in 1839 and could hardly be said to be new. There was one thing in its favour in Irving's eyes – everything was subordinated to the part of the Cardinal. Lytton's Richelieu was a curious mixture of Iago and Cardinal Wolsey, and even his contemporaries doubted whether it was true to history. Bateman, however, was not concerned with history but with box office, and Richelieu was known to be a draw.

Irving studied the part carefully. When making up he had pictures of the great Cardinal in his dressing-room. When, on 27 September 1873, he opened the autumn season in the role of Richelieu, both the study and the make-up produced another success for Irving.

But it was a success not without carping voices. Clement Scott, then only 28 and later to become one of Irving's most assiduous admirers, using the editorial 'we' said: 'It was but slightly to our liking. But we own we are in a serious minority. The old play went as it has probably never gone before. Hats and handkerchiefs were waved, the pit and gallery leaped upon the benches; the house shook and rang with the applause. It was the wild delirium of the revival meeting.'

The play makes difficult reading, and the plot is hard to follow. The verse is by turns bombastic or sentimentally obvious, except in a few passages from the Cardinal which have greater life. Thackeray found it little to his liking: 'It has always seemed to me as if one heard doors perpetually clapping and banging.'

But writing of a later performance the great French critic Jules Claretie brought the strength of Irving's performance vividly to life:

'*Richelieu* was the first play in which I saw Mr Irving in London. Here he is superb. The performance amounts to a resurrection. The great Cardinal, lean, worn, eaten up with ambition, less for himself than for France, is admirably rendered. His gait is jerky, like that of a man shaken by fever; his eye has the depth of a visionary's; a hoarse cough preys upon that feeble frame. When Richelieu appears in the midst of the courtiers, when he flings his scorn in the face of the mediocrity that is to succeed him, when he supplicates and adjures the vacillating Louis XIII, what a profound artist this tragedian is! The performance over, I was taken to see him in his dressing room. I found him surrounded by portraits of Richelieu. He had before him the three studies of Philippe de Champaigne, two in profile, and one full face.'

But many critics at the first performance found his voice monotonous, his long speeches oppressive, and his acting spiritless. The *Daily Telegraph* pontificated that this play would not secure the long run to which the Lyceum had grown accustomed. The paper was wrong. It ran for 120 nights and remained in Irving's repertoire as one of his great 'personations'.

During this run Samuel Brodribb, his father, fell seriously ill in Birmingham. Irving had always cherished an affection for the old man who had not disapproved of his career and had lovingly stuck his son's notices, good, bad and indifferent, into his book of memories. The iron rules of Irving's early acting days, and the 600 parts he had weathered, had produced a disciplined instrument. Humanity had to be fitted in between shows. Irving travelled to Birmingham on Sunday and was back in the theatre for the Monday night performance.

He had always worked hard, his only relaxation being to sit up till the early hours after the performance talking with his friends and cronies. Nothing – not illness, personal disappointments, the shipwreck of his marriage, or the loss of his children – was allowed to stand in the way of achieving what he had set out to achieve. Irving shared that uncomplaining endurance of the soldiers, explorers, and adventurers of his times. The end, the Holy Grail of achievement, was the sole criterion. The executant must ignore fatigue, illness, and disappointment. He was merely the means to that end, and his personal satisfactions ranked low in the list of priorities to be considered.

Philip, a farrago of Spanish honour and jealousy by the popular novelist Hamilton Aidé, out of a story by Balzac, was the next offering. It was admitted that the play owed any intellectual content which it had to the fine acting of Irving. His indignant rage, terror, anguish and remorse were all commended as showing a good deal of Latin heat. But the *Globe* critic, showing a little humour for once, remarked that the Lyceum audience had so often seen Irving suffering from remorse for murders he had actually committed that they 'found it a little difficult to believe in his innocence. When it was found that Philip had not slain his brother, the sense of relief was not wholly unmixed with a measure of incredulity.'

The rest of the season was taken up with reaping profits from established successes. But in the autumn of 1874 Irving persuaded Bateman to let him play Hamlet.

The testing moment had at last arrived.

Chapter 7

The Hundred Pound Hamlet

'Colonel' Bateman, who had listened to the merry clink of coin at the box office so easily produced by the gasps of horror at *The Bells*, was both unconvinced and uninspired by the idea of *Hamlet*. He did not intend to gamble heavily on art. All he would allow Irving for the production was £100.

Charles I, *Eugene Aram*, and even *The Bells* had been well mounted. The costumes had been lavish, but for Shakespeare the prospects were poor. Naturally, Bateman was not bruiting this fact abroad, and he banged his drum as usual, alleging months of careful preparation. This could hardly have deceived either public or professional critics. It was only too obvious that the graveyard was the self-same one in which Eugene Aram had expired nightly two seasons before.

The omens were not good for Irving, either. A feeling was about that this time he would overreach his powers. He may have played Hamlet in the provinces, but that was not the same as pitting himself against the toughness and glitter of a London audience.

But in his usual dogged way he began to reassess the part. In the theatre, where he had set himself to break the bonds of tradition, he was about to tackle the most traditional role of all. To mention *Hamlet* was to allow writers and public to people the stage not with one ghost but with a dozen: Burbage, Betterton, Garrick, Kean, Fechter, Macready – the list was endless. There was not one serious theatre critic from Hazlitt and George Henry Lewes, to the contemporary Clement Scott and John Oxenford who did not have a detailed conception of the real Hamlet. But, as Irving himself said, 'I am the last man to admire slavish or even unthinking adherence to tradition. Few characters or passages will not repay original study.'

And to this he gave his mind. 'I may not know all Shakespeare, but of any play of his which I present on the stage I know more than any man in England.'

His study of the part may have been deep, but so were the prejudices against which he had to fight. The soliloquies, the expected points, the traditional *coups de théâtre*, were all in the minds of the audience, and against these he must set his quiet interpretation of the essential *Hamlet*.

Bateman may have been uncertain and the critics trimming their pens to attack, but the public sensed that this was no ordinary theatrical occasion, and by three o'clock in the afternoon the doors of the Lyceum were crowded. Although Irving was greeted with warmth on his first entrance even his appearance caused consternation. It was simple. All the ideas of the past had been left aside. There were no funereal trappings, the fair wig affected by Fechter had been discarded. Irving wore his own dark hair, long and disordered. Clement Scott described his costume:

'We see before us a man and a prince in thick ribbed silk with a jacket or paletot edged with fur; a tall imposing figure, so well dressed that nothing distracts the eye from the wonderful face; a costume rich, but simple, relieved only by a heavy chain of gold.'

But the performance was quiet. This was the man whom Hazlitt had wished for, a man who was thinking aloud. Edward Russell of the *Liverpool Daily Post* wrote a long essay on Irving's Hamlet which grasped the essentials of his reading of the part:

'The root of all is a simple steady resolution on Irving's part to be what Hamlet must have been and let the rest take care of itself. To appreciate what Hamlet goes through without preconceptions is the best way of raising to the highest point the human interest in the character.'

Russell went on to write that it was laughable to hear Hamlet sneered at for infirmity of purpose by writers who never in their lives had a more serious question to settle than whether they should give up a house at the midsummer or Christmas quarter. Why should a modern writer sneer at Hamlet's dejection? 'As if having to kill your mother's second husband upon the injunction of your father's ghost were quite an ordinary piece of work by which no well-regulated mind would suffer itself to be disturbed!'

Irving's Hamlet was a man who fostered and aggravated his own excitements. It was life and death which Irving created when he was on the stage. He defined the temptations and the allurements of a text which invited declamation. He was never drawn out of the character, and 'in him lives the character as it probably never lived before'.

Even Irving's broken marriage lent pathos and bitter humour to his scenes with Ophelia.

In spite of the uncertain acting of some of his supporting players, in spite of the shabby scenery, he held the play in his firm grasp. Even Isabel Bateman managed to rise to the occasion, and was said to have 'crushed down the cruel scoffs by her true artistic impulse'. Perhaps the idea of getting her to a nunnery, a piece of advice which she afterwards took literally, inspired her.

Russell concluded his panegyric of writing:

'To Irving belongs the merit of snatching – with a hand feverish perhaps, but sure, graces which were not, and can hardly become traditional. He has made Hamlet much more than a type of feeble doubt, of tragic struggle, or even of fine philosophy. The immortality of his Hamlet is immortal youth, immortal enthusiasm, immortal tenderness, immortal nature.'

Irving had broken through at last to touch the hearts of men with the force of Shakespeare and his own imagination. And he had triumphed by the force of his own personality, had imposed himself and his own views on the critics and the wondering groundlings. It was like standing on the top of a great cliff watching the seas pounding below, and knowing that the seas were controlled by no one except oneself. It was a lonely moment, but a moment to be exquisitely savoured.

Hamlet became a cult. It attracted all classes to the theatre, including many who had considered the trashy representations on offer as beneath their cultured intelligences. The whole artistic life of the capital was drawn to the Lyceum. Tennyson and W. P. Frith, the painter, both considered that Irving's reading of Hamlet was far better than Macready's. It was a new, a modern reading – the heroics and histrionics had been cast aside. For a new generation Shakespeare's intentions shone out clearly. It became unfashionable not to have seen *Hamlet.* Even the Chevalier Wykoff, who had seen himself caricatured as Digby Grant, wrote to Bateman in terms of fulsome praise: 'Irving has gone at one bound to the very top of the ladder of fame. His Hamlet is beyond all praise.' Being unaware of the backstage economies and the second-hand scenery, the Chevalier also praised Bateman for the risks he had taken. Had these not been hazarded, 'you might have thrown a deep shadow over the rising fame of a promising young actor'.

Bateman had proved that Shakespeare could hold his own against *opéra bouffe* and French indecency. What a pity that the Princess of Wales was not present at such a memorable first night. When the Prince of Wales was finally dragged to *Hamlet,* he was heard to remark that the only thing worth looking at was the face of Isabel Bateman as Ophelia. Both *opéra bouffe* and French indecency were more to Bertie's taste. He had been satiated with culture from his early youth; oratorios, organ music, and orations, whether from Shakespeare or anyone else, could hardly be classed as entertainment. They fell into the category of compulsory culture, and were occasions to be avoided. But in spite of this royal indifference, *Hamlet* went from strength to strength. The 100th performance was celebrated with a grand supper in the saloon of the theatre, which was graced by an equal number of literary men and critics.

Irving had proved that Shakespeare did not spell ruin. Before the run of *Hamlet* ended, Shakespeare had ousted *opéra bouffe,* burlesque, and even equestrian performances at three of London's leading theatres. *A Midsummer Night's Dream* was playing at the Gaiety, *As you Like it* at the Opera Comique, and *The Merchant of Venice* at the Holborn Amphitheatre.

After the first night of *Hamlet,* Bateman had said to the audience: 'I have done all that man can do – I thank you for your support.' This he had had in full measure.

On 21 March Irving gave a supper party for Bateman at the Pall Mall Restaurant in the Haymarket. There was some muddle over an extension of the drinking licence, and the waiters, in their usual way, began to break up the party by putting out the lights and stacking the chairs on the tables. Bateman became furiously angry, and having a weak heart he became fatally affected by his choleric temper. The next morning he had a heart attack but recovered. He spent the day resting, but in the evening when his wife came home she found him dead.

Irving's greatest triumph had been the old showman's last presentation. Bateman's death was a great blow to the family and to Irving. He had lost a good friend who had proved a stepping-stone in his climb to fame.

But in his usual way Irving did not forget. When he spoke to the audience he said that in his pride and pleasure at their approval he must remember:

'the friend whose faith in me was so firm, a friend to whom my triumphs were as dear – aye, dearer than had they been his own. The announcement last autumn that I, a young actor, was thought fitted to attempt Hamlet came from a warm and generous heart, and I cannot but deeply feel that he to whose unceasing toil and unswerving energy we owe in great measure the steadfast restoration of the poetic drama to the stage – I cannot but regret that he will never meet me, as he has done on so many occasions to confirm your approval – with affectionate enthusiasm and tears of joy.'

Along the way Irving had met with many setbacks, but the 'Colonel', for all his faults, had always championed the actor he had promoted. He had not only given him enthusiasm in good measure, but he had protected Irving from unjustified critical attacks. Irving's friend Lady Pollock wrote of Bateman: 'Whatever faults he had, they were accompanied by many merits, and he was a man of force.'

Irving had lost not only a friend, he had lost a backer who was prepared to take risks, he had lost a good publicist, a real showman, the man who had strung bells across the Strand when the Prince of Wales drove to the City. He was left with Mrs Bateman and her economies.

It was sentimentally suggested that he could be a son and a brother to the family. It was a charming thought, but it was not the truth. Mrs Bateman had the theatre – and the daughters. Irving had the talent. Honours were not equally divided.

The American flair of 'Colonel' Bateman was a gap which would not easily be filled. But Mrs Bateman had determined to take culture by the horns – and provide good parts for her daughters. What had been well begun must be continued.

The run of *Hamlet* finished, and the next offering was to be *Macbeth*. Traditionally ill luck has always dogged runs of this play. Whistling in the dressing-room while making up for *Macbeth* would be regarded as a combination for attracting fires, broken legs, and the early demise of leading ladies. Irving was no less unlucky.

Macbeth to the contemporary critics was a noble and victorious soldier returning from the wars who had unfortunately met a coven of witches and who happened to be burdened with a wife who led him astray. Killing off contenders for promotion was no way to reach the top in the 1870s. The Victorians, fortunately for themselves, had clear and uninhibited views of human conduct.

Irving's reading of Macbeth was cloudier and more Celtic. He imagined that the idea of murder was already in the mind of the Thane of Glamis before he met the witches, who were the emanations of his own imagination. They merely gave a concrete form to his thoughts. The critics would have none of this. They demolished Irving's Macbeth as craven, cowardly, cringing, and unmanly. They stripped him of regimental honours. They talked of his mouthing mannerisms, of a voice which produced a most irritating effect upon the ear and destroyed the beauty of the verse, sounding, it was said, like the efforts of a ventriloquist.

Kate Bateman was castigated for whispering, but it was said that although her acting was conventional at least she provided a strong contrast to her feeble and over-lachrymose husband. Irving was not only lachrymose, he was nervous. It was remarked that his helmet shivered and rattled when he walked, which added to his pusillanimous rendering of the part.

The only scene which brought the critics any cheer was the fight at the end, with Macbeth hacking with desperate energy, his hair streaming in the wind. His death came, they said, as a relief. 'Nothing in his life became him like the leaving of it,' wrote the publication *Figaro*.

The scenery was much commended, and the witches like the scenery got good notices. Mr Mead, one of the male witches, was especially praised, but one witch does not make a successful production of *Macbeth*.

Macbeth was produced in September 1875, and, although some critics were gradually won over by Irving's reading of the part (the *Illustrated London News* featured a long essay on it in its Christmas number) the play had done little to advance either Irving or the Lyceum.

Mrs Bateman was undeterred. *Othello* would be her next offering. What better than a family double, with Isabel as Desdemona and Kate as Emilia? When the play was announced, the storm warnings were hoisted against it.

Fun, a rival of *Punch*, attacked the idea with particular venom in an open letter 'To a Fashionable Tragedian'. Signing himself 'A disinterested Observer', the anonymous writer begged the actor in the name of humanity to abandon the idea. Carried away by the fervour of his own words, he accused Irving of having a hireling press at his command and having focused the attention of the mob and debauched its intelligence: 'You have steeped it in an atmosphere of diabolical lust and crude carnage, casting around the foulest outrages the glamour of a false sentimentality.' Irving's evil influence was spreading through the whole of society, he went on. 'The deadly weeds whose seeds you have so persistently scattered' were causing 'men to revel in the details of the lowest forms of human violence; women to crowd the public courts to gloat over the filthy details of murder and licence. I maintain that for the disgusting bloodthirstiness and callous immorality of the present day you are in a great measure responsible.'

It was one thing to object to Irving's acting, his voice, his legs, and even his pronunciation, but quite another to accuse him of perverting the public. This time he decided to attack. He consulted lawyers, and on Christmas Eve, 1875, the printers were presented with an unseasonable gift in the form of a summons for 'scurrilous libel'.

On 2 January Irving appeared in court. The *Weekly Dispatch* reported that James Judd of the Phoenix Printing Office in Doctors' Commons appeared in answer to a summons taken out for publishing a libel on Mr Henry Irving. Judd stated that he was the printer of *Fun*.

Cross-examined, Irving was asked: 'Was *Macbeth* a failure as stated in the article?' He replied, 'Far from it – if we judge the play commercially – I can tell you what the profit was – if you wish to know.'

The magistrate did not press the point. Irving denied debauching the public, and to the charge that he paid reporters to puff him he said that he knew very few. He did know Dutton Cook, 'but he always cut me up'. (Laughter in court.)

On the first day of the trial it was said that there was no clear proof of authorship, but by the second day a Mr George R. Sims had nobly travelled 400 miles to admit authorship and answer the charges. His defence was that he felt it his duty to protect society against the production of Shakesperian plays. A curious point of view.

There had been cuts in the article? Certainly, he had to admit that it had previously been more ensanguined.

'"Bloody King" struck out?'

'Yes.'

'"Bloody brother"?'

'Yes.'

'And "bloody prince"?'

'Yes.'

'And even "bloody chieftain"?'

'Yes.' (More laughter in court.)

J. L. Toole, the comedian and old friend of Irving, gave evidence: 'It has been suggested that Mr Irving should not play in tragedy – this is most impertinent.' The magistrate, anxious to show his knowledge of the theatre, remarked, 'Perhaps it is quite out of Mr Toole's line. No one ever shed a tear who saw Mr Toole.'

This upset Toole's professional pride. 'I am sorry to hear you say that.' He shook his head sadly, saying that his Michael Garner in *Dearer than Life* had caused thousands to weep, and for thirteen years his *Caleb Plummer* had been noted for pathos.

The unfortunate Judd was dismissed from the case, both editor and writer apologised, Irving was awarded damages, and the case closed.

Macbeth ran for eighty nights, although *Figaro* published a last word or two in feeble verse:

> A popular actor H. Irving
> As Hamlet of praise was deserving.
> But he failed in Macbeth
> Being too scant of breath
> And most people thought him
> Unn-Irving.

As with Macbeth, the dice were loaded against Irving long before he attempted Othello. The previous year Salvini, a noted Italian actor, had impressed the town with his physical robustness and his acting, which was said to have raised the part to supremacy in tragic art. No doubt the fact that he was acting in Italian added to the impression of strangeness. There is always a tendency on the part of cultured audiences to appreciate plays in foreign languages. A thin actor, speaking in English, must obviously be prepared for equally thin houses and sour criticisms. These Irving obtained.

He had carried eccentricity to the verge of the grotesque. Even his costume was condemned as being entirely different from that which any student of Shakespeare could imagine Othello's to have been. Critics, while commending Irving's previous performances, then slipped a knife or two in his back, saying he had been given generous encouragement by the public but there was no reason for this to continue. They now referred to him as a young and untried artist. (He was 38 and had been on the stage for twenty years.)

But he was not to be put down so easily. He had no great regard for criticism. He said: 'Kean's may be called a posthumous reputation. If you read the newspapers of his time, you will find that during his acting days he was considerably cut up and mauled.'

Othello was swiftly replaced by Tennyson's *Queen Mary*. Mrs Bateman had been attracted by a play which provided a feast for the family. Queen Mary was played by Kate Bateman, Princess Elizabeth by Virginia Bateman,* and Alice, her maid of honour, by Isabel Bateman.

Mrs Bateman's devotion to her daughters was not equalled by their devotion to one another. Kate Bateman enjoyed acting and was jealous of Isabel, who was given showy parts although she loathed being an actress. Isabel was her mother's favourite. She had a pliable nature. The death of Bateman had removed a stable masculine hand from female jealousies, and Irving was not a father substitute. He did help the girls in minor ways, and was able to persuade Mrs Bateman to refrain from making their off-stage clothes. Would it not benefit the theatre more if they went to a couturier so that Mrs Bateman could give all her undoubted energies to the theatre?

* Virginia Bateman, the third and least admired of the Bateman daughters, married Edward Compton. Her small spark of talent she passed on, for her children were Compton Mackenzie and Fay Compton.

Apart from providing parts for three daughters in one play, *Queen Mary* was not a good choice. Irving did not appear until halfway through the second act and had disappeared by the beginning of Act V, which largely consisted of Mary's unending woes interspersed with a catalogue of wrongs done to the noble Protestants by the evil Catholic rule.

> The hands that write these words should be burnt clean off
> As Cranmer's, the friends that utter them
> Tongue-torn with pincers, lash'd to death or lie
> Famishing in black cells, while famish'd rats
> Eat them alive.

Mary takes twenty-five pages to die, and is succeeded by a radiant Elizabeth. 'If our person be secured from traitor stabs – we will make England great!'

> 'God Save Elizabeth Queen of England,
> God Save the Crown, the Papacy is no more!'

The piece was received in respectful silence and restrained enthusiasm as a poetic offering by the Laureate.

But Irving as Philip II received the critical acclaim he deserved. He presented a Titian-like appearance, and his performance was finished and subtle, the stiff and heartless Spanish grandee to the life. Ellen Terry, who saw him, said he had never played better and his Philip II was the perfection of quiet malignity and cruelty.

Browning, who was at the first night, wrote to Tennyson: 'Irving was very good indeed, and the others did their best. The love as well as admiration for the author was conspicuous.' But respect for an author does not fill a theatre. The play opened on 18 April and on 13 May Mrs Bateman was apologetically sending Tennyson £230 (the total of royalties for twenty-three nights at £10 a night).

Only one masterpiece remains to recall Irving's Philip II, the portrait which Whistler painted of Irving. When Whistler's goods were sold to pay his debts, Irving bought it for £30.

Queen Mary's woes were swiftly replaced by a double bill, *The Bells* and Mrs Cowley's old comedy, *The Belle's Stratagem*. Irving had to play Doricourt for the second time. He never excelled in eighteenth-century plays, but the comedy had been retailored to make a good setting for a leading actress, and Isabel Bateman acted Letitia Hardy in 'a very graceful and sprightly fashion'; Irving was commended for his finesse. He was able to lead Isabel Bateman forward to enjoy the honours of the evening with graceful complaisance.

Just before the production of Mrs Cowley's comedy, *The School for Scandal* was produced for one of those innumerable benefits in which the theatre regularly paraded with its heart on its sleeve. Sheridan's play was given for the old actor J. B. Buckstone, who had been fifty years on the stage. The cast included Samuel Phelps playing Peter Teazle, Buckstone himself as Benjamin Backbite, Lucy Buckstone, old Buckstone's daughter, playing Maria, and Adelaide Neilson as Lady Teazle. Irving did not show to good advantage as Joseph Surface. For once, his strange modern technique looked thin and awkward against the robust playing of the old-school actors who filled the rest of the bill. The eighteenth century, with its sharp, finished wit and polished mannerisms, was not the milieu for this actor of the new school. Or perhaps Irving was not a player for a team. He had been trained in a school where the visiting Titans expected actors of lesser breed to provide speaking scenery rather than solid support.

At the end of the summer season of 1876, Irving took his benefit playing *Eugene Aram*, in which he showed to advantage, *The Belle's Stratagem*, which gave Isabel Bateman the acting honours, while Miss Helen Faucit played Iolanthe to Irving's Count Tristan in *King René's Daughter*. It was her last appearance on the stage.

The following night Irving set off on a provincial tour. He went back to his beginnings, but this time to triumphant applause. In Manchester 18,000 people paid to see him. Everywhere the enthusiasm blotted out the failures of *Macbeth* and *Othello*. Birmingham, Liverpool, Newcastle, Edinburgh, Dundee, Glasgow – all cities in which he had suffered poverty and disappointment – now greeted him with acclaim. The past was forgotten.

The most glittering triumph of the tour was in Dublin, the city in which he had suffered his greatest humiliation. This triumph had been helped to its peak by Bram Stoker, who as an unpaid dramatic critic had said of Irving's Hamlet: 'There is another view of Hamlet which Mr Irving seems to realise by a kind of instinct . . . the deep underlying idea that in the divine delirium of his perfected passion there is the instinct of a mystic.' It was a notice which an actor could have written himself. As a result of it, Stoker and Irving met for the first time.

It was an odd encounter, and as Bram Stoker sat in Irving's dressing-room the actor suddenly began to recite *Eugene Aram*. Bram Stoker admits to having been spellbound, sitting as if carved from stone. Irving was inspired and at the end fell back half-fainting. Stoker himself then had hysterics.

This tribute to his powers left Henry Irving 'much moved', and he promptly went out, returning with a signed photograph on which he had written, 'My dear Stoker, God bless you! God bless you!! Henry Irving, Dec. 3rd 1876.'

Soul, said Stoker, had looked into soul. Irving had found a permanently receptive audience, a firm friend, and had given a promise that, when the time came, they would work together.

Meanwhile Stoker arranged a tribute to Irving to be given at a reception at Trinity College, Dublin. The address written by Stoker himself in his most eulogistic style, referred to Irving as a purifier of the passions and a nurse of heroic sentiments. He had even succeeded, said Stoker, in commending himself to a portion of society which, although large and influential, did not as a rule darken the doors of a theatre. He was presumably referring to the nobility, gentry, and hunting squires of the English ascendency.

To the fulsome compliments Irving replied equally fulsomely. He was embarrassed for words in the presence of so much learning, but for his profession he tendered gratitude, for his art he honoured them, but for himself he could only tender his grateful thanks. It was not insincere; Irving was always acutely aware of his self-education, and like many self-educated men tempered pride in his own achievement with a real, or temporarily assumed, humility in the face of true learning.

Stoker lyrically described the evening which followed. At the theatre most of the seats were taken by students, whose entrance was signalled by the blowing of horns. They called for Irving several times during the performance of *Hamlet*, and when the curtain finally fell 'the pent-up enthusiasm burst forth and the whole house rose to its feet. Cheer upon cheer swelled louder and louder as the player stood proudly before his audience with such a light upon his face as never shone from the floats.'

Irving spoke to 'the sea of upturned faces – clear strong young faces with broad foreheads and bright eyes'. He recommended honest steadfast work which brought rewards and honours, giving the happy recipient a new zest for existence. 'Such honours you have heaped on me. You cannnot think it strange that every fibre of my soul throbs, and my eyes are dim with emotion as I look upon your faces, and I must say good-bye. I only hope you have God's blessing – as you have mine.'

It was an emotional occasion which for a few blessed hours had dimmed the memory of the past – although, as Irving told Stoker, an actor never forgets a hiss.

Outside the stage door a hundred students waited for the triumphant hero of the evening; they had taken the horses out of his carriage and now they dragged it up Grafton Street, round into St Stephen's Green, and then to his hotel. With an expansive gesture of gratitude he tried to invite his escort into the hotel, but the hotel manager, much less moved than the actor, decided against it, and with an actor's wave of his hat he disappeared into the vestibule. The following day the Dean of Trinity expressed his gratitude to the students for their admirable behaviour, both at the reception in Trinity College, and afterwards at the Theatre Royal.

Town and gown may have responded eagerly, but the Protestant ascendancy were less enthusiastic. The Duke of Connaught did not put in an appearance until the second Act, when he arrived with the Lord Lieutenant, the Duke of Marlborough. Lord Randolph Churchill, Marlborough's son, went round to see Irving in his dressing-room to find out how *Hamlet* ended. Presumably he wanted to find out if it was worth staying till the end. Later he thanked the actor. He had had no idea of Shakespeare until he had seen Irving. Since that day he had seen *Hamlet* not once but twice, and even read four of the other plays. Irving, he said, had introduced him to a new world. It was a pertinent reply to the carping of the critics against Irving's popular performances. He had introduced a new generation to Shakespeare.

Invigorated by the memory of the cheers of his provincial triumph, Irving revived *Macbeth* for the Christmas season. It was received grudgingly; it may have been received rapturously in the provinces, but the London critics were not going to revise their opinions. Bram Stoker found the production both startling and romantic:

'Macbeth's soldiers were seen against a low dropping sun, with a vast expanse of heather, studded with patches of light glinting on water, and an endless procession of soldiers straggling – filling the stage to the conclusion of an endless array giving the idea of force and power which impressed the spectators and forced them to *think*.'

But Irving was merely reassembling his armament. He had decided to attempt *Richard III*, the part in which Kean had triumphed. But that triumph had been in Colley Cibber's travesty of Shakespeare which had held the stage for nearly two hundred years. Irving was proposing, with startling originality, to restore Shakespeare's play. The Lyceum programme stated boldly that 'the version presented was strictly the original text without interpolations, but simply such omissions and transpositions as have been found essential for dramatic representation.'

The Henry Irving Shakespeare outlines passages 'showing what portions of each play may be easily or desirably omitted without breach of continuity.' In *Richard III* they include many passages left out presumably for reasons of delicacy. Dead Henry's wounds no longer open their congeal'd mouths and bleed afresh, nor does the Lady Anne spit at Gloucester. The murder of Clarence gives the first and second murderers little chance to shine because most of their scene, except the stabbing, is cut. Whole scenes where the women are thrown into prominence are eliminated. There are few cuts in Richard's scenes, but then a leading actor likes to shine, and this Irving did.

The amazing idea of presenting *Richard III* in Shakespeare's own words was hailed on all sides. Garrick and Kean had acted in Cibber's version. Clement Scott made the point that because the original text was being used the audience attention was focused on the progress of the action and 'not distracted by watching for the mode in which the prominent actor will deliver his favourite points'.

It was a shining asset. Irving's Richard could be new-minted. Even his mannerisms worked to his advantage. 'His deformity is no more obtrusive than is needful to justify the references of the text, and the halting gait, appropriate to the character, absorbs a certain mannerism of movement which had occasionally an unplesant effect in previous impersonations.'

Irving's own humour, always more sardonic than benevolent, added that edge to the character which brought it to life. A long-forgotten newspaper called *Saunders News* made this clear: 'He very strongly brings out the cynical gall of Richard, his bitter irony, his scorn of mankind and his mockery of this world and the next.' From the heights and depths of personal success and failure, Irving had learned to transmute bitterness into theatrical effect.

The whole production was in the best realistic style, from the picturesque streets of old London and the gloom of the Tower to the scene in the Council Chamber (most substantially constructed with broad, massive stairs and a lofty gallery.) In the battle scene a tent occupied the whole stage, complete with luxurious couch, armour lying about, a coal fire burning in a brazier, and with a flap of the tent pulled aside to afford a view of the battlefield. A triumph for the art of Hawes Craven.

Irving knew his audience when he remarked that Shakespeare well acted on a bare stage could afford intellectual pleasure, but the pleasure would be greater if the eye were charmed. 'Many are thus brought to listen with pleasure to the noblest works of dramatic art who might otherwise turn away from them as dull and unattractive.'

Gradually Irving's productions, like modern productions of classics on television, revived interest in Shakespeare. An acting edition of *Richard III* was brought out with a preface, ostensibly by Henry Irving. In this he set down his views. *Richard III* was not a play 'for the closet', it was full of action; fashions may change but truth should remain unalterable, and the true words of Shakespeare be allowed to speak to the human soul.

Even Dutton Cook, who usually cut Irving up, had to admit that his first impersonation of Richard III was 'startling in its originality, and its power and completeness'. But Richard had to fight his battles alone; the remainder of the company afforded little opportunity for favourable comment. This included A. W. Pinero's playing of Lord Stanley. Kate Bateman played Margaret of Anjou, and Cook remarked that, 'there is sound judgement manifested in the elimination of that vociferous character from the later acts of the tragedy'.

When publishing his version of *Richard III*, Irving wrote that he felt he had been able to lay a laurel spray on the grave of his honoured and regretted friend, the late manager of the Lyceum Theatre, 'Colonel' Bateman. Few laurel sprays came the way of the Bateman girls. They had hardly garnered critical acclaim. Isabel had earned a few damp flowers as Ophelia, but all in all their notices veered from lukewarm praise to outright condemnation.

Irving continued to act under Mrs Bateman's management, but he was nearly 40 and thoughts of the future were in his mind.

Chapter 8

A Theatre ‘Where I Should be Sole Master’

Irving was now accepted by the fashionable as well as by the populace. He had become a figure in society. The man who for so long had been an unknown touring actor was described as one of the best known men in London. He did not underplay his off-stage appearance. He wore his dark hair long, he walked the streets with lengthy strides, a dreamy, absent manner adding to his artistic image. His cheeks were thin and wan, and round his tall, spare figure his stylish clothes clung with a negligent air. He may have been lionised by the fashionable givers of breakfasts, dinners, and receptions, but he himself was happier with his old friends, talking long into the night about the mysterious workings of the profession he knew and loved.

Appearing as a ‘Celebrity at Home’, his rooms in Grafton Street were lovingly described as being entirely different from those of the ‘wealthy wifeless which abound in the vicinity’. The study was sombre, the window-panes obscured by stained glass. Interviewers concluded from this that Irving preferred a Gothic gloom in tune with his character, but he confessed on one occasion that he had merely put in coloured glass to stop the neighbours peering in.

Interviewers bring their prejudices with them, and in Irving’s rooms they found a perfect example of the confusion and neglect of order of the artistic mind. The study appears to have been a jumble of tiger-skin rugs, books, prints, and boxes of cigars, with the tables, chairs, and piano covered with manuscripts. Even the broad sofa which had been a present to Irving when he moved in was, according to his interviewer, undecided whether it was intended for a wardrobe, a bookcase, or a portfolio.

It was the dressing-room of a touring actor transferred to the West End, and no amount of artistic trimmings, whether the clever sketches by John Tenniel or even medallions by Marochetti, could change a background which had been built up over more than twenty years.

Irving's contemporary fame can be measured by the fact that when these 'Celebrities at Home' interviews were published as a book he shared the honours with the Prince of Wales, Tennyson, John Bright, and Gladstone. He had come a long way.

Petticoat Bateman government was not to be allowed to impede him. But the time was not quite ripe for a break. All the publicity which followed him was strengthening his position. He had already brought in Henry Loveday to act as stage manager. Loveday had been the chief violin player at Edinburgh in 1858. Irving often chose men for their loyalty rather than for their expertise. He was gradually building up a team for the future. But in the meantime he had to placate Mrs Bateman and keep her daughters happy.

The London season began with the opening of the Royal Academy, and Mrs Bateman's new season on 19 May 1877 with a popular melodrama, *The Lyons Mail*.

The play was based on an appalling miscarriage of justice. An innocent man, Joseph Lesurques, as a result of a superficial resemblance to the real criminal, Dubosc, had been guillotined for a crime he did not commit. A marble monument in the Père Lachaise cemetery testified to the truth: *A la mémoire de Joseph Lesurques, victime de la plus déplorable des erreurs humaines*, 31 *octobre* 1796.

In 1850 three French writers, Moreau, Siraudin and Delacour, with the permission of the Lesurques family, turned the plot into a vehicle for a leading actor with the dual role of Lesurques/Dubosc. In France, where the real story was known, it was the custom to play it on alternate days with different endings. One day the innocent man was duly executed, and on the next a reprieve arrived at the last moment. In England there was always a reprieve.

Originally seen in London with Charles Kean and with Kate Terry playing the young boy Joliquet, it had been rewritten once more for Charles Reade. Irving did not receive universally good notices for his Dubosc/Lesurques. His drunken vicious Dubosc was found to be too crudely drawn to cause anyone to mistake him for the noble, wronged husband and father, Lesurques. Engravings of him in the dual role seem to prove this point. The first night was further marred by the fact that pit and gallery were incensed at being cheated of both farce and curtain raiser. They objected to a performance which ended at ten o'clock. The press sharply advised that for the enormous price of two shillings a pit seat, and a shilling for the gallery, 'Mrs Bateman will not fail to see that the prices charged for admission demand a longer entertainment.'

But *The Lyons Mail* was instantly successful, and Irving adopted it as his own, and twenty-eight years later it was still in his repertory.

The autumn of 1877 found him in Dublin again, playing his old successes and being received with the usual enthusiasm. He was entertained with supper parties of hot lobster, wines and grills – the male Victorian chop-house and club entertainment in which he delighted. He met his understanding admirer Bram Stoker again and after *The Bells* had supper with him in his rooms. There they talked about the future. Irving spoke about what he intended to do when he 'should have a theatre all to himself – where he would be sole master. He admitted to a feeling of limitation under Mrs Bateman.' He was quite frank about his difficulties, which included the three Bateman sisters. Musingly, Irving suggested that if his plans materialised there could be a future with Stoker 'sharing his fortune'.

Enchanted with the idea of giving up the Civil Service, on 22 November Stoker wrote in his diary three triumphant words – 'London in View!'

Stoker gave Irving not only admiration but understanding. He sympathised with Irving's liking for late hours. 'I well understood', wrote Stoker, 'that after a hard and exciting night the person most concerned does not want to go to bed.' At 3 a.m. Stoker and Irving were still talking and the next day the actor set out on a fifteen-hour journey to London.

Irving, still brooding darky on his future, and much irked by the necessity of providing parts for the Bateman girls, was hardly encouraged by the bad notices which the supporting company consistently received under Mrs Bateman. The 'Colonel' had tempered Irving's grand notions with down-to-earth common sense and a flair for publicity. Mrs Bateman had carried her sartorial economies into the theatre. The whole winter was to be taken up with revivals, in preparation for a new production of *Louis XI.* This was one of Boucicault's pieces of pastiche with a complicated pedigree – from a play by Casimir Delavigne, out of a character in Scott's *Quentin Durward.* The only virtue of the play was that it had an outstanding part for a leading actor, the rest of the cast providing mere wallpaper.

Louis XI was only 60 when he died; Irving made him into a senile 70. But the aged staggerings, the sudden quirks of sardonic humour, the irritable passion, the alternating cruelty and irresolution impressed as being nature itself. Even Irving's make-up was admitted to denote considerable research, the pale, cadaverous face, the unsteady hands, and the feeble gait being entirely in character.

There was a dissenting voice. One critic was anxious to rehabilitate the real Louis XI. This much-maligned king had done much good in uniting France after the defeat of the English, had reformed the judiciary, had introduced the printing press; and founded the post office. He had introduced standard weights and measures, and even begun a system of policing. None of these practical items would seem to contain good dramatic material, but possibly the writer was confusing Louis XI with Queen Victoria, for he concluded sourly that the play showed a republican spirit. Mr Irving's acting was said to have been marred, as usual, by the company which supported him.

The next play was a pious memory of the late 'Colonel' Bateman. He had commissioned Percy Fitzgerald and W. G. Wills to turn the story of the Flying Dutchman into *Vanderdecken.*

Percy Fitzgerald was one of those literary figures who make the best of small talents by attaching themselves to others whose gifts are more outstanding. At the beginning of Fitzgerald's friendship with Irving he had been drawn to him not only by the actor's fame, but by a genuine liking. Fitzgerald said of Irving that 'he had an unaffected gaiety – a merrier man, within the limits of becoming mirth, I never spent an hour with.'

During the course of the negotiations about *Vanderdecken* the letters which passed between the two men show Irving's attitude towards Mrs Bateman at a delicate stage of his association with her. Fitzgerald wrote to Irving with suggestions for the play:

'I quite see your idea of the whole as a play of high wrought romantic characters. The ending with the bodies at the bottom of the sea – they might descend slowly through the greeny water. My sisters on whom I experimented with it are enchanted with the flesh-creeping notion of casting the body into the sea.'

He added further ideas – old Crone's warnings, romantic pictures of old Dutch manners and customs on betrothal, and a church scene with hymns and plenty of local colour. He ended his letter by mentioning what an enjoyable evening he had passed with Irving.

The letter reached Irving when he was on tour and he wrote back:

'My dear Fitzgerald, Your suggestions and additions seem admirable but I would like the entrance of the Dutchman to end the first act.

My purpose in writing now is to ask you to re-write what you wrote to me – to Mrs Bateman. She would rather, I know, that you wrote your views of the play to her – especially as you had already had correspondence on the matter. This is a little pardonable vanity which you can thoroughly understand. I have not told her for this reason, the contents of, or the receipt of, your letter which I return to save you trouble in case you have forgotten anything. Her address is the Prince's Theatre, Bradford. After that Newcastle-on-Tyne until the end of next week.'

Irving's writing is hurried, illegible and old-fashioned, for he used the long eighteenth-century 'S' when writing the word 'address'.

Wills seems to have written most of the play, although some of Fitzgerald's first act remained. But Fitzgerald was enchanted with the play. There was nothing like the charm of the footlights, he wrote, or the exquisite sensation of 'hearkening to your own words and sentiments'. This naïve point of view is much dependent on the actors, and not shared by all playwrights, but Percy Fitzgerald was the starry-eyed triumphant amateur.

In spite of the wild romanticism of the phantom Captain, the scenery of the landing-place on the edge of the fiord lit by the cold steely blue of the north, not to mention a small brown foresail swaying in the wind, the play flopped. Irving acted with picturesque intensity, but there were flaws. Mrs Bateman had been economising: 'a fatal blemish was the unveiling of the picture, on the due impressiveness of which much depended. This proved to be a sort of picturesque daub greeted with much tittering.' The production was closed by a spell of sultry weather, a perennial excuse for theatrical failure.

Isabel Bateman played the lady destined to rescue the doomed Dutchman. In real life she also had doom hanging over her. She had become fatally attracted to Irving. This was embarrassing for him on several counts. He was not attracted to her and, although separated, was still married; most pertinent of all, he had no regard for her talents as an actress.

The constantly repeated chorus of praise for himself and denigration of the Bateman company led him more and more to the thought that he must free himself. He needed, as he said to Stoker, to be sole master. He was not afraid to strike, but he was unwilling to wound. Old loyalties were hard to break.

Irving, anxious to cast off his fetters and leave Mrs Bateman and her daughters, was in a delicately embarrassing situation. Isabel, never an outstanding actress, had become even more inhibited by her passion for Irving. Mrs Bateman, it was said, was quite willing to turn a blind eye to her daughter's forming a 'strict alliance of friendship' with Irving. She was a practical woman, and if that were the way to keep Irving in the family, and Isabel in work, she could see nothing against it. The religious-minded Isabel, shocked by her mother's eighteenth-century attitude, found herself in one of those situations which she was accustomed to mime on stage. Honour or dishonour? Love or duty? The Vicar of St Peter's, Eaton Square, advised her to stand firm against the dishonouring worldliness of her mother.

As Irving showed no inclination to become Isabel's protector or to fall in with Mrs Bateman's plans, the dilemma was hypothetical. His friends, companions and club cronies were constantly urging him to action. Labouchère wrote: 'Depend upon it, no actor in the world can carry a bad play *and* a bad company.'

Irving decided, at last, to express his dissatisfaction in a roundabout way. He suggested that he might have a new leading lady for the next season. Mrs Bateman's reply to him makes it clear that she already suspected that he had decided to break the partnership. There was only one thought in her mind. She did not want that break to cause the complete eclipse of her daughters as actresses. The theatre was their livelihood. Should the part of Ophelia be taken away from

Isabel, 'it would be an endorsement signed by you – the friend of her family and me – her mother, of her entire incompetency'.

Some accounts of the break with the Bateman family show Mrs Bateman insisting on Isabel remaining as leading lady, and Irving about to leave the theatre when, like a ripe plum, the theatre automatically falls into his hands.

The webs of human conduct are not simple to unravel. The official account was that to resolve all problems – Isabel's infatuation, Irving's dissatisfaction, and her own concern with the future of her family – Mrs Bateman had a simple solution. Irving should take the theatre from her. Perhaps he had effectively done that already, and she preferred to part as a friend. She could have made money from the remainder of the lease. Although he had no money, Irving had a reputation and that could attract finance.

A writer on *The Hornet* was in no doubt about the Bateman girls: 'Colonel Bateman may be said to have discovered Mr Irving, but it will be a great advantage to a new lessee if Mrs Bateman takes her daughters with her. They may be very charming ladies, but they are not altogether suited to the parts with which they have been entrusted.'

Mrs Bateman and Irving seem to have parted without bitterness. Perhaps even Mrs Bateman realised at last that her daughters did not have the qualities which Irving sought. He wanted a partner who could attract the public. Perhaps he instinctively realised that charm, lightness, and an essential feminine attraction were qualities which he needed as a complement to his own gifts. On stage he never played lovers with any critical success. He had the mesmeric gift, he needed a lure.

Once Mrs Bateman had decided to settle her affairs with Irving she set about planning the future of her family in an eminently practical way. She closed the theatre suddenly, in the third week of August 1878 and on the 31st issued a statement which combined dignity with pride. She announced that after seven years of being associated with the Bateman name she was handing over her lease to Mr Henry Irving in the confident hope that under his care it would attain higher artistic prosperity. She thanked the public for its support and kindness which had sometimes overlooked many shortcomings. During her time at the Lyceum she had given *Macbeth* and *Richard III* from the original text, and, while she may not always have attained artistic excellence, she had invariably, as she pointed out, ended with a profit.

Her letter to Irving, after the break, in which she outlines her plans, shows no rancour and is full of good practical ideas for investing her money and securing her children's future. She had bought the lease of Sadler's Wells and was going to work it as a country theatre which, with low prices, touring companies, pantomimes, and the occasional drama, should show a profit; the neighbourhood was much improved, was without any place of amusement, and trams and buses would bring in the customers. She had raised the money easily and when the building was finished it would be very pretty and hold 2,600 people. Even more important, the saloons alone would pay the interest on the loan, and leave her rent very low. 'The lease is for 34 years', she wrote, 'and I trust with some luck and a great deal of economy we may be able to make a living, and as no special gifts are required for the conduct of such a place the girls can make a living out of it when I am gone.'

And so with good wishes for his tour and admonitions about wrapping up against the cold, which is good for theatre business and bad for the health, she signed herself 'affectionately S. F. Bateman', making a dignified and sensible exit from Irving's life. The girls were not as enchanted as Mrs Bateman, and Isabel particularly harboured bitter feelings about Irving for many years.

He had already been in correspondence with Ellen Terry a month before his break with Mrs Bateman. Lady Pollock, one of his admirers, had been urging him to think of Ellen as the partner he had been looking for. It was not Irving's habit to watch other actors, and he seems to have relied on reports of Ellen's acting and the notices she had attracted. Ellen herself wrote: 'It was never any pleasure to him to see the acting of other actors and actresses.'

Ellen's idyll with Godwin was over. Bailiffs and lack of money for her children had driven her back to the stage. Charles Reade had offered her £40 a week if she would play in *The Wandering Heir*. The story is that he leapt over a fence while out hunting, to find Ellen as a lady in distress with a wheel off her pony cart. It is a charming tale, but perhaps not quite the whole of the story. Reade said of Ellen that she was such a character as neither Molière nor Balzac had the good luck to fall in with – soft and yielding on the surface, egotistical below, hysterical, sentimental, hard as a nail in money matters, but velvet to the touch. She had, said Reade, the great art of pleasing, and this was a quality which Irving needed.

In 1875, the year when Irving had failed as Macbeth, she had charmed as Portia. The Bancrofts at the Prince of Wales had made a great success of what were called 'cup and saucer' domestic comedies and dramas. Because of Irving's success in *Hamlet*, they decided on a change and their choice was *The Merchant of Venice*.

Ellen's account of her success brings her feelings vividly to life:

'My fires were only just beginning to burn. Success I had had of a kind, and I had tasted the delight of knowing that audiences liked me, and I had liked them back again. But never until I appeared as Portia at The Prince of Wales's had I experienced that awe-struck feeling which comes, I suppose, to no actress more than once in a lifetime, the feeling of the conqueror. In homely parlance I knew that I had "got them", at the moment when I spoke the speech beginning "You see me, Lord Bassanio, where I stand". "What can this be?" I thought! This is *different*. It has never been quite the same before.'

She had stretched out her hand to fame and was conscious of her power to charm. She remembered her appearance with pleasure; in the casket scene she had worn a dress like almond blossom. She recalled how thin she was, but Portia and all the ideal young heroines of Shakespeare ought to be thin. 'Everyone seemed to be in love with me! I had sweethearts by the dozen, known and unknown.' It could hardly be said that Irving was one of them.

The two actors proceeded with the utmost professional caution. Contacts had been tentatively made through third parties. Lady Pollock had told Irving that Ellen was the very person for him, all London was talking of her Olivia in *The Vicar of Wakefield*. She would bring to the Lyceum a personal following.

Irving, who had not seen her acting, was more impressed with the idea of her personal following filling the Lyceum. He sent a polite message saying he would wish to call on Miss Terry, who replied from 33 Longbridge Road, South Kensington, on 19 July 1878, saying that she was at home 'all these hot days from 11 to 3 and would be very pleased if you will call any day this week or next, or – if you can't come out in the heat, be kind enough to fix your own day and hour, letting me know, and I'll stay at home to see you.'

He replied the following day: 'Dear Miss Terry, I look forward to the pleasure of calling upon you on Tuesday next at two o'clock.'

Ellen admitted that she found a startling change in Henry Irving since the first time she had met him. She painted a picture of him which serves as a double vision of the man he was in 1867 and what he had become in 1878. At thirty he looked conceited and

'almost savagely proud of the isolation in which he lived. There was a touch of exaggeration in his appearance – a dash of Werther with a few flourishes of Jingle. Nervously sensitive to ridicule, self-conscious, suffering deeply from his inability to express himself through his art, Henry Irving in 1867 was a very different person from the Henry Irving who called on me at Longridge Road in 1878.'

In finding himself, he had lost the stiff, ugly, self-consciousness which had encased him. Even his physical appearance seemed to have changed: his forehead had become more massive and the outline of his features had altered. Ellen found him a man of the world whose 'strenuous fighting was to be done as a general – not as hitherto in the ranks.' There is no doubt that to a leading actress a general is of more use than a private. She found his manner very quiet and gentle.

One small incident broke the ice. Henry's dog made a mess on the carpet, and Ellen made a joke of it in her unselfconscious way. They became easier with one another, and Henry drifted off convinced that he had engaged her to play Ophelia at the Lyceum.

Ellen went off on tour. If her professional life was simple, her personal life had become tangled. Godwin had left her in the autumn of 1875. The following year Watts had decided to divorce her. Ellen's friends, admirers, and biographers put forward the view that Godwin was the only man whom Ellen ever loved. The belief that Miss Terry was a Virgin Mary who happened to take to the boards necessitates making her into a woman who loved but once. The reasons for this were her two children by Godwin, Gordon and Edy Craig. It is very hard to believe in as many *chambres séparées* as are envisaged by Ellen's biographers. Two large living children cannot be shrugged off as a medical phenomenon. Ellen herself liked to think Godwin was the great love of her life; yet shortly after he left her he married a girl of 21, which hardly indicates a permanently broken heart.

At this time Ellen saw herself as a wife and no wife, and her children as fatherless orphans. But Ellen's family were obliged to regard her as a fallen woman. Now that her career was re-established, she needed to polish up her public image: she must reflect bright virtue. When speaking of the part of Olivia which she played in *The Vicar of Wakefield* she wrote: 'I was generally weeping too, for Olivia, more than any part, touched me to the heart. It had a sure message – the love story of an injured woman is one of the cards in the stage pack which it is always safe to play.'

With all these ideas in her mind she promptly married an actor called Charles Kelly, whose real name was Wardell. He was an ex-soldier and appears from his notices to have been a wooden actor. Ellen, all her life, veered between artistic men like Watts and Godwin, who enlarged her view of life, and large beefy hunks of military-seeming manhood. Perhaps she felt that solidity of appearance indicated a solid character. But in Ellen's case the men she chose often suffered from both lack of brains and lack of cash. Ellen, looking on the sunny side of Kelly, described him as 'a manly bulldog sort of man, possessed as an actor with great tenderness and humour'.

What she did not say was that he was addicted to drink and was not especially useful as a father to her children. Gordon Craig described him as something very large and heavy-footed, 'a kind of stranger who growled and clumped his way along the passages'.

Ellen married Kelly a year or so before she met Irving. The marriage solved her problems with her family, who could now visit her; she had become respectable again. She was even occasionally received by Kate on the heights of Campden Hill. Her father, Ben Terry, did not share the general opinion. When she admitted her tenderness for Kelly, Ben reminded her that Kelly drank. She answered airily: 'Oh, I shall reform him.' Ben turned away saying, 'It's a Princess marrying a cellarman.' Her tender admirer, Forbes-Robertson, was equally horrified by the news of her sudden marriage. But Ellen was a creature of moods when it came to her private life, over-feminine and not given to reflection.

While Ellen was touring with Kelly, Irving seems to have thought he had made a firm contract with her. He wrote to his old headmaster, Dr Pinches: 'I have engaged Ellen Terry, not a bad start eh?' But

Ellen, who had been reared on the uncertainties of life as a touring child actress, took no manager's word for his bond and wrote from Liverpool where she was playing with the manly Kelly: 'I understand you would like me to be with you at the Lyceum next season,' adding that if Irving would make her a definite proposition she would answer him equally definitely.

The terms were agreed at £40 a week, and a half clear benefit. It was, after all, not to be Wardell who gave her security but Irving. When Irving finally agreed to her terms he asked her to come and see him play Hamlet. She saw on that night what she considered the perfection of acting.

More than any critic's account, more than painting or sculpture, Ellen's sympathetic description brings Irving's performance to life:

'There was never a touch of commonness in whatever he said or did, blood and breeding pervaded him. His make-up was very pale and this made his face beautiful when one was close to him, but at a distance it gave him a haggard look. He kept three things going at the same time – the antic madness, the sanity, and the sense of theatre . . . His melancholy was simple as it was profound, touching rather than defiant.'

His first entrance as Hamlet was dramatised first by music, and then by a great procession. He had always been a believer in processions. 'When the excitement was at fever heat, came the solitary figure of Hamlet looking extraordinarily tall and thin. He was weary, his cloak trailed on the ground, the hair looked blue black like the plumage of a crow, the eyes burning, two fires veiled as yet by melancholy.'

She added that many people thought her Ophelia had improved Henry's Hamlet, but this was not so, and she added a significant phrase: 'He was always independent of the people with whom he acted.' In his mind he had become the great visiting actor like those he had known in his youth. He was never to be an ensemble player.

The night when Ellen saw Hamlet in Birmingham was to be a high point in her life. If she had set out to charm him for financial reasons, he set out to mesmerise her for the good of his theatre. She wrote:

'The Birmingham night – he knew I was there. He played – and I say it without vanity – for me. We players are not above that weakness, if it be a weakness. If ever anything inspires us to do our best, it is the presence in the audience of some fellow artist who must in the nature of things know more completely than anyone what we intend, what we do, what we feel. The response flies across to us like a flame.'

It was a flame which was to guide Ellen and lead her into a safe haven – a safe haven from bailiffs, a living for her children, and freedom from worry. Craig, her son, says: 'Seldom has such an easy time been given to anybody as Irving gave to Ellen Terry. All financial responsibility removed. For the day Irving came to engage her, Ellen Terry knew perfectly well that her financial future was safe in his hands.'

In the autumn of 1878 Irving, like Ellen, was touring, and in September he was in Dublin for a fortnight. He was constantly in the company of Bram Stoker, lunching and dining with friends and relations. Stoker was allowed into the theatre to watch rehearsals.

As with Ellen, Irving left without making Stoker a definite offer. He always moved with a peasant-like caution, as if by making his motives too plain he might jeopardise some other option which he had in mind. But six weeks after leaving Dublin, Irving wrote asking Stoker to join him as Acting Manager at the Lyceum. The stage-struck Stoker, unlike the experienced and wily Ellen, agreed at once without waiting for a firm offer. He sent in his resignation to the Civil Service, got married, and immediately left for London. The dream he had nursed since he first met Irving had been realised.

The reality of his arrival at the Lyceum, when contrasted with the dream, did not disillusion him. Irving had taken over the theatre in August 1878. The whole building was a complicated jungle of activity. Builders were making structural alterations. Upholsterers, paper-hangers, and painters were working furiously on and off stage. The auditorium was a cat's cradle of poles and platforms. The paint room, the gas rooms and the property rooms were occupied in equally frenzied activity with the new production of *Hamlet*.

At last Irving had his theatre in which he was sole master. He had his old friend Loveday as stage manager and his admirer Bram Stoker as general manager. He had a sparkling leading lady with a following.

The one thing which he did not have was money. Because the theatre was dark from August till December there were expenses but no receipts. He was £10,000 in debt, and the redecoration was to cost some £5,000. During these months he was touring, trying to make up on the provincial roundabout the money he was losing on the swings at the Lyceum. Throughout his acting career, whether in England or later in America, touring was always to be the makeweight for financial overstretching. The days of careful Bateman housekeeping and home dressmaking had gone. There was to be no penny pinching.

Irving had gained control of the Lyceum at the right psychological moment. The prosperity of Victorian England was approaching its apogee. The taste for display and for entertainment was there to be satisfied. Buses and trains could bring the seekers of amusement from remote suburbs. No longer was the player dependent on the carriage and cab trade and on those within walking distance to pack the pit and gallery and fill the boxes. But this new audience, when they wanted an evening out 'up West', wanted to do it in some style. They wanted comfort in the auditorium and spectacle on stage.

The original Lyceum Theatre in which Sheridan's company had taken refuge after the burning of Drury Lane had in its turn been burned down and rebuilt in 1834. The decorations dated from the days of Charles Mathews and his wife, Madame Vestris. The colours were dull gold and crimson, the true theatre colours, and the panels of the boxes were painted with cupids and flowers. The theatre had an old-fashioned charm and was a living version of the tiny cardboard theatres sold by Pollock.

The paying customers of the 1870s wanted softer upholstered seats and a richer comfort. Henry Irving was spending a great deal of money to improve the auditorium, but the decorations were refurbished rather than totally changed. That was for the future.

The Lyceum had been the first theatre in London to be lit by gas. The gas lighting remained during the whole of Irving's time there. Ellen writes lyrically of the effect of the gas footlights and gas 'limes'. Gas had a thick softness with specks and motes in it, like natural light, and misted the imperfections of costumes and scenery, lending grace and beauty to the faces and movements of the actors.

Irving arrived back in London in the middle of December with only two weeks to rehearse and set *Hamlet*. Although he had played

Hamlet in London for over two hundred nights, he worked on it as if he had never played it before. He rehearsed in cloak and rapier, and at the first rehearsal read everyone's part except that of Ophelia.

Ellen described him at rehearsal: 'He threw himself so throughly into it that his skin contracted and his eyes shone. His lips grew whiter and whiter and his skin more and more drawn as the time went on, until he looked like a livid thing.' And Ellen added tenderly: 'Beautiful!' It was a similar strange performance of *Eugene Aram* that had reduced Stoker to hysteria. Irving rehearsed the actors over and over again, trying to instil into them the exact tone and timbre of a speech. Very often all this intensive work only produced colourless imitations of himself, often the weakness of the actor who directs.

Ellen had become more and more worried about her Ophelia. Up to ten days before the first night he had rehearsed no single scene with her. 'I am very nervous about my first appearance with you,' she said to him. 'Couldn't we rehearse *our* scenes?' 'We shall be all right! But we are not going to run the risk of being bottled up by a gas-man or a fiddler,' answered Irving airily.

There were other minor difficulties. As the former wife of one artist and the mistress of another, Ellen prided herself upon what she called her 'artistic and archaeological knowledge'. When Irving asked her what she was going to wear for Ophelia, she listed pink for the first scene, amber brocade to tone down the colour of her hair, and a transparent black dress for the mad scene. Irving listened to this dressmaker's list with patience. But one of the old actors who surrounded Irving and was acting as 'adviser' on the production was stunned. There was only one black figure in *Hamlet*, and that was Hamlet. And so it was. Ellen's black crêpe de Chine trimmed with ermine disappeared, and white sheeting with rabbit fur was substituted.

If Ellen was worried, Irving, well supported by his team of satellites and secure in his possession of his theatre, was conscious of no feeling of self-doubt. Hamlet was his part. He proposed to sell copies of the play in the auditorium, and for this Frank Marshall wrote a long introduction. But even this was amended. 'Cannot it be put down that I played Hamlet at the Lyceum for two hundred consecutive nights?' It must also be underlined that the alterations had been made by Mr Irving 'in accordance with the experience gained by frequent representations of the character of Hamlet'.

Worried about Ophelia, Ellen went to a madhouse to study – as she wrote – 'wits astray'. She was disheartened. She found no pity in the lunatics, they were too theatrical. Suddenly she noticed a young girl gazing at the wall. 'I went between her and the wall to see her face. It was quite vacant, but the body expressed that she was waiting. Suddenly she threw up her hands and sped across the room like a swallow.' Ellen found it pathetic, young and poignant. She had found her model, now she must transform it into a performance. But she still felt unrehearsed and unsure.

When the curtain went up on *Hamlet* on 30 December 1878, pit and gallery had been packed for a long time. Private boxes and stalls were filled with a glittering array of people who saw themselves as representative of art, fashion and literature. Irving had forged himself into an actor who gave the stage an intellectual flavour. He had come a very long way from *Black-eyed Susan* and *Sixteen String Jack*.

One contemporary writer said: 'For such a spectacle as the house presented we have no precedent in England. The great players of the past could rely for ardent support upon only one section of their audience. Mr Irving seems popular with all classes.' The theatre was filled with his admirers, and the slightest rustle was received with a frenzy of rage; not a syllable must be missed.

Even Irving's attackers, Dutton Cook and Joseph Knight, seem to have been silenced by the distinguished audience and the general acceptance. 'His proved devotion to his art and his determination to uphold the national drama to its utmost' were saluted by Dutton Cook. It was not a night for cutting Irving up. Joseph Knight admitted that 'the representation of Hamlet supplied on Monday night is the best the stage during the last quarter of a century has seen, and the best to be seen for some time to come'.

There was not a dissenting voice. Only Ellen was not there to take her curtain call. She felt she had failed, and sped off, like the mad girl she had studied, towards the Embankment with the intention of drowning herself. She was followed and brought back to her house at Longridge Road by Mrs Rumball ('Boo'), the wife of the doctor who had delivered her first child.

After midnight Henry Irving came back to reassure her. In the emotions of this moment she became his mistress. It was the beginning of a long professional and emotional partnership. Ellen needed Irving's drive and the stability which this gave her, and Irving needed her magic. Hamlet had rescued Ophelia. It was both an end and a beginning.*

* This story is given by Marguerite Steen and corroborated by Percy Fitzgerald, who wrote about Ellen on the first night of *Hamlet:*

'On this momentous night of trial she thought she had completely failed and without waiting for the 5th Act flung herself into the arms of a friend repeating "I have failed, I have failed!" She drove up and down the Embankment half-a-dozen times before she found the courage to go home.'

Victorian biographers and autobiographers always use euphemism. Jessie Millward, the acknowledged mistress of William Terriss, constantly refers to him coyly as 'my companion'. In Ellen's case the fleeing to the Embankment, and the flinging herself into the arms of a 'friend', came in the reverse order, and the friend was Henry – always referred to as her 'close friend and collaborator', as indeed he was.

Chapter 9

The Spirits of the Age

The public partnership of Ellen Terry and Henry Irving shines in the full glare of gaslight. Their private life has been successfully hidden.

Most of Ellen's biographers, with one exception, deny that Ellen and Irving were lovers. Their letters to one another when they were still in love are destroyed. Their descendants and admirers prefer to transform them into creatures of fantasy appearing only in a starlit Arden of beauty and innocence. But Ellen in her old age, when all bitterness had faded, and husbands, admirers, and lovers had all acquired the warm glow of the past, said that certainly she had been Irving's mistress. Most of theatrical London knew it. But it was tacitly considered to be their own secret.

Their relationship has to be considered from two aspects, the professed views of the society in which they moved and the parts Ellen played on the Lyceum stage. Heroines had to be spotless or, if they were betrayed, they had to suffer disgrace or death. Ellen suffered neither, and the nobility of the heroines she played inhibited her private life from becoming public knowledge. Morals and manners were of one piece, and one did not cause embarrassment to one's friends.

It is impossible to read the criticisms of Ellen without being made to realise the unacceptability of her name being openly linked with that of Irving except as a stage partner. She was described as 'exhibiting one of those happy natures which keep heart-whole without difficulty and whose tenderest springs of thought and action can be touched only by love, and by a love at once frank and constant'.

The women she played were identified with her, and her personality dominated the parts she played. She charmed and she disarmed. Actors transform themselves. They put on the persona which best fits the age in which they live. Ellen had to be womanly, pure and beautiful. It was no longer the age of Dr Johnson's actresses with white bosoms in candlelit dressing-rooms.

As a foil to the womanly woman, Irving had to portray the accompanying gentleman. He was constantly described as gentlemanly. This was his contemporary mask: the neat suit, the white linen edging the frock coat as in the portrait at the Garrick Club – all the trimmings which gave him the air of Soames Forsyte about to woo Irene. The Victorians appreciated a gentleman, and Irving lived up to this ideal in his off-stage persona. He had to be respectable and Soames-like in appearance.

And always watching was the spiteful, rejected wife of Irving, anxious to cause a scandal which could destroy a career so carefully built up over so many years and through so many hardships. A love affair in the seventies was not easily conducted. It was not simply setting-up house together with that very brave modern defiance of a conventions which no longer exist. It was a midnight affair of closing doors and footsteps on the stairs, when discovery meant social and financial ruin. It needed courage.

Occasionally they snatched holidays abroad together, often taking one of Ellen's children with them as a respectable cover. An undated newspaper account described one of these holidays:

'Last week in Brussels my eyes were gladdened by a sight they little expected to see. I had taken myself to an open air concert in the Waux-Hall and was listening to the music and indulging in the customary modest Bock, when a loud ringing laugh from a neighbouring table attracted my attention as being strangely familiar. I turned round, and to my intense astonishment found myself rubbing shoulders with no less personages than Henry Irving and Ellen Terry with the latter's eldest daughter (*sic*). Here was genius relaxing indeed. Miss Terry who was in such buoyant spirits as would surprise some of the Lyceum patrons and evidently acting on the principle that when you are in Rome you must do as the Romans do, divided her attention, like the rest of the company between her glass of drink, the performance, and light conversation. The great Henry, looking eminently picturesque in his soft felt hat, was graver, as if the whole affair was a little beneath the dignity of his genius. Miss Terry wore a large black hat and a long brown wrap which the Lyceum manager solicitously adjusted about the shoulders of his leading lady. I did not wait to see or hear more as eavesdropping is hardly in my line, but the penetrating quality of Miss Terry's voice enabled me to distinguish her musical laugh above the babel of voices after I had moved off to a far corner of the illuminated gardens.'

The unknown reporter gives a vignette of Ellen, happy, noisy and relaxed, with Henry in loving and assiduous attendance, but looking carefully over his shoulder.

There is a tendency to contrast the charming, outgoing nature of Ellen with the strange, inhibited and ambitious Irving. Yet both acted their chosen parts, and were equally as false, or as true, as the passing emotions of the people they played. Ellen was always the great actress projecting charm and loving kindness. Gordon Craig writes of his mother as having a face with a double look, and on another occasion speaks of her dual nature. He describes her setting out from her house to go to the theatre:

Here comes Ellen Terry out of her house and down the steps. Talking to a servant and to a child or two. Getting into the carriage, the great Ellen Terry drives off to rehearsal. Stops in Piccadilly and buys some fruit, is hailed by someone in Arlington Street, and someone near the Garrick, sees them, calls them by name, kisses them.'

But once in the theatre she has forgotten who the dickens she met near the Garrick Club, added Craig. To Graham Robertson she wrote: 'One's work is the best of us all, don't you think so? With most folks I've met, I've loved their work better than them.'

With Ellen, as with Irving, work came first and second, and private life was slotted in, as and when convenient. It was not a recipe for an easy love affair. If Irving was more openly ambitious than Ellen, he was perhaps less self-deceiving. Ellen was always playing some other part in her private life. When she lived with Godwin, it was the country idyll, like Marie Antoinette in the Trianon. Her son said that she had 'all the sensitiveness of those who love what is beautiful in nature, trees, and flowers growing in woods and lanes, old cottages, castle and rivers'.

This was Ellen playing the part of a country lady in her sunbonnet. She had depicted the loving, caring mother for a few years, and then become bored with the part, with Godwin's neglect and her lack of money. The theatre called her back strongly because it was to her, as it was to Irving, like oxygen used to revive. She needed the applause and admiration as he did. 'Everyone was in love with me' – it was that feeling which gave her the conviction that life was, worthwhile. Craig's description of Ellen as the great actress leaving her house is a perfect vignette of her chameleon nature.

She often asked herself if she had been a good mother. Perhaps, as she once said, 'if there had been no horrible theatre', and no public life apart from her children, all would have been different. She admitted that she was never entirely one, never entirely actress or mother. It was her great illusion. She was all actress. Irving did not share this illusion; he *knew* he was all actor.

It was only when she went through the private entrance into the theatre that she became herself. The artistic attributes on which Ellen prided herself, knowledge of colour, painting and architecture, were like the veins in a piece of marble, and represented phases of her life and the men with whom she had lived. She had a great talent for admiration, for respect, and for learning from others. She said, 'I learned from Mr Watts, from Mr Godwin and other artists.' She was often praised for being the living embodiment of the pre-Raphaelite woman, but even this was an image created by G. F. Watts. He took the child of touring actors and turned her into a living, breathing legend. When she went to live with Godwin she learned ways of building, decorating, and arranging her house, and adopted her 'simple' style of dress, leaning towards linen and simplicity in the 'greenery, yallery' way of the artistic fringe of her day, unfashionably conformist.

When Ellen joined Irving at the Lyceum she was thirty years old, and at the peak of her charm, her beauty and her power. Like Watts the painter, Irving the actor took the material, and in return gave her financial stability and world fame. He has been blamed for failing to let Ellen's genius shine out in the full brilliance of its glory, for using her as a charming foil to his own egotistical representations. Actors are the prisoners of their age and of popular fancies, and Ellen was as much a prisoner as Irving.

Yet in the spring of their relationship, she who had been a professional since a child gave him much in return – her artistic knowledge, her unstinted admiration, and her professional dedication. The deep admiration she felt for him shines out through all the pages of *The Story of My Life*. She praised so many things about him. 'I watched him one day in the train, always a delightful occupation for his face provided many pictures a minute.' She was struck by a half-puzzled, half-despairing look, and asked him what he was thinking about. He replied slowly that it was strange that a man such as himself, with no equipment, legs, voice, walk, everything against him, had done so well. 'And I looking at that splendid head, those wonderful hands, the whole strange beauty of him and thought: "How little you know."'

It is not the remembered feeling of a great stage partner, it is the remembered feeling of a woman who had loved the man, and in spite of all cherished the memory.

She helped him on technicalities. Even the critics noticed his intense nervousness on first nights. Ellen, in her practical way, said that if she were to wait ten minutes in the wings and allow the acute consciousness of the audience to overcome her she would be paralysed with fright. 'I suggested a more swift entrance from the dressing room.' He pondered her suggestion, and in the end adopted it, 'as he told me with great comfort to himself – and success with the audience'. He was always ready to learn, to improve, and to change. His stage portraits were never finished.

After the triumph of *Hamlet*, his next production was *The Lady of Lyons*, that well-worn piece of fustian by Bulwer Lytton, written in the 1830s and set in post-revolutionary France. Irving tricked the play out with much artistic scenery and dressmaking, and hordes of marching men passing the window (played by selected men from the Brigade of Guards, at 1s 6d an hour). This phantom army does not appear in the printed script, but, as Ellen wrote, 'the march past the window of the apparently unending army – that good old trick – which sends the supers flying round the backcloth to cross the stage again and again created a superb effect.'

The play had originally been seen in London with Helen Faucit playing Pauline Deschapelles to the Claude Melnotte of the Anglo-French actor Charles Fechter. When Helen Faucit heard that Irving was to produce it, she wrote warning him against the feeble language and false sentiments. But as Ellen once remarked, Irving revelled in fustian, it was a legacy of the twopence coloured days of his beginnings. The speeches were long and colourful, and most of all it gave Ellen a chance to display her beauty.

The play was Irving's gift to his lady. Like many gifts it did not quite achieve its purpose. Ellen admitted that although she had played the part before she had not done so well when playing with Irving. There were reasons for this. Ellen no longer took the part seriously, and Henry Irving never shone brightly as a stage lover. There were other difficulties. Ellen later said that, once they had become lovers, when they played love-scenes together she felt stiff and self-conscious. She found herself blushing from head to foot 'which was *very* difficult for Henry'.

Ellen and Irving made all the mistakes which Helen Faucit had warned them against. Ellen was tearful and charming, and Irving played Claude as his usual tragic, haunted hero. In his careful way, he had based his clothes and make-up on pictures of the young Napoleon.

Ellen did not like the part, and it is difficult not to feel sympathy with her. The heroine constantly refers to herself as Pauline, as if to emphasise her name in case the audience had no programmes. Melnotte, as drawn by the playwright, seems to have more *rapport* with the white man disappointed in love going out to shoot big game than with the eighteenth century.

The plot hinges on a revenge taken on the haughty Pauline by her unsuccessful suitor, Beauséant, who persuades Melnotte (the low-born hero) to masquerade as a Prince of Como and marry her. But before the bedroom door is crossed, Melnotte repents: 'Here at thy feet, I lay a husband's rights. A marriage thus unholy, unfulfill'd is by the laws of France made void and null.' He proposed to lead her 'pure and virgin as this morn' back to her father. Having renounced his bride, Melnotte announces his intention of going to a distant land 'where I may mourn my sin'. He gets an instant commission in the Army, which fortuitously happens to be marching by.

In the last act he arrives back loaded with military honours – and money, in the nick of time to save Pauline from marrying Beauséant to pay off her old father's debts. Melnotte tears up the fatal contract and produces a wallet full of money: 'I outbid yon sordid huckster for your priceless jewel.'

The curtain came down on rapture all round. This was not shared by the critics. Ellen had turned the proud Pauline into a tender, sympathetic, tearful lady, and Irving was too tragic. Scrutator wrote: 'I do not think I ever so thoroughly enjoyed a burlesque as I did the sight of Mr Irving and Miss Terry unconsciously burlesquing as Claude and Pauline.' Clement Scott wrote that even those who found the sentiments old-fashioned were able to 'gaze contentedly at faultless pictures, and at costume raised to the dignity of art'.

The play ran for forty-one nights and the receipts were not disappointing. 'I suppose', said Ellen, 'even at our worst the public found something in our acting to like.'

The Lady of Lyons closed in June 1879 and Irving never played Melnotte again. It was a gesture to Ellen which had not quite succeeded in spite of its expensive setting. The rest of the season was given up to successes in which Irving knew he would shine, and to parts the public knew and appreciated: *Louis XI*, *Hamlet*, *Charles I*, *Eugene Aram* and *Richelieu*.

In *Charles I* Ellen played Henrietta Maria. She admitted that in the last act she cried too much, nor could she emulate Isabel Bateman and use a French accent. Ellen's real tears were much admired, but in *Charles I* they were a tribute to Irving's acting. He was not a man coming on to the stage but a king going to the scaffold. However often she played that scene she knew that 'when he first came on he was not aware of my presence. He seemed to be already in heaven.'

Irving's make-up as Charles I was much praised, but Ellen shrewdly remarked that he was not building up his face with wig paste. His art of make-up was lit by the expression from within. 'He had the most beautiful Stuart hands. Unlike most stage kings, he never seemed to be assuming dignity. He was very, very simple.' The public took Henrietta's tears to heart, and Oscar Wilde in a romantic sonnet described Ellen as 'like some wan lily overdrenched with rain'.

Eugene Aram was Henry's play, and as Ruth Meadowes, the vicar's daughter, Ellen had little to do. If Irving liked gloomy parts, he also liked gloomy effects to highlight them. In the last act he used a cedar tree, with a dark overhanging branch which seemed, he said, 'Like the cruel hand of Fate stretched out'. When the curtain went up he was lying beneath the Fate tree in a black cloak and only when the light of moonbeams touched the dark mass was it discovered to be a man. When she wrote about the play Ellen remarked: 'Melancholy and the horrors had a peculiar fascination for him – especially in those early days.' But her admiration of Henry shone out. His recitation of *Eugene Aram* was far finer than anything he did in the play. 'Especially when he did it in a frock coat – no one ever looked so well in a frock coat!' But Ellen, with her sure professional touch, told him that the way he recited it was *too much* for a *room*. He took her advice and toned it down.

The first season of Ellen and Irving's partnership closed with one of Irving's double acts. He played the first act of *Richard III* and Jeremy Diddler in the farce *Raising the Wind*. This performance was received with no relish by Shaw, who happened to be present:

'I remember years ago going into the Lyceum Theatre under the impression that I was about to witness a performance of *Richard III*. After one act of that tragedy, Mr. Irving relapsed into an impersonation of Alfred Jingle. He concealed piles of sandwiches in his hat; so that when he afterwards raised it to introduce himself as Alfred Jingle Esq. of No Hall, Nowhere, a rain of ham and bread descended on him. He knelt on the stage on one knee and seated Miss Pauncefort (the spinster aunt) on the other and then upset himself and her, head over heels . . . he inked the glimpses of shirt that appeared through holes in his coat, and insulted the other characters.'

Shaw remarked that Irving was not creating Dickens, he was simply taking his revenge on Shakespeare and himself for months of sustained dignity.

In looking back over his years of playgoing, Shaw appears to have merged in his mind the characters of Jingle in *Pickwick* and Jeremy Diddler in *Raising the Wind*. Both characters were played by Irving in the same eccentric way. *Raising the Wind* was the old James Kenney farce, first produced in 1803. Shaw was right in remembering the rolls in the hat and the spinster aunt, both of which do occur in Kenney's play, but not in *Pickwick*.

This does not invalidate Shaw's very perceptive criticism, which pinpointed the strange split in Irving's character. Although he loved practical jokes, he found it difficult to relax from his appearance of dignity. Ellen said that in the Hamlet days Henry's melancholy was appalling. 'I remember feeling as if I had laughed in church when he came to the foot of the stairs leading to my dressing-room and caught me sliding down the banisters.'

On the last night of the season, Irving made the usual speech in front of the curtain. For nearly eight years the audience applause had thrilled him again and again. 'We have taken since the 30th December the large sum of £36,000. I can give you no better proof than this of your generous appreciation of our work.' The speech had the right mercantile approach. The audience would not wish to be associated with a financial failure. Applause followed financial success.

When all salaries were paid, including Irving's and Ellen's, he had been able to reduce his debt by over £6,000, and an old friend of his, a Mrs Brown, had died and left him £5,000, which also went to swell the theatre's funds. He had good reason to be content.

In the ordinary way he would have set out on tour with Ellen and reaped a golden harvest from the provinces while the dazzling success of his first season was still fresh. But there were impediments. The heaviest of these was Charles Kelly, Ellen's husband.

Although her marriage to Kelly had been slowly breaking up during the first year of her engagement at the Lyceum, he remained a liability. He had become jealous and was touchy about his situation as a second-rank actor compared to the brilliance and acclaim which his wife had earned. His drinking had not improved his temper. Whether to placate him, or because she had previously agreed to do so, when the Lyceum season closed Ellen set off on a tour with her husband. Watching Ellen's attachment to Irving growing, Kelly had good reasons for his jealousy. During their tour of *Much Ado* they quarrelled with much greater bitterness off stage than on.

Ellen described Kelly as a male Julia (in Shaw's *The Philanderer*) and wrote to Shaw: 'I should have died had I lived one more month with him. I gave him three quarters of all the money I made weekly and prayed him to go.'

When Kelly suggested a divorce Ellen, with her strange double standards, was shocked. She had no intention of going through that kind of scandal again. In any case, in her practical way she could not see any reason for it. Irving was married and his wife had set her bourgeois mind totally against divorcing him.

In 1881 a judicial separation was arranged. Irving had managed to silence his wife by threatening that, should any breath of scandal sully Ellen's fair name, Florence's allowance would be stopped.

Florence was content to live comfortably from the proceeds of a profession she despised and a liaison which she heartily condemned.

Four years after the judicial separation, in 1885, Ellen's own marriage difficulties were solved. She was called to Kelly's deathbed by his current mistress. Ellen was always content to accept facts as they were, thanked the girl for looking after Kelly, and went up to see the dying man. 'When I went upstairs I could not feel it was Charles, but I had the strangest wish to rehearse Juliet there by the bed on which he was lying!'

But in the summer of 1879 Kelly was still living, breathing, making a nuisance of himself, and on tour with Ellen. Irving realised that without Ellen a tour alone would have lost a great deal of its pulling power, and he decided to accept Baroness Burdett-Coutts's invitation to cruise round the Mediterranean in the steamer *Walrus*. The press had a holiday too, with caricatures of the tragedian and the banking heiress sailing across the wine-dark seas of the Aegean together. This was the only time since he began his stage career in 1856 that he had had a holiday. For the first time in twenty-two years gaslight and canvas had been changed into the reality of sun, sea, and the moving panorama of classic landscapes.

Yet a month after he set out he was already writing to Loveday: 'I hope to be with you on the 12th September – at the latest – and glad I shall be to get back.' His letter is full of plans for the new season. He talks of putting on either *Venice Preserv'd* or *Othello*. But when he arrived in Venice itself he was immediately attracted by its charm and strangeness. He became aware of the way in which the city's old trading links with the East had made it a melting pot of races, and was particularly fascinated with the Jews he saw there. This put the idea of *The Merchant of Venice* in his mind – a part for himself, and a part for Ellen which she had already played with success. All the ports around the Mediterranean showed him different aspects of the Levantine Jew – his dignity, his sharpness of trading, and his anger at being cheated of the smallest bargain.

Hawes Craven, with the idea of *Venice Preserv'd* in mind, had already made detailed sketches of Venice – street scenes, buildings and romantic views of canals and churches. Everything was prepared to re-create Venice on the Lyceum Stage. By the time Irving had reached London his mind was firmly set on the idea of *The Merchant of Venice*. Hawes Craven had not wasted his time.

1. (a) Richelieu (1873): 'The performance amounts to a resurrection. The great Cardinal lean, worn, eaten with ambition is admirably rendered.' *Jules Claretie.*

(b) *Hamlet* (1874): 'Nothing distracts the eye from the wonderful face; a costume rich but simple relieved only by a heavy chain of gold.' *Clement Scott.*

2. (a) Romeo and Juliet (1882): The Balcony scene. 'His clothes were as Florentine as his bearing. He had no feather in his cap, but wore a sprig of crimson oleander.' *Ellen Terry*.

(b) Tomb Scene. A steep staircase and gallery lead down to the burying place, and down these steps and along the gallery Romeo dragged the body of the murdered Paris.

3. Ellen Terry by Edouard Rischgitz. A previously unpublished drawing of the actress circa 1874.
Rischgitz was born in Austro-Hungary about 1840. His family were exiled after the Kossuth Rebellion. He is best known for his country landscapes painted for Minton.

4. (a) Harvard Night at the Tremont Theatre, Boston.
Ellen Terry in *Nance Oldfield*. 'A brilliant audience received the play with intense enthusiasm–students and friends giving a Royal Welcome.'

(b) Becket at Windsor Castle. 'Becket is a noble and human part, full of the noblest thoughts and elements of introspection that may come to us in this life of ours.' *Henry Irving*.

5. (a) Shylock. 'He was old, haggard, halting, but represented the dignity and intellect of the play.' *Dutton Cook*.
(b) Richard III. 'He very strongly brings out the bitter irony of Richard, his scorn of mankind, and his mockery of this world and the next.' *Saunders News*.
(c) Ellen Terry in *Becket*. 'Fair Rosamund in a dream-like robe of tender salmon and ruby brocade embroidered in gold, silver and pearls.'

6.(a) The Audience. *The Pit*. 'When ribs and breastbone were on the verge of collapse, my hopes of a place in the front row ran high.' *Bernard Shaw*.

(b) *The Stalls*. Ladies and gentlemen expected to be received at the theatre as in their own drawing rooms – even programme sellers wore the apron of a parlourmaid.

7. (a) *Faust*. The Brocken Scene – vast, chilling and strange with its atmosphere of dizzy heights shrouded in mists hovering above tortuous crevasses was judged never to have been surpassed.

(b) Irving watching a rehearsal. 'But he never grew weary of coaching them, down to the minutest detail. I saw him growing more and more fatigued with his efforts.' *Ellen Terry*.

8. Irving making up at the Lyceum. 'His art of make-up was lit by the expression from within.' *Ellen Terry.*

However, Irving's first new offering was to be *The Iron Chest*, an old melodrama which had been worked and re-worked. Founded on a novel by Godwin called *Caleb Williams*, John Philip Kemble cobbled it together for himself, much to the dissatisfaction of George Colman (the younger) who had written the play. When the play failed Colman blamed Kemble's monotonous delivery which the author compared to the buzzing of a fly in a bottle. Why Irving chose this play is difficult to understand, except that it bore many likenesses to his early successes with Aram and Mathias. Actors are not always given to originality, and Irving was drawn, as Ellen said, to dark and gloomy parts. Kean had made a moderate success of it and was supposed to have reduced Byron to hysterics when playing Sir Edward Mortimer in 1816. Irving loved to re-create Kean's successes, and Sir Edward was a man with a guilty secret, a bloody dagger in a locked chest; added to which the play ends with him sinking in convulsions on stage and being led away gibbering noiselessly.

Irving, over-satisfied with the audience's wrapt attention to the gloom and revenge of *The Iron Chest*, made a complacent speech on the first night, giving a fervent promise to his audience that the play would be added to his permanent repertory. It lasted four weeks, and was never played again on the Lyceum stage, thus proving that a first night audience is about as reliable a guide to success as a racing tip.

This failure made a new production essential. Ellen came back from her stormy provincial tour with Charles Kelly and was immediately asked to rehearse for Portia. The slow audience decline was propped up with a revival of *Hamlet* with Ellen as Ophelia.

From the moment of its planning to the opening night on 1 November, the whole production of *The Merchant* took less than two months. This time the arrow hit the target. Pit, dress circle and gallery rose for Mr Irving, and the roar of applause was said to have been heard in the streets around the Lyceum. The rising of pit and gallery is the actor's dream, the ultimate accolade. Irving came before the curtain and bowed:

'This is the happiest moment of my life, and I may claim for myself, and those associated with me in this production, the merit of having worked hard – for on the 8th October not a brush had been put upon the scenery, nor a stitch in any of the dresses.'

With another humble inclination he retired behind the curtain. But this humility was another part he played. Ellen remarked that he had never forgotten the bitterness of the weeks of booing he had endured in Dublin. It coloured his whole attitude, and when he made his humble little speeches before the curtain there was always a pride in his humility. Perhaps, she said, he would not have received adulation in quite the same dignified way if he had never known what it was to wear the martyr's shirt of flame. He realised that a mob is as quick to lynch as to cheer. It had not been an easy lesson to learn.

The Merchant was acclaimed with few dissenting voices; both audience and critics took it to their hearts. Although the production was said to be lavish, it had cost less than £2,000. But the Hawes Craven backcloths had evoked the spirit of the Queen of the Adriatic. Gondolas moved along canals, merchants and citizens in colourful clothes mingled in streets and market places. Against these sunlit scenes moved the beautiful Ellen in her pre-Raphaelite poses, radiantly beautiful in her Venetian robes of gold-coloured brocaded satin, with the look of a picture by Giorgione. Ellen Terry, whose first acting of Portia caused her to remark 'everyone was in love with me', had charmed for the second time: 'Miss Ellen Terry is pre-Raphaelite, what others seek to imitate she *is*, as Portia she was perfect.'

Even Irving's attackers turned to praise. Dutton Cook called his performance consistent and harmonious, displaying that power of self-control 'which has come to Mr Irving this season as a fresh possession. Every temptation to extravagance or eccentricity of action was resolutely resisted. I never saw a Shylock that obtained more commiseration from the audience.' He was old, haggard, halting and sordid, but represented the dignity and intellect of the play. 'Beside him, the Christians for all their graces of aspect and gallantry of apparel seem but poor creatures.' Joseph Cook, Clement Scott, and even the sharp-penned Scrutator of *Truth* could scarce forbear to cheer.

The most curious part of this portrayal in modern eyes is that the idea for a more human Shylock came, according to Irving's contemporary critics, from Germany, the country later most notorious for the persecution of the Jews. This new Shylock was not to everyone's taste. One anonymous critic took exception to Irving's new modern theories. Shakespeare was a practical man of the theatre; in his age Jews were regarded as a race to be detested for their usury. 'All the modern twaddle about Shylock being a martyr or the spirit of toleration is leather and prunella.'

In the chorus of praise and adulation of the genius of Irving and Ellen, a few carping voices were raised. One critic anxious to display his specialised knowledge of gondola craft wrote: 'Why does the gondolier imagine he is in a punt, and push his bark along instead of pretending to row it in the graceful Venetian mode?'

Blackwood's Magazine attacked Ellen's Portia, saying that she showed too much of a coming-on disposition in the Casket scene. This upset her; any suggestion of indelicacy, she said, 'always blighted me'.

On other occasions Ellen was castigated for kissing and touching her fellow actors. It was her nature off stage to be demonstratively affectionate and she carried this into her stage parts. With a prudish clutch of critics and an audience ever on the look-out for suggestions of moral decay, leading actors had a thin tightrope to walk. Plays were apt to be criticised on suggestions of impurity, and leading actresses had to portray charm and affection, remain attractive, and keep their hands to themselves.

This view was endorsed by an anonymous American writer. Miss Terry may have been regarded as an actress of exquisite genius in England, but that was not his opinion.

'Miss Terry has too much nature and we should like a little more art. She arranges herself wonderfully well for the stage. She is not regularly beautiful, but a face in the taste of the period which Burne-Jones might have drawn. She has perception but lacks acuteness, her execution is rough, and her expression frequently amateurish . . . as Portia she giggles too much, is too free, too osculatory in her relations with Bassanio.'

Taste, concluded the critic censoriously, is not an English quality.

But these were solitary voices. *The Graphic* said:

'From Kean's time all succeeding personators have been weak imitators until a new and original Shylock has appeared in Mr Irving. The striking departure with the burgess's belt and pouch, the comparatively listless air of his performance in the trial scene, relieved once or twice by bursts of ferocious eagerness. The mood of a mind which has brooded over vengeance until the sleepless eyes have grown hollow, the mind become vacant, the outward world endowed with a weird unreal aspect and vengeance itself like the predominant image of a dream.'

Ellen, more intimately concerned with the practical acting of the play, said that Henry's Shylock meant an entire revision of her conception of Portia, who in the trial scene ought to be very quiet. But Henry's heroic saint, although splendid, upset the balance of the play.

The rest of the cast were considered to be weak. Critics spoke of the utter misery of listening to them, especially Florence Terry as Jessica. 'Handsome Jack' Barnes played Bassanio to little effect. It was said of him that he thought more of the rounding of his legs than the charms of his affianced wife, and 'in the love scenes he appeared to be taking orders for furniture'. But the enthusiasm carried the play forward triumphantly. It remained in Irving's repertory and little by little over the years he improved and added to his conception of Shylock. He had a childlike eagerness to learn from the smallest things. On one occasion he had acted Shylock when a blind man was in the audience. The blind man remarked that he could hear no sound of the usurer in the phrase, 'Three thousand ducats'. It was spoken with the reflective air of a man to whom money meant very little. The blind man was right, Irving had very little sense of the value of money as a commodity for its own sake. But he revised his reading, and remarked that he saw now that he had not been enough of a money-lender.

All Irving's parts were like paintings which were continually to be touched and re-touched, or gilded anew so that they should remain ever fresh and lively to his audiences.

With Ellen at her most decorative and charming, Irving at his mesmeric best, and the sunlit backcloths of Hawes Craven, the play pleased and enchanted, filling the Lyceum for many months. The hundredth performance was celebrated with the first of those vast Lyceum banquets where the guest list was as distinguished and celebrated as the menu was long and heavy.

From the obscurity of shivering without a coat in a northern winter, Irving had at last become a public man.

Chapter 10

The Public Image and the Private Man

When the curtain fell on the 100th night of *The Merchant of Venice* the scenery on the stage was struck, and Benjamin Edginton (of 2 Duke Street, London Bridge) was engaged to turn the stage into a banqueting hall suitable for 350 gentlemen, all of them outstanding in the fields of the arts, science, law, medicine, the army, commerce, literature, politics – and society.

Mr Edginton, naturally proud of this achievement, advertised his magical transformation scenes on a little calendar with coloured engravings showing ladies and gentlemen being entertained under various marquees, magically turned into glittering rooms by the addition of mirrors, chandeliers, rich carpets, and banqueting tables loaded with napery, china, and crystal. 'Mr Edginton had the honour of supplying and fitting up the spacious marquee erected on the stage with something like magical celerity (*Era*) for the Entertainment given by Mr Henry Irving in commemoration of the 100th performance of the Merchant of Venice.' The time given for this feat varies, but Percy Fitzgerald who was present and should have known puts it down as twenty minutes.

All the scenery was whisked from the stage and over the whole vacant space of some four thousand square feet rose an immense pavilion of white and scarlet bands, looped around the walls with tasteful draperies, and lit by two gigantic chandeliers 'whose hundreds of lights in lily-shaped bells of muffled glass shone with a soft and starry radiance, and by the twinkling gleams of many hundreds of wax candles which rose in clusters from the long tables'.

The guests entered through Irving's and Ellen's private doorway, along a crimson-carpeted passage flanked with palms and flowers, ascended the flower-decked staircase, and passed into Irving's armoury. This was a room which his contemporaries, with their fascination for the medieval, found especially impressive. Over the years, as the productions mounted, the heavy weight of authentically reproduced breastplates, halberds, swords, and rapiers was augmented until walls and floorspace glistened with metal.

On this the first of Irving's public celebrations of his fame and status, his flair for grandeur came as a surprise. From the armoury they went into the reception room which was the old room of the original eighteenth-century Beefsteak Club. This had been enlarged and its oak-panelled walls were decorated with portraits, notably one by Long of Irving himself as Richard III.

At midnight the guests moved into the supper room, the glittering marquee which had been erected with such remarkable speed by Edginton and his technicians. The house lights had been kept full on and they 'shone dimly through the canvas like starlight upon a summer sea; the great banner with its legend of crimson on a ground of grey velvet – "At first and last a Hearty Welcome" – hung on the tent wall opposite to the dais table'.

The tables were surrounded with heavily scented hot-house blooms and each of the guests was presented with a copy of the play (as arranged by Irving) bound in white parchment and lettered in gold. The supper was provided by Messrs Gunter, as all Irving's banquets were to be in the future.

Percy Fitzgerald, that assiduous collector of Irvingiana, was accustomed to paste selected menus in his book of memories. This. a typical example, is written in the worst of catering French:

Potages
Tortue Clair
A la Bagration

Poissons
Filet de Truite Grille Sauce Tartare
Turbot Sauce Hollandaise
Blanchaille Frits

Entrées
Supreme de Volaile aux Truffes

Relèves
Poulardes et Langue à la Montmorency
Hanche de Venaison
Jambon aux Epinards

Rot
Cailles Bardées

Entrements
Tomates Farcie a l'Italienne
Chatreuse de Pêches a la Crème
Macedoine de Fruits

Relève
Croutes de Jambon au Parmesan

The menu is elaborately designed in the Japanese taste with pictures of leaves, kingfishers, and butterflies, and Mr Fitzgerald has scrawled across it 'By Gunter P.F.' When it is borne in mind that the distinguished gentlemen who were present at Irving's celebrations had already eaten dinner it is not surprising that Baden-Baden in August became a necessity.

It was a good moment for the touring actor as he looked round the candlelit tables and saw the outstanding men of his time come to do him honour in his own theatre. Yet there was to be a skeleton at this feast – Lord Houghton. He rose to give the toast: 'The health of Mr Henry Irving and the Lyceum Theatre'.

That was merely the cream on the top of the dish; the rest of the pudding was more bitter. Houghton proceeded to launch an all-out attack on long runs; for his part, looking back on the days of his youth, he preferred the arrangement by which the same pieces never came on more than twice a week, when one could see various actors in various roles, and added that he was not at all sure that the present system did not expose actors to personal exertions which could injure their health. Having put long runs in their place, he gave a small pat on the head to the actor-manager. Irving had come, he said 'when the stage was purified very much from the impurity and scandal attaching to it before, so that the tradition of good breeding and high conduct was not confined to special families like the Kembles, or to Mr Irving himself, but had spread over the larger part of the profession so that families of condition were ready to allow their sons – after a university education – to enter into the dramatic profession'.

Having bestowed a cursory compliment on Irving for the white flower of his supposedly blameless life, the noble guest then launched a further attack on his misinterpretations of Shakespeare's characters, including Richard III and Shylock, and suggested that if Irving played Iago he would make him sympathetic.

The supper was given solely for male celebrities, but Ellen, who heard the details from Irving at first hand, said that they were all surprised by this sarcastic speech. It may have been more interesting than the usual 'butter', but it was considered discourteous to abuse long runs when the company were celebrating their 100th performance. Irving replied with a speech full of good sense, good humour, and good breeding. His speeches were always so much better when he spoke spontaneously, or prepared them himself, wrote Ellen, than when he was helped by 'literary hacks ignorant of the facts'.

When the gentlemen relaxed with their cigars and brandy, Irving's old friend J. L. Toole made a cheery speech to try to remove the sour note from the evening's entertainment. With his comedian's good humour, he did this very effectively and the party did not break up till daylight.

In an age of grand and lavish entertainment, Irving was not to be outdone, and with his sense of showmanship he could stage-manage the grandeur of the period better than most of his contemporary hosts. For his own supper he was content with a kipper and some champagne, but for public occasions it was grandeur by Gunter. The Victorians were gluttons for long and involved menus, for public entertainment, and for public speeches which were as long and heavy as the menus. Irving needed them all, for he had become a splendid social and public figure, and had made the Stage a part of Society.

His demanding work of acting and managing a great theatre was interspersed with these public occasions. The engravings in newspapers and periodicals show him laying foundation stones of theatres, unveiling memorials, and speaking at seemingly endless dinners, luncheons, clubs, and universities.

Nor was the cause of charity and the deserving poor ignored. His patroness, Baroness Burdett-Coutts, lured him into giving literary readings for the improvement of the lower orders:

'On Wednesday evening Mr Henry Irving entertained the Costermongers Club in Brown's Lane, Spitalfields by reading a story of Mrs Gaskell's. The mise-en-scene consisted of the identical paraphernalia used by the late Mr Charles Dickens on his reading tours. By employing a peculiar lighting apparatus Mr Dickens contrived that the light instead of springing upwards should be thrown down upon the reader in such quantity as to make every movement of the facial muscles distinctly visible. The effect on Wednesday night was perfect.'

One part of his past always remained with Irving. He had a deep feeling for people in his own profession. He performed in endless benefits for any and every retiring actor and actress. This affection for his profession was not always shared by his audience.

'Mr Henry Irving at the Theatrical Fund dinner seems to do his utmost to invest the actor's lack of necessary care with a kind of poetry; and talks about improvidence being the actor's badge in quite an exultant strain as though there were something absolutely heroic in a man squandering his earnings at the risk of dying and leaving his tradespeople unpaid and a widow and orphans destitute.'

Victorian sympathy could not be wasted on the improvident.

Irving, not as provident as he might be, also gave benefits for himself from time to time, and not always to the delight of the press.

'Mr Henry Irving took a benefit – and apologised for it. Quite right. The Manager of the Lyceum cannot plead poverty as his reason for taking a benefit, but he fondly clings to the Benefit Night as a sort of good old genial theatrical custom which serves him as an excuse for gathering about him a dress circle of admirers who will listen to a speech from the throne.'

He and Ellen were always ready to give their services for charity, whether it was to aid widows, orphans, needy musicians, or starving dogs – both of them shared the great English attachment to furry friends. Irving was invariably accompanied by a current canine favourite. A touching account is given by one periodical of Irving's dog Trin being rescued by a shepherd's collie in the Highlands.

This was illustrated by a full-page engraving of the 'Noble Dog Rescuer'. The account ended: 'Since the above account was written the poor little fellow (Irving's Trin) has died from too eagerly swallowing a bone.' As Trin was constantly mentioned as burrowing into and swallowing the entire contents of wastepaper baskets this early demise should not have come as a surprise to Trin's friends.

Irving's character as a public man was blazoned over columns of newsprint. His doings were recorded in cruel caricatures, romantic engravings, and in stiff photographs. His recitations like *Eugene Aram* and *The Uncle* were published as musical monologues. He sponsored the tonic wine Mariani (alleged to maintain health at its highest pitch), and recommended Marsuma Cigars. His fame was used by advertising pirates. A huge engraving of him as Hamlet bears the legend: 'To Beecham or not to Beecham that is the question, methinks I've heard they are worth a guinea a box (with apologies to our most renowned actor).'

His Shakespeare productions, like a modern TV serial, boosted the sale of the book of the play. No review of the year, with its engraved panorama of current celebrities, was complete without a picture of Irving. One edition of the periodical *Society* gives a double spread in which the apex of the mountain is Queen Victoria and the Prince of Wales, but also gives great prominence to the lean figure of Irving.

His 'rooms' in Grafton Street were described over and over again. The years and his increasing fame merely added to their confusion: more and more mirrors, busts, pictures, and books, but always books connected with past or future productions. They indicated a mind which was entirely absorbed with theatre. His home was a reflection of his dressing room, which was also described in great detail. ('Where is a more picturesque room than that which Irving enters nightly?') The walls are covered with pictures, scarcely a dozen inches of wallpaper are to be seen. The floor is covered in oilcloth and his chair repaired again and again. For he had a reverence, it was said, for anything which was a connecting link with old associations. His way of life was entirely bounded by his profession, but he had made himself into a splendid and respected public figure.

His private character, when the curtain was rung down, is more difficult to define. With his friends and cronies he would sit up till dawn smoking cigars, drinking, and relaxing after the play. He had a mordant humour when he wished to use it. Yet all agreed that no one could be more raffish and mischievous than he in his off-duty hours. He would joke and tease his assistants, Bram Stoker, and especially Loveday, who followed him like a dog. At the height of Irving's success, Loveday described to an interviewer how he had come from the provinces 'and settled for life, as seems to be the habit of those who serve Mr Irving. Mr Loveday is so proud of the Lyceum, which is to him as the Great Pyramid must have been to the ancient Egyptians, a thing apart from the ruck of mushroom managements – an immutable, solid, and everlasting fact.'

Loveday had been discovered in the orchestra pit. Howson, Irving's 'Treasurer', was another of his strange promotions. Howson had played Harlequin in pantomime, had been a violinist and was eking out a living copying band parts at sixpence a time when he was suddenly given the job of keeping the Lyceum Theatre accounts.

Henry Irving always had this softness towards old actors. He was often blamed for employing people who were obviously inferior. His enemies said it was because he preferred to shine in dull company – an easy accusation.

However, it is fairly well established that a handsome leading man, if he had talent, would not last very long under the Lyceum banner. But when it came to small part players he had immense sympathy for them. Their salaries were much higher than the salaries at other theatres, and he would employ their relations in various capacities about the theatre.

Howson's family, who were all good-looking, if histrionically untalented, were given non-speaking parts in the grander productions because Irving liked to 'dress' his scenes with striking and handsome people; even one of Howson's youngest children appeared as a cupbearer on the Lyceum stage. Word-of-mouth accounts of Irving's generosity came down to Howson's granddaughter, the authoress Pamela Hansford Johnson. They paint Irving as lavish with free boxes at the theatre, an inexhaustible source of books, and generous with properties – furniture, chandeliers, and the rings, necklaces, and sparkling shoe buckles which a later generation used as playthings.

Howson may have presented his visiting card as 'Charles E. Howson – Mr Irving's Royal Lyceum Company', wearing a correct frock coat, and felt the full dignity of being Irving's treasurer; but backstage he was extremely hot-tempered and jealous of Stoker. For it was Stoker who was closeted with Irving and who knew the secrets of the theatre's finances. Howson was merely the official treasurer. It may have been that the expenses were heavier and the profits less dazzling than public reports assumed. Or perhaps Irving, while giving an impression of bonhomie, yet kept his projects, financial, social and amatory, as an uncut book.

Ellen knew him as actor, lover, and friend better than anyone and wrote: 'Stoker and Loveday were daily, nay hourly, assistants for many years with Henry Irving. But after all – did they or anyone else really know him?' She thought that he never wholly trusted his friends and never admitted them to his intimacy, although they thought he did, which was the same thing to them.

Ellen, obviously an early follower of the psychological school, put Irving's distrustfulness down to the fact that when he was a child in Cornwall he had seen a sweet little lamb gazing at him from a hedgerow. Equating the fluffy creature with the innocent lamb in his Bible, Henry had scrambled up a bank, thrown his arms round its neck – and the lamb had promptly bitten him. This story has many affinities with Henry's marriage. He had embraced a soft, loving girl, and found a vixen.

Early struggles do not always produce an easygoing personality. It may have been that Irving had struggled too long in his early days for his later comfort. It was more than twenty years before he finally walked into the sunlight of success. He had had a romantic, grandiose view of the theatre. The Terry family had been brought up in it; it was neither new nor exciting to them. When he was dreaming in the rocky fields round the tin mines they were already memorising parts, rehearsing, and peering through the curtains to see if a full house was going to produce a good Sunday dinner. To the sons and daughters of the arts – writing, painting, or the theatre – art is a means of earning a living. It never has that bloom which the man who comes to it with an innocent mind can see. Irving had the endurance of the men of his age. They hacked their way through jungles and floods to discover a new continent or bring back a new flower to Kew Gardens. He had a human jungle to contend with, and a human audience to tame.

He had succeeded in replacing Mrs Bateman and had become sole master in his own theatre. It had not been done without cruelty. He had discarded the stodgy Isabel Bateman for the sparkling Ellen.

Sentiment for old actors and old associations, ruthlessness towards rivals, and a mind constricted by his profession made Irving a strange split character. His iron will stood out as his most enduring trait. He was, as Ellen remarked, a monument to show the power of genius of will:

'For years he worked to overcome the dragging leg, which seemed to attract more attention from small minded critics than all the mental splendour of his impersonations. He toiled and overcame this defect as he overcame his disregard of the vowels, and the self-consciousness which used to hamper and incommode him.'

He was at his simplest and most charming with Ellen's children, who called him Henry and were allowed to be both cheeky and precocious. They would interrupt abstruse theatrical discussions to put forward ideas of their own, to which Irving would listen with patience. When Irving revived *Olivia* and played Dr Primrose, Ellen's daughter Edy told him she disliked the way he played the part. 'At home,' she said, 'you *are* Dr Primrose.' Irving took note of her remark, he had taken notice of the blind man speaking of Shylock.

When Tennyson was reading his play *The Cup*, Edy was sitting on Irving's knee and giggling. After the reading there was some discussion as to whether the names of the characters Synorix and Sinnatus would muddle the audience. Ellen told Tennyson soothingly that she did not think they would. Dear little Edy (aged nine) piped up: 'I do! I haven't known one from the other all the time!'

'Edy be good!' said Ellen.

'Leave her alone', said Henry, 'she's all right.'

He was no less indulgent with Ellen's son, Gordon Craig, to whom he gave a golden sovereign with the instructions 'Make good use of your time, for fast time flies – therefore spend this sovereign as quickly as possible.' In view of Gordon Craig's subsequent history, it was an unnecessary piece of advice, for he went on to spend everyone's money – his own, his mother's, his wives', and his mistresses'. But Craig always cherished the thought of Irving, who to him in his childhood was not an actor but a very dear figure, 'sometimes appearing here, sometimes appearing there – generally bestowing a gift'.

Henry was indulgent towards Ellen's spoiled children and he was equally indulgent to small part actors. Craig remarked on this trait of Irving, and said that Henry thought that fat cats hunted better than lean cats. Irving had been a lean cat once, and wanted to cushion others against poverty. This was an innocent way of looking at things, wrote Craig, for the 'good old actor, the fat old matter-of-fact buffer of those days was little troubled, what he troubled about was to do as little as he possibly could manage – and get a rise of salary for doing it.'

But in his theatre Irving demanded obedience, sparing no one, not even himself. Rehearsals would last all day and sometimes half the night. There were no lunch breaks or tea breaks; actors could nibble a sandwich as and when they could. The driving will demanded sacrifice, human sacrifice, in the temple of the theatre. Here everything was held in reverence, there was to be no facetiousness. The theatre was a serious matter. Ellen sliding down the banisters had shocked him – how could an Ophelia or Portia show such a lack of dignity?

This total dedication of Irving amused Ellen. 'Yes, yes, were I to be run over by a steam-roller tomorrow, Henry would be deeply grieved; and would say quietly "What a pity!" and then add after a moment or two's reflection "Who is there – er – to go on for her tonight?"'

The infinite patience of his productions was like the old way of painting – first the drawing, then the sepia paint, and finally the careful painting of the colours, layer by layer. First he studied the play to be produced, by himself for three months, until every detail of it was imprinted on his mind. A Shakespearian scholar once asked him some abstruse question about Titus Andronicus and Irving answered, 'God bless my soul, I've never read it, so how should I know?', shocking the questioner. Later he said, 'But when I *am* going to do Titus Andronicus, or any other play, I shall know more about it than any other student!'

When he called the first rehearsal, the play was set in his mind. He knew what he was going to do the first night. Ellen remarked that the company would have done well to notice how he read his own part, for he never again, until the first night, showed his conception so fully and completely. It was as if he were constrained to keep his views secret lest anyone should choose to out-dazzle him.

The first reading of the play was carried out solely by Irving. He read all the parts, never faltering or allowing the company to confuse the characters. He acted every part in the piece as he read, and in his mind the tones of his actors' voices, the moves of the characters, the processions, and the order of the crowd scenes were already set. All the actors had to do was to come up to the expectations which lay in his mind. He spent no time on the women in the play. Occasionally he asked Ellen to suggest a move or two for them, or to coach them as he coached the men. To the modern mind, it was a curious way of proceeding.

Possibly Irving regarded the women in the play solely as decorations, like flowers to be placed here and there once the room was furnished. He lived in a male-dominated society and the action of most of the plays he produced was concerned with male passions. Such few plays as he produced where the female element predominated usually had Ellen as their guiding star, and he knew that she could sew the material of her part into suitably glittering raiment.

The men, the 'table legs', as Gordon Craig called them, were coached in the most intricate detail. On one occasion he wanted one actor's voice to ring out like a pistol shot with the words 'Who's there?' Fatigued by the constant repetition, Ellen finally told Irving, 'It's no better.' He said, 'Yes, it *is* a *little* better, and so it's worth doing.'

On and on, day after day, year after year, the iron will drove his motley company as near to perfection as he and they could reasonably reach. Scene painters, designers, gas men, stage carpenters – all were harnessed to the chariot driving towards the dream. The cost of the dream was considerable. For there were 600 people employed at the Lyceum itself. These included 40 musicians, 60 gas and limelight men, 60 carpenters, 250 extras and supers, and 40 artists and artisans in the property room under the property master, Mr Arnott. The permanent core of 600 did not include outside specialists, technicians and experts like wigmakers, dressmakers, or armourers. A report dated 1881 stated that Fox (the theatrical wigmakers and costumiers) of Russell Street 'thatched' the Irving company, making them 347 wigs. This was presumably for one season.

Nothing escaped the attention of Irving. Unsuitable scenery was turned down with the contemptuous words: 'Is *that* what you think you are going to give *my* public?' Dressmakers were reduced to tears or despair or both, and made to re-dress Ellen, or anyone else whose costume did not fit into the general picture of the play which existed in the mind of Irving. Everything extraneous to this vision was scrapped, no matter what the cost.

His infinite patience and care of his staff sometimes had a dark and callous streak. His old dresser had been with him many years. Irving told the story of his sacking:

'The poor fellow was given over to drink at last. I said to him, "I wonder you do not reform, you look so ridiculous." Indeed, I never saw a sillier man when he was tipsy. His very name would set children laughing – it was Doody. In response to my appeal, with maudlin vanity, and tears in his eyes, Doody answered, "They make so much of me."'

It was an insensitive age. Irving had forgotten his own recourse to drink after the break-up of his marriage. Doody and his weakness had become surplus to requirements, like Irving's wife. He engaged as dresser the wigmaker Walter Collinson, who stayed with him for life.

Even the descriptions of Irving's face vary. He is described by one interviewer as having a strong jaw and thin lips, while another found gentleness rather than strength in his face. Only his tall, spare figure, black hair, and bushy eyebrows remain constant. One writer, in a sudden romantic flight of fancy, was so carried away as to write: 'There is nothing brighter than his smile. It lights up his face and reveals his soul in his eyes, but like the sunshine, that bursts for a moment and disappears to leave the landscape again in shadow.'

He preferred the private man to remain in shadow. He disliked his portrait by Bastien Lepage which lit up his face with sardonic humour. The correct respectable image of the frock-coated gentleman had been created by himself from humble material. It was not to be dented by levity.

The *Sporting and Dramatic News* remarked that Henry Irving had been allowed a position infinitely above, and far removed from, his contemporaries in the more serious walks of the drama. When he had taken over the Lyceum he had announced that he was not actuated by the desire to make money, but by the ambition to drag the dramatic art from the slough into which it had fallen, to elevate it, and to make it generally respected.

Nothing was to get in the way of that goal. Neither his own humour, his domestic comfort, nor his love of a woman. The iron will controlled the whole man.

Chapter 11

A Feast of Spectacle

The seasons at the Lyceum were governed by the unwritten laws of the society round. The banquet at the Royal Academy on the first Saturday in May opened the summer theatre season; Goodwood closed it at the end of July.

Irving's actors were paid about forty-six weeks' salary, so that the season of harvest in the fields was a fallow season for them. The luckier and better known of the actors went touring. The month of August and the beginning of September were Irving's weeks of planning new plays or refurbishing old triumphs.

When the theatre season opened in September 1880, Ellen was on tour again with her husband Charles Kelly. She was not needed at the Lyceum because Irving had decided to open his autumn season with *The Corsican Brothers*, a full-blooded melodrama with rich and spectacular effects, in which he played one of his favourite dual roles – that of the twin brothers Dei Franchi.

The scene opened in the hall of the Dei Franchi château, a magnificent room leading on to a porticoed terrace. In the distance the trees silhouetted against the light and air of the beautiful island of Corsica were darkened by the advancing gloom of evening, that suggestion of sombre fate so beloved by Irving. Into this richness (after a suitably pregnant pause) strode the Corsican, Henry Irving, in a costume of lustrous emerald green, a coloured sash at his waist, and on his face a complicated expression compounded, it was said, of earnestness, tenderness, and deep feeling. This was to contrast with his portrayal of the Parisian twin – anxious, lovestruck, and nervously susceptible. Apart from the château, other grand settings included the Paris Opéra during a bal masqué: real private boxes, real curtains, real people in the loges, real trees and flowers, the floor of the mimic opera-house literally crammed with dancers, dominoes, merriment and masks, pierrots and pierrettes, ballet girls, monks, pilgrims, and comic dogs.

It was remarked that such a sound of revelry went up at the rise of the curtain on this scene that not a word of dialogue could be heard. Not all these merry-makers were paid. Anyone who happened to be about the theatre could join the dance by taking a domino out of a rack full of masks, cloaks, and slouched hats. A troupe of clowns was engaged to add a note of the genuine circus to the scene.

Through this *galère* strode Irving as Louis dei Franchi, with relentless face, pursuing his enemy, the dastardly villain whose murder of his twin brother he had seen in a vision.

The supper party at the Baron de Montgiron's house was equally richly appointed, although the courtesans proved disappointing: extreme difficulty was experienced in getting girls to play fast young persons. The actresses engaged would not behave as was required of them. One critic remarked that 'they would have set an example to a confirmation class.' This view was not shared by Disraeli when he saw the play with his friend Monty Corry. The old-fashioned setting revived the gaieties of the statesman's youth, and he asked Corry: 'Do you think we could have supper somewhere and ask some of the Coryphées to join us – as we used to do in Paris in the fifties?' On another occasion Gladstone appeared in one of the boxes on stage, and was cheered and applauded by the real audience.

The illustrations of these splendid scenes in the souvenir programme show the stage at its most Victorian. The hall and terrace of the Dei Franchi château appears like a Gothic country house, a romantic dream of the past; the Opéra is a mirror picture of the Lyceum itself.

The last act received the most acclaim. This was the duel in the forest of Fontainebleau, set against the bare, leafless trees of the forest, the frozen lake, the slowly descending snow, and the orange and red bars of the setting winter sun, with the two duellists, swords raised, in their dramatic white shirts. The practicalities of these scenic effects were thousands of feet of gas pipes for the masked ball scene, and dozens of bags of salt, which were shovelled out of trucks for the 'snow' scene and then smoothed evenly over the stage with wooden shovels.

The public flocked to the spectacle, as people flocked to spectacular films at the height of their money-making success. Irving was the Cecil B. de Mille of his age. When reading the contemporary descriptions of Irving's most spectacular productions, it is difficult not to come to the conclusion that he was the theatrical manifestation of Victorianism in its most obvious form. He had managed to lift the theatre into the respectable, he had provided the rich settings and the velvet background necessary for his prosperous public. The ultimate seal of royal approval, royal attendance at his performances, had been vouchsafed to him.

The Prince and Princess of Wales came to enjoy the spectacle of *The Corsican Brothers*, and on that night the elaborate scenes were changed in a mere minute or two, hardly time for the Prince to take a few puffs at his cigar or to survey the female talent in the stalls. Like his fellow citizens the Prince enjoyed these rich scenic effects and the reproduction of nature on the stage. With the coming of the cinema and television, audiences have lost that breathless wonder with which they viewed such remarkable scenes from pit, stalls or gallery.

The critics proved to be less enamoured of spectacle than the paying public. Anachronisms were noted. In 1840 there were no cigarettes, nor did the gibus hat exist in the D'Orsay period. Others said that the play had been acted to death since its first production in Paris in 1850. There was some truth in this. The original idea of the play was a short story by Dumas called *Les Frères Corses*. It had been turned into a play for the Paris stage and then adapted for the London stage by the ubiquitous Dion Boucicault. Charles Kean, Fechter, and Hermann Vezin had all played the Irving part.

Ellen came up from her tour with Charles Kelly to see the revival, and she said that Irving was acting against the memories of Kean and Fechter. He had set the play back in time to emphasise its old-fashioned atmosphere, but to his contemporaries, the modern 1880 audience, the costumes of the 1840s seemed antiquated. But Ellen remarked on the grace and elegance of Henry as the civilised brother. There was something in him to which the perfect style of the D'Orsay period appealed: 'He spoke the stilted language with as much truth as he wore the cravat and the tight-waisted full-breasted coats.' Such lines as "Tis she! Her footstep beats upon my heart!' were never absurd from his lips.

In spite of the critics, Irving's blend of spectacle, romance and revenge kept the theatre satisfactorily filled until the beginning of 1881.

Ellen returned from what was to prove to be her last tour with the clumping Kelly. The next Irving play was to be devoted to culture, purveyed by the Poet Laureate, Tennyson. *The Cup* was a short but heavy piece in dramatic, poetic, classical style. Clement Scott kindly gives a quick sketch of the setting for his less erudite readers:

'In order to be thoroughly sympathetic with the spirit of Mr Tennyson's new tragedy, *The Cup*, which last night was the occasion of so much interest and enthusiasm at the Lyceum Theatre, it is necessary to throw our minds back to the third century before Christ, and become familiar with that strange country called Galatia. This done, we may revive old recollections of its people, half-Greeks, half-Gauls.'

The story is concerned with the love of the lecherous Synorix, an ex-Tetrarch, half-Greek, half-Gaul. He announces his character in no uncertain terms: 'Tut, fear me not, I ever had my victories among women, but I am most true to Rome.' To which statement the Roman Antonius remarks (aside), 'What filthy tools our senate works with!'

Tennyson was not at all pleased with Irving's view of Synorix. Ellen loyally said: 'How he failed to delight in it, I can't conceive, with a pale face, bright red hair, and very thin crimson lips, Henry looked handsome and *sickening* at the same time. Lechery was written across his forehead.' Presumably Tennyson wanted a noble lecher and Henry had done his homework too well.

The settings were vast: a Greek hillside in which the huge cast operated on three levels, a hunting party sweeping by on one level, the entrance to the Temple of Artemis on another, and somewhere in the distance a goatherd playing his pipes.

The temple itself caused gasps of astonishment. 'A solid reproduction of one of the accurate pictures of Alma Tadema,' wrote one delighted critic. 'The altar fire burns on a tripod on the centre stage, the columns are of creamy marble with figures in relief, incense perfumes the air, and groups of lovely women are ranged under the countless columns.' Irving was dressing his stage with his statuesque beauties. At the far back, seen through a tactful blue mist, was the vast statue of the many-breasted Artemis.

The tragedy wound to its inevitable end, the noble husband of Camma (William Terriss) is duly killed, leaving the way clear for the lecherous Synorix. With much chanting of priestesses – 'Artemis, hear him, Galatian Artemis!' – and rhythmic movements of white arms, Synorix, gold-crowned and purple-robed, is led towards the wedding ceremony planned by the High-Priestess Camma (Ellen Terry). She pours out the wedding libation, remarking: 'I will be faithful to thee till I die,' a remark to which he should have paid a little more attention.

Camma then drinks the fatal cup, and hands it to Synorix, who drinks and says with every satisfaction: 'The sovereign of Galatia weds his Queen!' He is immediately struck by the poison.

'This pain? What is it? Again?' He staggers, and then says, 'I had a touch of this last year,' as if recalling a quick cure at Harrogate. Finally the thought strikes him that perhaps all is not well, and he denounces Camma as a madwoman, bids her goodnight, and dies. After a fourteen-line speech (making her position clear), Camma also dies.

Some critics found this tragedy uplifting if distressing.

Many showed amazement at the spectacle. Others were less indulgent. In spite of his laurels, the plays of Tennyson were thought to be poor. '*The Cup* may sound suggestive of the Turf, but there is nothing racy about this tragedy in two acts. This cup does not cheer. It lacks that one touch of human nature which has given life to worse plays,' wrote one critic.

Ellen was praised. 'Her sweetness and light classic grace are truly Burne-Jonesian.' But Irving was said, 'not to convey the idea of being such a dog as to have got himself kicked out of all decent Galatian society and had his licence withdrawn by the Roman Governor'.

Ellen's poetic appearance was heightened by her costumes. She had remained on good terms with Godwin, the father of her children. For Camma he had designed a series of Grecian gowns which fell into graceful white or seaweed-tinted folds about her tall elegant figure. These gave Ellen the freedom to drape herself in poses about the hillsides and temples of the far-off land of Tennyson's Galatia before sinking to her death in a final charming pose.

After the first night Ellen sent cheering messages to the Laureate about Henry's brilliant portrayal of Synorix, but feared that she herself had disappointed. She received a suitably honeyed reply from

Hallam Tennyson: 'Dear Camma – I have given your messages to my father, and said that he will thoroughly appreciate your noble, most beautiful and imaginative rendering of Camma.' He added that his father hoped to be able to see the play soon, when the present bitterly cold weather had abated, and added a PS that he agreed with Ellen about Irving's rendering of Synorix. It was the least he could do after the heavy libations of money which Irving had contributed to the lavish production of his father's play.

The Cup astonished rather than succeeded. But as it ran in a double bill with *The Corsican Brothers* it is possible that the audience had merely subsided slowly under the weight of so much scenery. In spite of the heavy labours of dozens of gas men, carpenters and scene shifters, the performance lasted from half past seven till nearly midnight.

In the spring of 1881 *The Corsican Brothers* was replaced by the old comedy *The Belle's Stratagem.* Irving had already acted in this twice before, once when he had first come to London in the sixties, and once with Isabel Bateman, who had received polite notices. The reason for the revival was pinpointed with truth: 'Presumably Mr Henry Irving was moved by a wish to provide Miss Ellen Terry with more employment for her talents than that admirable actress has of late obtained.'

She took Henry's gift of this part with both hands, and showed singular freshness, true humour, irrepressible skittishness, and passionate energy as Letitia Hardy. Clement Scott was enchanted:

'Words fail me to express the charm and spell of Miss Ellen Terry, as Georgian in her comedy graces as before she was pagan in her rites as the priestess Camma, she trips, floats and glides through the scenes with no effort, and coquettes round Doricourt, until one understands what Circe might have done to Ulysses.'

Others were not so overcome by Ellen's airs and graces, one writer remarked sourly: 'Ellen Terry is quite too too. In fact the tooest too we have ever seen. We could hardly refrain from repeating to ourselves the dying hero's words "Kiss me (Letitia) Hardy".'

Sharp-eyed students of 'old comedy' were quick to notice that Irving had cut the play to ribbons. The minor characters might just as well not have been seen, they had so little to do. Doricourt was one of the first hits which Henry Irving had made, and it was difficult to imagine anything in better taste than Mr Irving's expression of dismay as the man of fashion at the behaviour of his bride. Miss Terry played Letitia Hardy, not particularly well; the scene in which she assumed vulgar and countrified airs was indisputably overdone. William Terris was acceptable as Flutter, but one critic complained that he fell into ugly and ignoble attitudes.

In general, Irving's Doricourt was disliked; there was a lurking cynicism in his portrayal of the character: it was too strange and too subtle. In the minuet he was stiff, and stalked across the room to invite the fair Mask to join him in the dance as if he were a Dei Franchi sweeping to his revenge. Neither Ellen nor Henry had enough of the grace and bearing of the eighteenth century. The supporting cast was bad, untrained to the finesse required for old comedy. Even the furniture received critical blame – why concave mirrors with eagles, which did not appear until the French Empire? The shape of sofas, chairs and fire-screens was declared anachronistic. The passion for absolute realism fell heavily on the design staff of the theatre.

Only Ellen was delighted with Henry as Doricourt. He was immensely funny, she said.

'We had sort of Beatrice and Benedick scenes together and I began to notice what a lot his face did for him. There have only been two faces on the stage – his and Duse's. My face has never been of much use to me, but my pace has filled the deficiency in comedy at any rate. In *The Belle's Stratagem* the public had face and pace together. There was one scene in which I sang "Where are you going to, my pretty maid?" I used to act it all the way through, and give imitations of Doricourt – ending up by chucking him under the chin. The house rose at it!'

The critics may not have appreciated a romp, but Ellen enjoyed it, and so did the audience.

Two weeks after the opening of *The Belle's Stratagem*, Irving played Othello, interchanging the part of Iago with the American actor Edwin Booth.

Othello
Poor Fello

Twice killed
The part filled
By the deserving
Mr. Irving
And the smooth
Mr. Booth

A cartoon showed Booth saying, 'What does all this tarnation civility mean I wonder?' Mr H. Irving (aside) replied, 'This move will be certain to pull me through when I visit America.'

This was unfair, as it was Booth who had approached Irving and suggested that they should play together. Irving had rescued the American actor from an unsuccessful season at a rickety theatre, the Princess's in Oxford Street, by proposing not a series of matinees as suggested by Booth, but a proper month's run, which played to packed houses.

It is difficult to recapture the immense pulling power which Irving had. One small incident may give an idea of this. A provincial theatre manager had achieved a seat in the gallery. When he came out for a breath of air at the interval he was offered £10 by an American for the opportunity to see one act of the play. It was more than his weekly salary, but he refused. Irving had presented Edwin Booth with a chance to act to full and enthusiastic houses.

Othello, as a play, was not well received by the Victorian audience. *Punch* wrote that there was one thing which Shakespeare could not do – write a tolerable play for a nineteenth-century audience. Scrutator in *Truth* agreed with this view: 'For my part I should be by no means sorry to hear that the plays of Shakespeare had been banished from the stage for a term of 10 years.'

With these opinions to contend against it is surprising that the actors received the acclaim they did. Booth's own Othello was scholarly, but failed to convince. Not only was he acting against Irving at his best as Iago, but the contemporary audience considered Salvini to be the only possible Othello, presumably because Salvini acted in Italian. There is always a tendency to prefer foreign acting in a tongue imperfectly understood to the native product.

Irving's mannerisms were attacked too:

'I have all along contended that Irving's forte lies in comedy, and it is the comedy side of Iago's character that he makes prominent.

I should like to give Henry two or three hints – don't stroke your moustache so much – it might come off and do let that back hair of yours alone. I noticed you had a go at the rear of your cranium exactly 56 times.'

Somehow, in spite of some detractors, Irving seized the very essence of Iago and played the part with an airy kind of callousness which convinced. A. B. Walkley described him as daringly Italian, a true compatriot of the Borgias.

Ellen suffered her usual first-night nerves, and although she was good in the pathetic passages her caressing nature was considered unsuitable. With Henry playing Iago she appears to have used him as an emotional bolster.

'Miss Terry should be cautioned against permitting her Desdemona even in her moments of severest suffering to fling herself upon the bosom of Iago and to accept the consolation of his embraces and caresses. The wives of commanding officers should not be wont to accept comfort at the hands of subalterns.'

This was judging Othello by the standards of officers and gentlemen who had suffered from wives in the foothills of the Himalayas.

Irving's Othello was almost universally condemned. He was caricatured as an infuriated Sepoy, and a sooty warrior. 'He carries himself with a travestied majesty that is often preposterous,' reproved one writer. 'Mr Irving's creation is a person no retinue of human beings could walk behind with gravity.'

Irving's Othello was a sootier warrior than the critics realised. Booth had said to Ellen, 'I shall never make you black, when I take your hand I shall have a corner of my drapery in my hand. That will protect you.' Ellen missed the courteous Mr Booth the next week when she played Desdemona to Henry's Othello. 'Before he had done with me I was nearly as black as he!'

But whatever the critics said, the theatre was full and *Othello* brought in the customers. The season closed. Irving announced to his public with heavy humour that they would be sorry to hear that he was going to spend thousands of pounds on improving the theatre for their comfort. The Lyceum would be closed for five months (groans) but some parts of the house, especially the pit, would be enlarged (cheers and bravos). He and Ellen then set off on a five months' tour of the provinces which netted Irving a two-thirds share of some £24,000. The old days of the leading actor joining the local stock company were over; now the full West End production was loaded on to special trucks and was brought along, like the mountain to Mahomet.

Irving's financial success was resented. *Punch* remarked that he had felt it to be a public duty to chronicle his triumphal march through the provinces. 'An illuminated balance-sheet with gilt edges will be handed free of charge to every visitor at the Lyceum Theatre.' A Belfast newspaper, determined not to be impressed, wrote:

'To illustrate the lavish nature of Mr Irving's genius we mention the fact that two special trains are necessary in order to meet the requirements of travel, one train being set apart for the distinguished Tragedian himself, the other conveying the costumes, which are the most expensive that can be procured for the money, the scenery (being designed by Royal Academicians at immense outlay), and the company engaged to support their chief, the properties, and the Acting Manager.'

Another paper, commenting on the last night at the Lyceum, hoped that no block will 'cause any interruption of the coronetted carriage traffic in the Strand'.

Irving's path had been hard and when he had succeeded more brilliantly than perhaps even he had dreamed the pens were sharpened and the detractors found grist for their denigration. It might be that Irving's achievement in lifting the stage to a pinnacle of success was felt to be the action of a parvenu – someone who had arrived from the sordid world of the strolling player on to a glittering stage and who did not deserve, in view of his lowly origin, the admiration and acclaim which he received. The eye of envy is keen.

But with two-thirds of £24,000 in his pocket from his provincial tour he could afford to ignore the sneers and plan his next triumphal production. This was announced as *Romeo and Juliet*, which opened on 8 March 1882. With profits rolling in, like golden corn in a sunlit September, horizons opened and no expense was to be spared.

The idea of Italy appealed to the Victorian soul. It was an old country, flower-filled, romantic, full of hot passion, and divorced from the everyday world of the plain men who were building up the fortunes of Britain. It had a particular appeal for Irving, and with *Romeo and Juliet* he gave full rein to his imagination.

Clement Scott wrote over seven thousand words (equal to a very long short story) about the production. He praised the restored text. The David Garrick version had been thrown aside, and now the play shone forth in the glory of Shakespeare's thoughts.

Chorus was dressed as the poet Dante, and after the introduction to the star-crossed lovers and their death-marked love the curtains parted to reveal the market place at Verona. Donkeys, children, a picturesque conduit, a sloping bridge in the background, life, animation and colour – into all this Italianate charm swept the warring Montagues and Capulets, turning the fair scene to disorder and fear.

In *Romeo and Juliet* Irving exercised to the utmost his mastery of crowds. Mercutio and Romeo walked through an avenue of torches into Capulet's house, and suddenly the curtain lifted on the banquet. Serving men removed peacocks from the table, Rosaline was seated on a throne of blue and silver flanked by silver draperies and surrounded by scarlet oleanders, while in the foreground moved richly clad pages and serving wenches. The minuet began and crowds of youths and girls moved slowly and rhythmically, displaying their rich Renaissance brocades and satins. The music had been specially composed by Sir Julius Benedict and unseen singers added their voices to the dance melodies.

The balcony scene was as richly apparelled as the dancers. Juliet stood on a marble terrace of an ancient palace, beneath a roof supported on huge pillars which had the appearance of a temple. Her garden below was filled with real trees, the moon shone on a little rivulet, and around the water grew real lilies, tall and white in the moonlight.

The death of Mercutio took place outside the city walls of Verona in the glaring white heat of the sun, darkened by long lines of cypress trees, and with the red-tiled roofs of buildings stretching away into the distance. The monastery scene was resonant with distant monks chanting and monastery bells punctuating the action.

The most elaborate scene of all was Juliet's bedchamber: golden lattices, foliage in the garden, and the sky, like an Italian ceiling, blue with the rosy fingers of dawn breaking across it.

Nothing was left out of the picture of Renaissance Italy – an old street in Verona, a street in Mantua, and the ancient apothecary's shop were all there. The tomb scene satisfied everyone. A steep staircase and gallery led down to the burial place, and down these steps and along the gallery Romeo dragged the body of the murdered Paris.

Against these splendid settings moved Irving as Romeo. Ellen wrote: 'In Iago he had been an Italian of Venice, as Romeo, it was the Italy of Tuscany. His clothes were as Florentine as his bearing. He had no feather in his cap which was the tradition, but wore a sprig of crimson oleander.'

After the dress rehearsal Henry wrote to Ellen: 'Beautiful as Portia was, Juliet leaves her far, far behind. Never has anybody acted more exquisitely than when I saw part of the performance from the front. The play will be, I believe, a mighty "go" for the beauty of it is bewildering. We are in for a long run.'

Ellen had moved among the pageantry in her clinging gowns of gold, or blue, or white, cunningly designed to make her stand out in innocent beauty. It was not surprising that Henry was dazzled and enchanted. He added a PS: 'I have determined not to see a paper for a week. I know they'll cut me up, and I don't like it.' In spite of the years, and his success, the hisses of the past remained in his mind.

He was quite right. The critics did cut him up. Some few praised him for the spectacle, for the handling of the crowd scenes, some for the intelligent new ideas he had put into the production. That was about all. Even Ellen did not receive her usual acclaim. But the public flocked to the play, to the disgust of the critics. One wrote:

> Too much ado about the whole affair,
> No standing room or sitting anywhere,
> Each who upon the sight would be a feaster
> Will have to wait his chance until next Easter.

Another writer was more brief: 'C'est magnifique mais ce n'est pas l'amour.'

It is often supposed that Victorian critics treated Irving with respect and dignity; to read the contemporary cuttings and gossip columns of the period is to be disabused of this idea. Romeo found the caricaturists and satirists in full cry. One gossip columnist reported having heard two ladies in the stalls discussing the play.

'How old is Romeo supposed to be?'

'About 18.'

'And Juliet?'

'15 or 16.'

'Dear me, Mr Irving is 43 and Miss Terry 30 – they are old enough to know better.'

The rhymesters joined in:

Oh Henry, we heard with a flutter
You would not spare any expense
To make Romeo and Juliet 'utter'
And all your supporters 'intense'.
But if you yearn after successes
In the juvenile tragedy line
Make your face young,
As well as your dresses,
Your Romeo *looks* forty-nine.

Others quoted, 'Romeo, Romeo! Wherefore art *thou* Romeo?' One caricature has Irving drawn at his worst with the caption 'Rummy-o'.

The jokes were not subtle. Irving himself knew he was too old for the part. He had read the play to Walter Pollock and his wife:

'He read at half-tone, yet gave its full force and meaning to every character, and it was evident throughout that his conception of the part of Romeo was instinct with beauty and truth. He put down his book, looked round at us, and said with a half-humorous sigh, "There is what I want to make of Romeo. Unluckily I know that on the stage I cannot come anywhere near it."'

Pollock and his wife tried to reassure him, but he repeated: 'No, no. I know. I know I can't do it. How I wish I could! But I must do the best I can.' After he had gone, Pollock's guest, a naval officer, said: 'If only he could play Romeo as he read it he would set the town ablaze. But what a Mercutio he would make!'

In spite of his misgivings, Henry was drawn to Romeo. And to his Juliet. For Ellen was on her own again. Kelly had clumped out of her life. 'One cannot live with a steamroller,' she said, and now she was free. Irving perhaps saw himself and Ellen as star-crossed lovers. They may have been no longer in the blush of spring-time, like the lovers they portrayed, but their feelings were as strong.

Watched by the public, and the jealous Florence, how could their path of true love run smooth?

An admirer annotated a copy of the play describing the performance from the point of view of the audience. Throughout the balcony scene, Irving 'used rich, soft, low tones, full of tenderness, to Ellen's bell-like clear ones. I should never hope to see a sweeter or lovelier Juliet than in this scene.'

Ellen herself wrote of the beginning of the play, when Romeo seeks out Rosaline, how he turned away completely disheartened and stood spellbound, motionless, entranced by the loveliness of the vision. 'Can I ever forget his face when suddenly in pursuit of her he saw *me*. . . . ?'

If Irving did not succeed as Romeo, Ellen understood his feelings about the part: 'I know they said he looked too old, but according to his imagination Henry Irving *was* Romeo.'

In spite of the cutting-up and unkind references to his age, Irving's Romeo was a financial success and it ran until the end of the season, making £10,000. One hundred and thirty performances to full houses did not alter the critics' opinion but it had improved the bank balance of the theatre.

The winter season opened as Irving had promised with *Much Ado About Nothing*. Ellen knew the play well and had played Hero as well as Beatrice. It was to please her that Henry decided to do it. It was a nice gesture, but she was not at home playing against Henry's Benedick, which she found too 'finicky'. Beatrice should be swift, swift, swift! Henry slowed her up. Nor did his using an old gag in the church scene please her:

'When I was told that we were to descend to the buffoonery of:
Beatrice: "Benedick, kill him, – kill him if you can."
Benedick: "As sure as I'm alive – I will."
I protested.'

She protested loud and long and, as usual, lost the battle. But when the first night came none of the critics noticed the gag, and it was even commended.

All her protests and criticisms were stilled by the acres of praise which the play received. From the moment when in her rich russet-red robe and coquettish little ruff she descended lightly from the steps of Leonato's palace, she stepped into a warm bath of praise and adulation. It was judged to be a matchless performance, radiant with good humour and instilled with grace. How true, said Clement Scott, was the description, 'for look where Beatrice, like a lapwing, runs close to the ground'. This was the way that Ellen did run. Even Dutton Cook found Irving as Benedick a valorous cavalier, and of his witty encounters with Beatrice, where presides a spirit of pleasantness, he wrote that, 'his rudest sallies are so mirthfully spoken as to be deprived of all real offensiveness; he banters like a gentleman, and not like a churl'.

The settings were richly Italianate, in the grand Lyceum tradition. Irving was judged to have made the church scene beautiful without falling over into the mistake of too much popery. There was danger in an Italian church scene; he could have used crucifixes, a red sanctuary light burning, vestments, and an excess of genuflexions, but he had contented himself with a little incense and a discreet choir. The garden scene was particularly commended – dim arcades of green, an old marble moss-eaten seat, and the yellowing brown foliage of a rich autumn tint.

The costume which Irving wore as Benedick still exists. It is of a rich cut velvet, and, even allowing for the fading of time, its muted russet colours strike the modern observer as richly Victorian rather than swashbucklingly Elizabethan. Ellen's equally russet robe has the air of a discreet and ladylike afternoon dress.

On 7 May 1883, when the Prince of Wales graciously decided to view the bickering of Beatrice and Benedick, Irving gave a banquet after the play. It was a small supper party for fifty, but with a royal setting. The stage was transformed by a vast tent through which hung glittering chandeliers; three sides were draped with crimson plush and painted satin, and on the side of the proscenium arch a forest of palms and flowers hid the orchestra which played soft music. When the Prince entered he politely remarked on the beautiful decoration of the table. It was a bouquet thirty feet long and a foot high, delicately constructed from golden flowers for a golden occasion.

Much Ado ran from October 1882 to June 1883, and the smiles and pleasure which the play brought to the audiences netted an equally golden return – £26,000 clear profit. It was a good augury for the tour of America which Irving had been planning.

Chapter 12

America! America!

Henry Irving took his theatre companies to the United States on eight different occasions between 1883 and 1904. He had always been drawn towards America. The idea of the country and its people was often on his mind.

The man who had put the weapons of success into the actor's hands, 'Colonel' Bateman, was American. After the failure of *Fanchette*, Bateman, disillusioned with London, had proposed to Irving that they should seek their fortune on the other side of the Atlantic. This project had been seriously considered, and then suddenly Irving had brought *The Bells* to Bateman's reluctant notice. The brilliant and unexpected success of this play had filled Bateman's pockets and put the American idea into the distance. Yet Irving himself, schooled by Bateman in American ways of publicising his plays, had always kept the thought of an American trip in his mind.

As early as 1878 he had taken the trouble to write to *The Theatre* to deny that he had ever written: 'I am not foolish enough to consider my success certain among American people of whose taste I know nothing. In England I know what I am about.' Irving's retort to *The Theatre* was short and sharp: 'This extract is pure fabrication and I shall be glad if you will let me say so. Far from not wishing to visit America – I earnestly look forward to going there, for I love the country and have troops of friends in it.'

Both Irving and Ellen had been tempted on various occasions by American managers who had come with these tentative approaches. American correspondents and newspaper critics had written a great deal about Irving. Gossip paragraphs of the period depict a writer on the *New York Times* making wristband notes in which he tells some marvellous stories of our social manners and customs. Reams of criticism of Irving's performances had been relayed across the Atlantic. Other writers drew intimate portraits of Ellen and Irving in their private capacity. In the days before actors became a commonplace, to be turned on in the sitting-room like taps, Irving and Ellen were news of a more exciting world.

The impresario Henry Abbey had finally persuaded Irving to test his company in America. The resultant explosion of tears, tributes, dinners and emotion engendered in London could hardly have been greater if Gladstone had decided to emigrate. The last night at the Lyceum was drowned in cheers and tearful farewells, and the stage thick with laurel wreaths and bouquets. Irving, who had taken his benefit that night with a programme of snippets including condensed versions of *Eugene Aram* and *The Belle's Stratagem* (between which was sandwiched *The Death of Nelson*, rendered with wonderful effect by Sims Reeves), appeared in his costume as Doricourt, pale and emotionally affected: 'Soon an ocean will roll between us, and it will be a long time before we can hear your heart-stirring cheers again,' he said.

He announced that he would be touring the United States for six months, and that in his absence Mary Anderson and Lawrence Barrett, both American actors, would be playing at the Lyceum Theatre; but he left the theatre, he said, knowing that his friends would give them the usual warm Lyceum Welcome. (Cheers.)

Before he sailed a public dinner was given for Irving at the St James's Hall, London, on 4 July 1883, a date chosen, it was said, as a slight compliment to the American people and to the American Ambassador, who was present. The five hundred distinguished guests included innumerable peers, baronets, and honourables, and prominent men from all walks of life – from Parliament, society, the law, art, science, and literature. This glittering company was presided over by Lord Chief Justice Coleridge. Even the learned judge was overcome by the occasion. He remarked that no man could come to such a meeting as this, and bring together such an association of men as he saw before him, unless he had great and remarkable qualities.

The menu was long and complicated, and written in a curiously faulty 'franglais', each dish being appropriately named as a compliment to Irving's stage impersonations.

Mayonnaise à la Dubosc
Navrins de Volaille à la courrier de Lyons
Tartelette de peaches à la Mathias
Gelée à la Digby Grant

And finally, and sadly, Glace Pouding 'Bon Voyage'.

The toasts began with Lord Coleridge proposing the Queen (coupled with H.R.H. the Prince of Wales, and the entire royal family). Other toasts by Lord Coleridge, during the evening, included one to the President of the United States and another to Irving himself, to which Irving gladly responded. These speeches and toasts were followed by Lord Houghton, who proposed Literature, Science and Art, which speech was answered by Mr Alma-Tadema (for Art), and the Hon. J. Russell Lowell (for Science and Literature). Toasts, speeches and replies were punctuated by a large-bosomed lady called Mme Antoinette Sterling singing several songs, and Mr Sims Reeves, who sang several other songs. Mr Charles Santley obliged from time to time with musical interludes on the piano. The ladies (God bless them!), including Ellen, were graciously allowed to look down on these grand masculine proceedings from the balcony where their charming toilettes were discreetly shielded by potted palms.

The *World*, reporting these solemn tributes to Irving's fame, remarked: 'We are, above all things, an earnest and serious people.' The guest list proved the statement. One flaw darkened the evening – the Prime Minister, Mr Gladstone, had been unable to be present owing to pressing political duties, although this was mitigated by the presence of Lord John Russell and five distinguished judges.

This was only the first of a number of dinners given for Irving's departure to the United States. He was invited to Hawarden by Gladstone, and to Knowsley by Lord Derby. All these junketings caused one unimpressed reporter to write in the *Referee*:

'What gives him the powers of endurance for the Big Feeds? No matter where he goes a dinner or supper must be prepared in his honour, and he, poor fellow, not only has to eat it, but is compelled to sit up till three or four o'clock in the morning to listen and contribute some post-coenal oratory.'

Henry Irving's departure to the United States took on the appearance of a national event, like a small coronation or even a national catastrophe: one drawing pictured a weeping Britannia drawn on a penny inscribed 'One Henri', with a distant sail marked 'Far West'. Special cards were printed with the picture of a sailing ship and thirty-two rhymed couplets which ended emotionally:

> The fetters of friendship are free, but unbroken,
> The chain round the heart that is link'd with a sigh,
> Not a word of farewell from our lips shall be spoken
> But a strong 'God be with you!' – an honest good-bye!

The words of farewell had, in fact, run into thousands.

Irving's last engagement in England was in Liverpool, where making yet another of his farewell speeches he quoted Sir Peter Teazle and said that he and Miss Terry left their characters behind them: 'but we are more confident than Sir Peter that they will be taken care of, and so with full hearts and big hopes we wish you an affectionate farewell.'

The air of national mourning continued till they left. When Ellen and Henry sailed together in the *Britannic* hundreds of well-wishers, including Oscar Wilde and Lily Langtry, gathered on the shore to wave a last fond farewell. Ellen was bathed in tears when contemplating this departure from her country, her children, and her past. She felt as if she would never see the shores of England again, and the English seemingly felt that they would never see Ellen again.

On the ship the quarters of Irving and Ellen had been arranged as if they were members of a reigning European royal family. A quarter of the ship's main drawing-room had been cut off and partitioned for Ellen's use. Two cabins had been made into one to give her the proper setting for her status. Irving's quarters were equally princely. They had both come a long way from theatrical 'digs'.

History does not relate whether their palatial suites had communicating doors. No doubt the official reason for their travelling separately from the company was a question of rest for Irving and a chance of recuperation from emotional strain for Miss Terry.

While Ellen and Henry could enjoy some days of quiet and peace in the privacy of their drawing-rooms and staterooms, the rest of the company, the tons of scenery, the hundreds of costumes, the 1,200 wigs, the small-part actors, the supers, and Bram Stoker, had sailed to America in a slow boat called *The City of Rome*.

In New York the ticket speculators were busy and all the best seats at the Star Theatre had been bought by touts. There were other troubles.

Joseph Hatton, a friend of Irving and a New York correspondent of the *Tribune*, had gone ahead, like John the Baptist, to make smooth the path of the actor. Terrible rumours of the ferocity of American reporters had reached London. Irving was amazed. He had always found American correspondents well informed and pleasant. 'Ah', said a much travelled person to Irving, 'here under your own control, and probably smoking a cigar in your own room! Wait until he boards the steamer, off New York. *Then* you will see the sort of fellow he is, with his string of questions more personal than the fire of an Old Bailey judge at a hostile witness under cross-examination.' And he added that the Inquisition could learn nothing from American reporters.

To counteract these terrible travellers' tales, Joseph Hatton was busy in New York. He found that, although no man was more written of or talked about in America than Henry Irving, most of the tales had suffered a sea change on crossing the Atlantic. Irving was credited with owning a palace on the Thames, where he spent most of his time entertaining the Prince of Wales and assorted Dukes, his success as an actor being due mostly to lavish spending on chicken and champagne.

All these reports could be brushed aside with a light laugh, but the report which had been cabled to the *New York Herald* from the London *Standard*, was less easy to wave aside:

'American audiences have a favourable opportunity of showing that they can think for themselves, and not slavishly echo the criticisms of the English press. . . . Are we indulging the vain imaginings if we hope that our cousins across the water will forget all that has been said or written about Irving and the Lyceum company on this side of the ocean . . . and send us a true, independent – and unconventional – account of his gifts and graces or the reverse.'

Disingenuously, the *Standard* added that, of course, Englishmen would be delighted if the Americans endorsed the general opinion, but let the American voice, above all, show independence.

It was an invitation to New Yorkers to give an adverse verdict.

Hatton draws a charming picture of late nineteenth-century New York. At four o'clock in the morning he and some guests from the Lotos Club made their way down Fifth Avenue to the Brevoort House, where they had ordered a carriage. The 'electric arcs' made deep shadows, and the Edison lamps threw the buildings into silhouette. The carriage with its flickering lamps was found, and the convivial clubmen made their way to the 22nd Street Pier. 'Want the *Blackbird*?' asked an officer. 'This way!' They made their way to the river steamer, where they found all the intimidating reporters sleeping on the floor in the ladies' cabin. Hatton remarked that, with their slouch hats covering their faces, asleep they looked like brigands. But when they woke up and started to talk he took an entirely different view:

'These gentlemen of the Press, who are going out to meet Irving are reporters – socially they occupy the lowest station of journalism, intellectually they are capable men. Theirs is the best of education – they have chatted on familiar terms with Lincoln, Grant, Garfield, Patti and Bernhardt, and they will add to the long list of their personal acquantances Irving and Miss Terry.'

There was a shout of '*Britannic* ahead!' and clubmen and reporters clambered on board the *Blackbird*.

The *Britannic* was sighted, flying the Stars and Stripes at her topmast and the Union Jack at her stern. Mr Abbey had thoughtfully brought along a fine military band from the Metropolitan Opera House and a team of waiters from the Brunswick Hotel.

Irving was sighted on the *Britannic* looking pale in the cold, raw light. He waved his bowler to the *Blackbird*. A cheer of welcome went up. Two of Irving's friends steamed up in their private yacht to meet the actors. A gangway was thrown out, the band played 'Hail to the Chief' and 'Rule Britannia', and Irving and Ellen boarded the yacht *Yosemite* to be thrown as lambs to the American reporting lions. The lions seem immediately to have fallen under the spell of Miss Terry.

The *Tribune* waxed particularly lyrical:

'As she stepped with a pretty little shudder over the swaying plank upon the yacht she showed herself possessed of a marked individuality.

Her dress consisted of a dark greenish-brown cloth wrap lined inside with a peculiar shade of red; the inner dress, girt at the waist with a red, loosely folded sash, seemed a reminiscence of some 18th century portrait, while the delicate complexion caught a rosy reflection from the loose flame coloured red scarf tied in a bow at the neck. The face itself is a peculiar one. Though not by ordinary canons beautiful, it is nevertheless one to be remembered, and seems to have been modelled on that of some pre-Raphaelite saint, an effect heightened by the aureole of soft golden hair escaping from under the plain brown straw and velvet hat.'

The scene round the ships was said to be essentially American – the broad river, the gay wooden villas ashore, the brown hills, the bright steam craft on the river, the fast rig of the trading schooners, and above all the Stars and Stripes of the flags and 'the triumphant eagles that extend their golden wings over the lofty steerage turrets of tug and floating palace'.

Ellen's approach to her trip had been intensely emotional. She had wept copiously at every farewell performance and set out feeling that she would never return. She had left her children, her bullfinch, her parrot, and her housekeeper Boo, in order to face unknown dangers in the United States. She was convinced that all American women wore red flannel shirts and carried bowie knives, an idea she had probably culled from some old melodrama. But by the time she arrived in New York she was crying again – this time at the beauty of the harbour.

Henry had an immediate success with the reporters, offering them cigars, chicken, and glasses of champagne, and putting on what Ellen called his best Jingle manner, 'full of refinement, bonhomie, elegance, and geniality'.

When Henry's health had been drunk by the press in his stateroom he said:

'Now gentlemen, I shall be glad to answer any questions, but I approach this interview with a great deal of apprehension. I have heard that you New York newspapermen are a terrible set of fellows. Only one thing I beg of you – don't ask me how I like the country. I'm sure I *shall* like it, but I haven't seen it yet. There now – I'm at your mercy.'

And then he used an eighteenth-century phrase: 'Have at me!' Irving, skilled in duelling, was equally skilful at handling the newspapermen of the New World.

The reporters' questions, to a modern interviewee, would seem to have been excessively polite and refined. The senior reporter announced how pleased they were to welcome Mr Irving. He was asked which plays he was going to produce and how, and why, and he was given immense acres of space to express his views. Irving said that he had been invited to America as a solo performer, but he was not interested in making money; he wanted to have the pleasure of seeing the New World, to win its favour and friendship, and to show some of the work which he did at the Lyceum. 'I have brought', he said, 'my company and my scenery – and Miss Ellen Terry, one of the most perfect and charming actresses that ever graced the English stage. And so', he added, with an actor's flourish, 'I bring you – almost literally, the Lyceum Theatre!'

Other small items he had brought were sixty or seventy artists, several tons of scenery, hundreds of costumes, and the 1,200 wigs. Irving and Stoker and Abbey had embarked on a very complicated and hazardous theatrical enterprise, but the first interviews went well. Henry was voted gentlemanly but human. He had carried off his interviews triumphantly, put over his points, and softened the hearts of the reporters who were now on the very best of terms with him. He then turned to Ellen, and said: 'These gentlemen want to have a few words with you.' With a mischievous expression he whispered in Ellen's ear, 'Say something pleasant – merry and bright.'

Ellen was promptly overcome by the fact of being in a foreign land, and was again thinking of her children, her parrot, Boo, and her bullfinch. One reporter asked, 'Can I send any message to your friends in England?'

'Tell them I never loved them so much as now!' said Ellen, and promptly burst into tears. She was labelled as a woman of extreme nervous sensibility. Her figure, in the days when a plump and comfortable armful of woman was admired, was described as spare 'almost to attenuation'.

Irving and Ellen were staying discreetly at different hotels. Irving's hotel was the Brevoort which was, he said, more like an English house than any other in the city. 'The genial proprietor evidently desires to make his guests think so. Portraits of Queen Victoria, the Prince Consort, and pictorial reminiscences of the old country meet you at every turn.' If the proprietor extended these delicate compliments to all his foreign guests he must have had quite a gallery of pictures in his basement.

Ellen was driven to the Hotel Dam, named after the Dutchman who ran it. Here she cried for two hours. Then, suddenly, her room was filled with roses, and she wrote: 'My dear friends in America have been throwing bouquets at me in the same lavish way ever since.' Her spirits speedily revived, and Henry came round to the Hotel Dam and bore her off to see some 'nigger minstrels'. Like all actors, as soon as he had a night off he liked to be amused. Ellen found the jokes difficult to understand, but her professional eye approved of the comedians' cool and dry way of putting them over.

The pictures which both Ellen and Joseph Hatton paint depict an old, simple New York, jingling with the bells of private carriages, horse trams plying between the various parts of the city, muddy sidewalks, and the curious costume of the women. They are described as wearing Indian shawls with diamond earrings, as dressing too grandly in the street and too dowdily at the theatre. But the girls in the stores looked trim with their white shirtwaists, so different from the blowsy dresses worn by English women. Ellen liked the classlessness of New York. It seemed to her a land of sunshine, light, and faith in the future. There was no misery or poverty. Everyone looked happy. In America the barrow boy of today might be the millionaire of tomorrow.

Irving was a pioneer in America. While there had been English actors who had toured the States, none had brought an entire company and scenery. He was an innovator in England and the same applied to his approach to production in America.

American actors were accustomed to play either Shakespeare or what was called old comedy, that is Sheridan or Goldsmith. There was an indigenous theatre, but at that time it was much given to domestic plays concerned with the differences between the States, and comedies of manners concerned with the simple American life. The reverence for and canonisation of young women, which struck the English visitors, was transferred to the stage and depicted in the action of the plays.

Nothing had ever been seen in New York on the lavish scale of the Lyceum productions. Irving had only to put out his hand to shake the tree and the dollars of success were ready to fall for him. He had chosen just the right moment to arrive. Both he and Ellen were at the apogee of their powers. All his future tours in America were to be financially successful, but none was to achieve the fascination or the acclaim of his first arrival. Never again would any English actor achieve such applause or be received with the wonder of the first Lyceum tour.

The coverage from coast to coast was unprecedented: 'Irving – Terry – Arrival of the Famous Actor and Leading Lady of the Lyceum.' The *Sun* was less impressed and more colloquial: 'Up early to Meet Irving – a Business-like Hamlet and a Jolly Ophelia arrive.' Columns and columns were devoted to the mere arrival of Ellen and Henry. The *Tribune* drew a very vivid picture of Irving as a tall, spare man wearing a short blue pilot-cloth overcoat and a broad-brimmed soft felt hat, with his long grey hair thrown carelessly back. 'He is clean shaven with features remarkable for their delicate refinement, united with a suggestion of virile force.' The *New York Herald*, on the other hand, found that the actor looked like Oscar Wilde, a comparison which did not please Irving.

In his interviews, Irving tactfully emphasised the help given to him by Bateman. It was nevertheless true, he said, that Bateman had lost a lot of money and intended giving up the Lyceum. 'He proposed to me to go to America with him. By my advice and against his wishes *The Bells* was rehearsed.' The rest was the history of the Lyceum, and now here he was at last bringing *The Bells* to New York in remembrance of Bateman.

The first week of Irving's stay in New York was devoted to preparations. Ellen and Henry were showered with invitations, but between rehearsals they accepted only two, breakfasts given by Mr Vanderbilt and Judge Shea. The hospitality of the Americans overwhelmed them. One man lent Irving a carriage, another offered a house, and a third a steam launch. Ellen attended an elegant party at Delmonico's. Joseph Hatton took Irving to Sieghortner's in Lafayette Place, formerly the town house of one of the Astor family. It was said to be typical of New York's early millionaires' houses, with marble steps, heavy mahogany doors and rich Moorish decorations. Herr Sieghortner himself welcomed Irving and suggested a simple meal of Shrewsbury oysters, gumbo soup, canvas-back ducks, a soufflé, Stilton cheese, an ice, a liqueur, a dish of fruit, and a bottle of hock. The meal finished, Irving thanked the restaurant owner: 'It was perfection, Mr Sieghortner.' Irving may have crossed the Atlantic, but he had not escaped the 'big feeds'.

Between all these junketings, the real business of the trip went on. The theatre proved to be spacious enough in respect of the stage itself, but the dressing-rooms were small and poky. There were other little local difficulties. It was the custom to play the audience out as well as in. 'I understand that,' said Irving, 'but what sort of music do you usually play?' The Star Theatre manager said succinctly: 'A march.' Irving tactfully pointed out that jolly marches did not always fit the mood of the play. A cheerful march certainly did not fit in with *The Bells*, which was to be the first production. The rehearsals were completed, and all the arrangements made. But the result, as always in the theatre, was a huge question mark.

Irving was worried. 'The wild manner in which the speculators in tickets are going on is enough to ruin anything.' A man called McBride had put twelve men on duty in front of the Star Theatre box office three days before the tickets for Irving's season were to go on sale. The men stayed there day and night until the tickets were at last for sale. The rates for this vigil were: district messenger boys thirty cents an hour, older men five dollars a day (plus meals and cigars). Every one of the men bought ten season tickets for the whole of the Lyceum company's New York season. The canny McBride had made a nice killing of more than three thousand tickets.

Irving, always careful of his customers' pockets, had wanted to play at Lyceum prices, but he had been told that if he did he would simply put even more money into the pockets of the speculators. He pinpointed the trouble as he saw it: if playgoers had to pay ten or twenty dollars for a three-dollar seat they would not come to the house in a contented frame of mind. It was a strictly practical actor's viewpoint, and he was nervous of the outcome. A stranger in a new land, he did not want to set his audience against him.

The Bells opened on 29 October 1883. It was a night of torrential rain, with the modern electric lights flashing on unmetalled roads, and the press of vehicles churning up rivers of mud. The elegantly appointed carriages contrasted strangely with the broken, muddy streets. The tropical rain splashed on the pavement, and, blown by the wind, drenched the intrepid theatre-goers in sheets of water. The horses were protected by huge rubber cloths, and the elegant men and women were also shrouded in larger waterproofs as they pushed their way into the crowded theatre. They were pursued by crowds of ticket touts doing business right up to the entrance to the stalls, and sometimes with success.

Outside the theatre, in spite of the rain, the distinguished audience had attracted a crowd of sightseers who huddled in the shadows thrown by the electric lights at the entrance to the foyer.

The audience, distinguished and expectant, included eminent Americans from all walks of life – judges, Vanderbilts, generals, and Ellen, who was escorted by Mendelssohn's godson, Felix Moscheles.

She watched nervously from her box. She had very good reason to be nervous. The first half-hour of the play was constantly interrupted by latecomers who had managed to get cut-price seats from the touts, causing a double annoyance to prompt arrivals who had paid double and treble for the privilege of seeing Irving.

The curtain went up on *The Bells*. Irving spoke the opening words: 'It is I!'

He remembered the moment vividly:

'When I first stepped into view of the audience and saw and heard the great reception it gave me – I was filled with emotion. I felt it was a great epoch in my life. The moment I looked over the footlights at the people, I knew we were friends. I knew they wanted to like me, they expected something great, and would go away if I disappointed them, saying, "Well, we wanted to like him and can't." Who could stand before such an audience on such an occasion – and not be moved deeply?'

He did not disappoint them. The reviews and descriptions of his performance and the brilliance of the audience were fulsome. The Americans received Irving with unstinting praise and generosity. The carping and sniping which sometimes greeted his London productions were almost totally absent. No one took the London *Standard*'s advice and cut Irving up. His acting was described as electrical, and the audience paid him that supreme compliment of a complete and hushed silence. Only one thing puzzled Irving. In England the audience had laughed a good deal at the beginning of the play in some of the comedy scenes. In New York he found people followed the plot with an anxious attention.

The following night Ellen appeared for the first time in America in the play *Charles I*. This play was equally warmly received – astonishingly so, in a country where the woes of a hereditary monarch might be thought to be pointlessly of his own making. Irving's impersonation was considered fine and subtle. The *Tribune* praised Ellen, her dazzling beauty, strange personal fascination, and above all her sweet voice: 'She possesses a sweetness that softens the hard lines of ancient tragic form and leaves the perfect impression of nature.' Ellen, always self-critical, did not think she had done well. She had cried too much in the later scenes, but Henry always touched her greatly in his rendering of Charles I, every inch a king and a martyr.

The company played in New York for four weeks, giving, apart from *The Bells* and *Charles I*, *Louis XI*, *The Merchant of Venice*, *The Lyons Mail* and *The Belle's Stratagem* (mis-spelt in the programme as 'The Bell's Stratagem'). A varied selection to allow both Henry and Ellen to show their paces in a new country.

There were a few criticisms. Some of Irving's methods with Shakespeare were found to be low-key. His modern methods of naturalistic acting were not entirely accepted. The Americans liked a little robust action, proved by the fact that on one occasion the American actor Edwin Forest had knocked down all the supers in a stage fight and been received by loud applause – from the audience.

The Merchant was the most triumphant of the New York productions. The spectacle, the gondolas coming and going with lanterns and song, and above all the sparkling Ellen in her Venetian costumes delighted everyone. One writer described the play as a poem seen with the eyes as well as the ears. If only, added the critic, Charles Lamb, and of course, Gulian C. Verplanck, those lovers of Shakespeare, had been present! The name of Charles Lamb lingers in the memory, but Mr Verplanck seems to have failed to achieve universal acclaim.

William Winter, the eminent American writer and critic, summed up the season. He said that every artist has a way of his own. Irving's way may not be the best way for everyone but 'undoubtedly it is the best way for him'.

'As far as he now stands disclosed upon this stage Mr Irving is a thorough and often a magnificent artist, one who makes even his defects help him, and one who leaves nothing to blind and whirling chance. If the light that shines through his work be not the light of genius by what name shall it be called?'

It was a generous and wholehearted tribute.

Before the curtain fell on 24 November, Irving thanked his generous hosts in New York, saying that he and his company were only bidding 'au revoir'; they hoped to be back in April with *Hamlet* and *Much Ado*. They left New York with the cheers of the New Yorkers ringing in their ears.

The opening weeks had fully justified Irving's optimism and allayed his secret fears. Financially, the season brought in nearly $76,000, or £15,600. But the ticket touts had been equally successful. It was estimated that with some three-dollar seats being sold for ten dollars, the public had paid more than double the sum which Irving had received for his appearances.

It had been a triumphant beginning. From the first Irving carried the American public by storm. Cables had been sent to London by some people with an axe to grind alleging that he was playing to empty benches. But never in the history of the American stage had an actor had such success as Irving on his first American tour. He was lavishly entertained. The whole of New York society set themselves out to show their appreciation. One of the big occasions was a dinner for 500 people given at the Lotos Club in New York, where Irving was reported as having made a speech of 'considerable length'. The Americans were obviously not such gluttons for the punishment of long speeches as the clubmen in London.

Henry Abbey's presentation of Irving and Ellen had been abundantly justified, but some plans were less happy. He tried to force the Lyceum company to play 'one night stands'. Irving, always conscious of the necessity of good presentation, especially in a new country, rejected the idea. Abbey's arrangements were haphazard. In America, in the depths of winter, the company journeyed backwards and forwards over thousands of miles, from Brooklyn to Chicago, from Chicago to Cincinnati, and then back to Chicago and from Chicago to Toronto. With the numbers of people and tons of scenery, the costumes and the special trains, this not only added to the fatigue of the actors but added considerably to the expense.

But the long journeys were in the future. The next town after New York was Philadelphia. Here they opened at the Chesnut Street Theatre, described as a handsome brick building which seated 1,500 people. Irving had been warned that Philadelphians 'claim to occupy the highest critical chair in America – and that of all other cities they would be the least likely to accept a new Hamlet'. His reaction showed his courage. The warning decided him to play Hamlet in America for the first time in Philadelphia. 'I never played it to an audience that entered more fully into the spirit of my work,' he said later.

The Philadelphians were astonished at their own fervour. So were the reporters. 'I have never seen an audience in *this* city rise and cheer an actor as they cheered Irving when he took his call after the play scene in *Hamlet*. Such enthusiasm is unknown here,' wrote one. This first performance of *Hamlet* in America drew curious critics from New York, from Boston, and from further afield. Their criticisms were strangely out of key with the acclaim of the audience.

Irving, inured but not impervious to the blows of fortune, discussed the phenomenon with a dispassionate analysis. There were three kinds of critics – those who wrote their criticism before they had seen the play, and peppered their writing with erudite historical references; those who brought their preconceived ideas of Hamlet or Shylock to the theatre with them; and those who judged the play according to the night's performance, and interpreted the feelings of the audience. No doubt he felt that many of the out-of-town critics had written their pieces on the train.

Irving found Philadelphia quieter than New York and the homely red-brick houses with their white marble steps and green blinds pleased him. On Sunday the streets were bright with people going to church and chapel, the women much better dressed than in England. He found the newspaper much more lively than at home, and full of amusing snippets. A theatre-goer complained that Irving, in moments of deep emotion, was inclined to loosen a scarf round his neck. A local scarf manufacturer replied that it was very good for *his* business; half a million amateur actors would all be imitating Irving and buying scarves to do so. Not that it appeared that amateur actors received much acclaim or encouragement. A Mr James Malley had announced in the paper that he wanted to become a professional; the *Evening Call* suggested he should wait until a drastic fall in the price of eggs.

The same local newspaper boasted a band of eighty-six performers, who marched down Broad Street to serenade Irving outside his hotel, ending up with a spirited rendering of 'God Save the Queen'. They then set off at a smart pace to Miss Terry's hotel and after a short street parade serenaded her. As might be expected, she cried to hear the strains of the national anthem of her own dear land.

As in New York, the big feeds began. One of these was given at the Clover Club, which planned a splendid breakfast. This club had taken over the Hotel Bellevue and turned it into a 'fairy bower'. The central pillar had been turned into a huge camellia tree. At the base, amongst moss and ferns, hundreds of lilies and trails of smilax 'covered the entire board, furnishing a radiant green setting for the dazzling glass and silver and handsome plaques of flowers and fruits'. The room was darkened and lit by hundreds of candles, and in the centre of the table the words 'Henry Irving' were spelt out in flowers.

Irving found the speeches at these club affairs in America wittier and less pompous than in England.

The feast ended with a generous gesture. Mr Donaldson, a well-known Clover, got up and said that America boasted 1,800 theatres, 20,000 actors and actresses, and spent forty million dollars a year on going to the theatre. On behalf of this great art the Clovers wished to present to Mr Irving the watch of 'the greatest genius America ever produced – Edwin Forrest'.

It was Irving's turn to be moved to tears: 'I shall wear this watch close to my heart. It will remind me of you all, and with all my heart I thank you.' He kissed the watch and put it in the upper left-hand pocket of his waistcoat. It was the gesture of an actor, but genuinely felt.

Chapter 13

Blizzards and Shakespeare

Henry and Ellen were seasoned touring campaigners, but as is so often the case with travellers the winter they had chosen to tour America proved gruelling even for them. When they journeyed to Boston the fields had been brown and stubbled and a mild winter forecast by the weather prophets. All seemed set fair.

The company were nervous of their reception in Boston because there had been difficulties with the scenery. After the Philadelphia engagement, Irving realised the impossibility of transporting so many tons of scenery over hundreds and thousands of miles. Perhaps, like many Englishmen, he had not entirely understood the reality of the vast distances to be travelled, nor the depredations of what he called the 'baggage wreckers' on the American railways. From Boston onwards he employed local carpenters to build the scenery, and used the Lyceum draperies, dresses, and props to re-create the reality of the original productions.

The Boston audience was a challenge. The *Post* remarked that it was not made up of average theatre-goers, but 'a very large majority of those present were people of wealth, who go to the theatre comparatively little'.

Yet even the upper-crust Bostonian audience was stirred to enthusiasm. They showed no doubts, no desire to conceal their pleasure, and laughed and wept with the actors, and listened wrapt to the poetry of *Hamlet*. All the plays Irving gave in Boston from *Charles I* and *The Bells* to the heights of *Hamlet* were praised. To modern eyes and ears the prototype of the old-time 'actor', Irving was received in Boston as a pioneer of new methods. Gone were the old barnstorming ways, the making of points, and the ramming home of soliloquies.

Irving managed by some magic to get over the full meaning of almost every sentence. The *Boston Transcript* said: 'He made *Hamlet* more of a convincing reality to us than any actor we can remember.' The theatre had come a long way since Edwin Forrest had knocked out the supporting cast.

Audiences were enthusiastic but the weather became less kind. Overnight the blizzards struck, and suddenly Boston was transformed into a city of sleighs and sleigh bells. Coming from a country where the climate was less dramatic, Irving said: 'Yesterday autumn winds, bright streets, and a rattle of traffic, and today, snow and sleigh bells. The omnibuses are sleighs, the grocer's cart is a sleigh, the express wagons are sleighs.'

The snow was soon a foot deep, but it made no difference to the audiences at the theatre. Irving was amazed: 'It would have ruined business in London.' Fired with enthusiasm, Irving asked Brooks, his coloured attendant, if he could find him a sleigh and two horses. Wrapped in rugs Irving enthusiastically toured the city and the surroundings, a Napoleon of the theatre, driving rapidly in his sledge across the fine streets of the Back Bay district, crossing the Charles river with its long lines of red-brick buildings, seeing the heights of Brookline in white, green and grey against a startling blue sky. Through Cambridge and the colleges he went, noticing all the wooden villas, and the fact that they lacked the picturesque touch of blue wood-smoke curling up against the blue sky, for they burned smokeless coal. Irving commented: 'What a blessing it would be if London were to use nothing else.' It was to take eighty years for this idea to cross the Atlantic.

On the way back to his hotel Irving found the streets merry with stylish sleighs and gay driving parties. The Boston winter had begun cheerfully out of doors. Indoors the lavish entertaining began as usual. Irving was fêted at the University and entertained by the Somerset Club, where he met Mark Twain. The Boston ladies of the Papyrus Club entertained Ellen, escorted by Joseph Hatton, who remarked that 'she captivated the women, all of them'. He noticed the sharp difference between the American attitude towards women and that prevailing in Europe:

'A woman who adorns and lifts the feminine intellect into notice in America excites the admiration rather than the jealousy of her sisters. They share in her fame; they do not try to dispossess her of the lofty place upon which she stands. There is a sort of trade unionism among the women of America – they hold together in a ring against the so-called lords of creation, and the men are content to accept what appears to be a happy form of petticoat government.'

The applause died away and the really hard journeying began – first to Baltimore. Hatton, waiting at the 'depot' under the spluttering electric lights, was told that the Irving train had been delayed. This was not surprising. The snow was falling more thickly than ever in the chilly darkness.

The baggage train consisted of eight enormous cars which had to be transported by boat, the raft and train being attached to a tug-boat. The train was then run on to a floating track at Harlem and reconnected at Jersey City. All this had to be achieved in a blizzard.

Through the heavily falling snow the ferry-boats' hooters were heard at last. People came and went covered in snow, bent against the bitter wind. Eventually the floating train arrived, and Hatton with his family were escorted by the light of flickering lanterns to the raft and eventually into the tropical heat of the railway car. Ellen greeted them and provided hot tea and sympathy, while Irving, Stoker, Loveday and Hatton sat down to a very excellent supper of oyster pie, cold beef, jelly, eggs, coffee and cigars. The contrast between the bitter weather which swirled around the train and the home comforts provided within could not have been greater. What modern travellers have gained in speed of transport, they have lost gastronomically.

After his long hard journey Irving settled down to sleep in his bunk next to the drawing room where the supper was served. The train ground slowly through the snow and eventually came to a standstill. The coloured waiter regaled the nervous Hatton with tales of armed attacks on trains.

But the lanterns seen against the falling snow were only carried by the train staff trying to find their way through the snowdrifts. The passengers' worries were not without reason. One train had blown up on the same track after running into a deep drift. The fire-man and stoker were both killed.

One of the linesmen boarded the train and was revived by Hatton with a drop of brandy. He had been on the track for nearly two hours; there were trains in front, trains behind, and a gang of men trying to clear the track ahead. It had taken three hours to go twenty miles. There was no other sign of life, not a house nor a person. In the darkness the bells of approaching trains were heard. One right in front of the heavy baggage wagons.

Fortunately it was a freight train come to the rescue of the Lyceum company. Then other trains were heard, whistling and bellowing, obscured by the falling snow. Meanwhile the train conductors were out on the track trying to clear the points in the constantly drifting snow and the freezing wind.

Inside the cars the heat was ninety degrees.

'What's going on?' said the voice of Mathias, as in *The Bells*.

'Getting another engine.'

'What for?'

'To check our speed, we have been going too fast.'

'You astonish me,' said Irving sarcastically, going back to his bunk and promptly falling asleep.

Eventually the train arrived at Baltimore where they were to play for a week, including a performance on Christmas Day.

Baltimore was a bustling, picturesque city. The streets filled with blocks of ice, melting snow and sloppy snowdrifts, were busy with buggies, wagons, carts, carriages, and tram-cars. The women getting on and off the cars plunged courageously into the snow heaps and gutters deep with melting snow. They all wore black waterproof capes, sometimes enlivened with a bright feathered hat. The 'carriage ladies' were enveloped in furs, wearing those diamond earrings that marked their status. The shops displayed shop signs as in the early London streets – a gilded horse's head indicated a saddler, the watchmaker hung out a clock, the glover a hand. The bright piles of tropical fruits astonished the travellers, and the men were attracted by glimpses of the bright blonde beauties passing by, enveloped in their waterproof hoods.

At the theatre things were not so picturesque. The white workmen refused to work for Irving. Such heavy manual labour, they said, was for the coloured men. But the coloured men refused to work after dark. The night, they said, quite logically, was for sleeping – and for actors.

Irving had been told that audiences in Boston and Baltimore were cold. He said he found them extremely warm: 'I had more applause from them than I have had in my own country.'

The applause again died away and the long and gruelling travels began once more. The scenery was packed into the freight cars with the greatest possible speed and the train set off at midnight. From Baltimore they steamed to Brooklyn, and from Brooklyn to Chicago, over one thousand miles. Their journey was made as pleasant as possible. The President of the Erie Railroad had sent Irving a parlour car which had once belonged to the financier Jim Fisk. Miss Terry had a private reception room with two easy chairs, a settee, tables with periodicals, and a buffet. There was a private sitting-room and smoking-room for Irving, and a kitchen was attached to these grand travelling apartments. This special train cost Abbey three thousand dollars. Miss Terry was reported as having spent most of the journey reading, singing and eating grapes. She must have been an unrestful companion.

Irving, always the actor, was more worried about his reception in Chicago than the fatigues of the journey. He felt that they should have played there for four weeks instead of two, and their success would have been more assured. There were the usual rumours of the American reporters ready to board the train before it arrived. Irving laughed off this idea. He had been told of worse dangers than reporters. During Madame Bernhardt's tour, one of Abbey's special trains had been attacked by armed robbers and the conductor badly wounded. But then Bernhardt would insist on carrying all her diamonds with her. In the end the armed guards had beaten off the robbers. The wild West was not far away, either in time or distance.

One reporter (alleged to be a genuine German baron) did manage to board the train and drew a realistic if unflattering picture of snoring actors and actresses and jumbles of women's clothes on chairs. He did a rapid hunt through the train to get an interview with Irving. Flinging through a large array of British beauties in different stages of undress, the reporting baron proceeded to interview Irving – before breakfast – about everything from the state of the stage to uncut acting versions of Shakespeare, and then to ask very direct questions about Miss Terry.

Irving was charming and circumspect. He had the highest respect for Miss Terry and her talents, he said. Personal matters were not to be discussed. Unfortunately Miss Terry was not to be seen. But suddenly the door opened and there she was: 'Lustrous eyes of a rare azure, a profuseness of wavy blonde hair, and a lithe form, every motion of a natural supple grace.' Miss Terry had made another conquest. But she held up a 'round well-shaped arm'. No, she could not be interviewed, but she was prepared to admit that all American women were both nice and pretty. Miss Terry's charm broke through the most difficult barriers.

When the baggage train arrived in Chicago, they found the city snowbound. Within a day or two the thermometer had fallen to thirty degrees below zero. Huge storms of wind and snow had been followed by frost, which closed the rivers, and even Lake Michigan was solid for nearly twenty miles out. Railway tracks had been swept away and outside Chicago hundreds of hogs had been frozen to death on freight trains.

For his tour Irving had chosen the bitterest winter for more than twenty years, but like most actors he was undeterred by climatic conditions and concerned only with audiences. He surveyed the city and came to the conclusion that it had something of the 'go' of Manchester and Liverpool about it. 'One is forced to admire the pluck of Chicago, twice burnt down and twice built up, and now to be laid out anew. A people who can do that must be great – broad-minded and ready to appreciate what is good. We have something to show them, and they will catch on!'

The cold would not break Irving's spirits, though men went about the frozen streets totally muffled in furs, and the shores of Lake Michigan were barricades of ice, like palisades of marble. The 'ice boats' skimmed along the edges of the lake while beyond ships lay anchored in the ice. Irving and Ellen went sleighing along the fine streets which were being made. The forty-mile drive through these wide boulevards amazed Irving. Both he and Ellen were struck by the revival of architectural art in Chicago. The chaste decorations of cream-coloured marble pleased them, and the marble fronts of the palaces on Michigan Avenue reminded Ellen of Regency Brighton.

Irving opened at the Haverley Theatre with *Louis XI*, *The Merchant of Venice*, *The Bells*, *The Belle's Stratagem*, and the romantic drama *The Lyons Mail*. He was received with rapturous applause from the audience and discerning praise from the critics. Backstage, the theatre staff were less impressed by Irving's finished productions. 'You haven't an idea what an amount of *stuff* these people carry around with them,' said manager Will Davis to the *Tribune* reporter. He took the reporter backstage to show him the enormity of the burden which his scene shifters had to carry.

If the bustle and 'go' of Chicago impressed Irving, the theatre programmes were less tasteful. At the Lyceum he made a point of plain programmes with no advertising. Sometimes, on special occasions, they contained artistically produced notes on the production and the souvenir programmes were adorned with engravings of the play. But in America they were scraps of paper with the cast list printed very small in the middle of advertisements for 'Pansy Corsets', Oyster Saloons, Dressed Beef, Baking Powder, Ladies Perforated Chamois Vests, Ostrich Feathers, and appeals to use the Erie Railway. Advertising was all part of the 'go' which Irving admired.

The two weeks at Chicago came to a triumphant conclusion with Irving making one of his usual last night speeches. He thanked the press of Chicago for its sympathy, and its eloquent and ungrudging recognition of a 'sincere although incomplete effort to bring the dramatic art abreast of the other arts, and not leave it behind in the cold, out of the general march of progress'. He ended by announcing that the company would be returning in the following month and hoped 'that we may live in your memories as you will live in ours'. (Thunderous applause.)

The applause from the box office was equally pleasing – nearly forty thousand dollars.

On a cold Sunday morning, the company now set out for St Louis. William Terriss and Tyars walked up and down the platform without overcoats to indicate the intrepid nature of Englishmen. Ellen Terry was not far behind in her attitude towards cold, and it was recorded on many occasions that she complained of the heat of hotel rooms, trains, and restaurants and remarked that American women were unable to move about without being muffled in furs – even when out in the nice brisk air – and travelled in closed carriages, covered in rugs. The British talent for discomfort was greatly in evidence in the nineteenth century.

A few miles out of Chicago the train ran into high snowdrifts again, with snow piled on both sides of the track to a height of eight or ten feet. They travelled through a complete world of snow; the only signs of life were occasional skating parties gliding along the great silent waterways. The sun lit this strange landscape with icy reflections, dazzling the eyes, and at sunset the whole landscape was filled with a red glare, soon to be snuffed out as the lamps were lit in the parlour cars on the train.

The travelling actors arrived in St Louis at three o'clock in the morning. The following day they found they could walk across the Mississippi. Near the quay they saw the remains of a hotel which had been burned out, and from the windows, like spilling bales of cotton, were festoons of ice flowers and sculptures in ice – the frozen remains of water pumped into the building in an attempt to put out the fire.

A procession of carts and wagons with their mule teams crossed the bridge over the river, laden with cotton, corn, and hides. The drivers were all wearing old army cloaks, greyish blue with scarlet linings, which heightened the colours of the winter landscape, the snow-laden sky, and the red setting sun. Smoke hung like a pall over the city and the winter mist crept along the icy river to shroud the scene in a curious harmony.

Harmony also greeted the actors when they unrolled their wares on the St Louis stage. All the flower and chivalry of St Louis had turned out for this 'meeting in St Louis'. Five hundred ladies and gentlemen, 'representing the most exclusive and aristocratic circles of St Louis Society', and, added the *Post Dispatch* with sly sarcasm, 'a number of the most liberal and eminent of the clergymen were there also. Society in St Louis has more good sound commonsense than in any other city in the union.'

The audiences were not disappointed and the St Louis *Post Dispatch* did Irving proud:

'To the delighted audience which hung with wrapt attention last night on each word and look, each tone and motion of Henry Irving, there was only one element of disappointment – that they had not been prepared for any such magnificant revelation of dramatic genius. As far as the people of St Louis are concerned, we have only to say that those who *miss* seeing him will sustain a loss that can never be made good.'

Off stage, they were entertained by the Elks, their lodge and club rooms artistically decorated with drawings of Ellen and Irving, hung with the arms of England, and framed in flowers with the words 'Our Guests' picked out in purple blossoms. The supper rooms were 'decorated with dainty flowers interspersed with culinary trophies'.

All this splendour awaited the actors when they came from the theatre at about eleven o'clock. Mr Irving's face was found to be rather sombre and solemn when in repose, but Miss Terry was the life and soul of animation. Her dress was commended – white silk trimmed with Spanish lace and a brocade train of white and crushed strawberry; no jewellery, just gold bracelets and a pearl necklace, with a simple bunch of natural flowers tucked into her bosom.

'Miss Terry was surrounded by a gay throng of young folk and appeared the youngest and gayest of them all. A number of beautiful roses were taken from the table and presented to her by ardent admirers, for all of whom she had some little coquettish reply to their gallantry.'

While Irving represented the dignity and nobility of his profession, Miss Terry's charm could be dispensed like sunshine to open the flowers of approval amongst the paying customers. They formed a powerful public relations team for the theatre they loved. After a week in St Louis they moved on to Cincinnati. The city seemed to Irving to be picturesque – had he been able to see it. During his week there it was choked with snow and shrouded in mists and fog. In the German quarter Irving found all the characteristics of the Fatherland, transported thousands of miles across the ocean: beer-gardens, concert rooms, theatres, and German language newspapers with gothic printing. But the criticisms of the German Americans, as Irving called them, proved to be as friendly as in other cities. The *Tägliches Cincinnati Volksblatt* soared into lyrical passages of praise over *The Merchant of Venice*. Irving's reading of Shylock was found to be the same as that of Döring, who ranked as the best Shylock in Germany. 'This was the Jew that Shakespeare drew,' said the *Volksblatt*. Miss Terry took the public by storm from first to last. 'She is one of those endowed actresses who shine so completely in the character they represent that the spectator forgets the actress, and only sees the person represented in the piece.'

As the Lyceum company left Cincinnati after their week's successes, Irving was impressed by the splendidly dramatic sight of the frozen river breaking up, a great rising flood of ice and snow, and along the wharves the silent ships and steamers. It was less impressive for the local population, because a few days later the city was flooded; thousands of people were made homeless and saw their belongings float away on the floodwaters. Riots broke out. 'The objective point of the mob was the jail and the murderers it contained whom they meant to hang,' said the New York *Sun*. The local population had taken exception to the maladministration of justice in the city and the press of the country warmly supported the cause of the rioters. As the floods rose over Cincinnati the theatrical circus rolled out of town, taking with it the light, the colour, and the charm.

In Indianapolis, Irving again found the audiences very friendly, but he was somewhat put out to find that his noble art had some keen competition from attractions such as the Fat Lady, the Two-Headed Pig, the Tattooed Man, and the Wild Man of the Woods. Nor was the orchestral accompaniment what he was accustomed to in the West End of London. The violoncello had only two strings. Ball, the orchestral leader, chaffingly said: 'I suppose you will consider two strings sufficient for tonight?' 'No,' said an indignant musician, 'I stick to three – on principle.'

Irving was always interested in every aspect of the life of America, and in Columbus he went to the State House where he was introduced to many members of the General Assembly and to the Governor. He was amazed at the free way the American papers criticised their politicians. There had been some scandal in the oil world and the Columbus *Times* linked it with Irving's visit:

'The members of the General Assembly who looked upon the Standard oil, when it flowed with unction in the recent Senatorial struggle, might get a few points on the effects of the remorse of conscience by seeing Henry Irving in "*The Bells*".'

Irving, with the typical actor's reaction, was delighted to be linked with local politics.

They spent two nights in Detroit, and then a great concession from Mr Abbey – a day off to see Niagara Falls. The river banks were corrugated into lines of ice, ice blocked the channels, and the horses splashed through the snow and icy water at the approaches to the falls. Suddenly the sun came out, the wind changed, and a rainbow stretched over the American side of the falls. The company arrived prepared to be astonished and amazed.

Irving and Ellen drove with Joseph Hatton in a closed carriage. When the driver pulled up Irving was able to see the falls for the first time. Immediately the fatal accident to Webb, the first Channel swimmer, came into his mind, and the whirlpool where he had disappeared was duly pointed out. 'Imagine the coolness, the daring of it! He takes a quiet dinner, rests a little, then hires a boat, rows to the place where the rapids begin, strips and dives into this awful torrent. A great soul – any man who has the nerve for such an enterprise,' said Irving.

Walking back, he noticed the changing light, the bluish-purple horizon, the golden yellow of the water and the creamy whiteness of the foam. 'A great stage manager, Nature! What wonders can be done with effective lighting!' And then, turning, he said to Ellen: 'Do you remember the lighting in the garden scene in *Romeo and Juliet*, the change from sunset to night, from sunset to moonlight, from moonlight to morning and the motion of the sunlit trees, as if a zephyr had touched them?' People, places, senates, sunsets, and the thundering of the falls, everything turned to theatre in his mind.

Meanwhile William Terriss and some of the others were exploring the regions below the falls. The ice had made this descent slippery. Terriss fell, and only saved himself from being swept away by clutching a jagged rock. He had to play with his arm in a sling for several weeks. Breezy Bill was as courageous off stage as in the Adelphi melodramas in which he was to star later in his career, and about as accident-prone as their heroes.

The holiday over, the actors returned to their journeyings – Boston, Washington, Philadelphia, Brooklyn, and then finally back to New York.

Irving said finding himself in New York again was like going home and as if suiting the action to the word he immediately began to rehearse *Much Ado About Nothing*, 'as completely as it is possible for us to do it outside our own theatre'. The supers were rehearsed again and again. 'No – no, there must be no wait. The second procession must come on promptly at the cue.' Even the halberdiers did not escape his notice: 'Hold your halberd like this, my boy, not as if you were afraid of it.' The wedding procession entered. '*Bow, bow* – don't nod! Too much light at the back there! No – the blue medium!' The orchestra began again. 'No, no, the basses are too *loud*!' On and on in the dark theatre he worked until the spring daylight had faded and it was already five o'clock. At seven he must be ready to begin his night's work.

'Yes,' he said to one of his staff, 'I *am* rather tired, feel inclined to sit down – hard work standing about all day.' He was 46 and had been standing about at rehearsals since he was 18 – nearly thirty years. But his vision was still as fresh as on the day he had begun. He turned to the setting of the garden scene in *Much Ado* and pointed: 'This is the reward!' He was back in the make-believe of the only world he loved and really knew.

Much Ado opened on 31 March 1884 and played for three weeks to crowded houses. The press was ecstatic:

'Mr Irving and Miss Terry were welcomed by a brilliant company with the heartiest admiration and goodwill. The applause upon the entrance of Beatrice, a rare vision of imperial beauty, broke forth impetuously and continued long. Upon the subsequent entrance of Benedick it rose into a storm of gladness and welcome.'

Irving's first tour of the United States ended on 26 April 1884. The *Tribune* loaded the actor with flowery prose:

'Honour goes before him, and affection remains behind. Fortunate for the world as for the actor that this should be so. The history of the dramatic art presents many examples of men with faculties of a high order who had spent long years of toil in intellectual pursuits whose efforts have passed without recognition – and without reward.'

Irving's efforts had certainly not been without reward; the total takings of this first tour were over $400,000, a huge sum at the time. 'Thrice happy he', said the *Tribune*, 'to whom nature has vouchsafed the investiture of genius, so that his labour becomes glorified in all eyes, with the mysterious radiance of divinity!'

On 25 April, by way of returning some of the hospitality which had been so freely lavished on him, Irving gave a breakfast at Delmonico's – a small intimate breakfast for several hundred of his personal friends. William Winter had welcomed Irving to America with a poem, and he read another of sixty-four lines at the farewell breakfast.

Farewell, thou child of many a prayer,
Thou pride of her that bore thee!
All crystal be the seas that bear
And skies that sparkle o'er thee!
Thy mother's heart, thy mother's lip
Will soon again caress thee –
We can but watch thy lessening ship
And softly say, God bless thee!

Irving's mother, who hated the theatre and regarded it as an invention of the Evil One, would have been astonished at these eulogies of the profession she feared and despised.

Thus canonised and loaded with dollars, on 30 April Irving sailed for his native land.

Chapter 14

Home to Cheers and Hisses

Loftily ignoring the harvest of dollars which Irving had brought home, *The Times* welcomed him back, saying that the remarkable success he had achieved was the gratifying sign of 'the willingness of public opinion in America to co-operate with that of England to rescue the stage from the lower level to which it has sometimes sunk'.

Ellen and Irving arrived at Euston about five o'clock on a May morning in 1884.

'Both Mr Irving and Miss Terry were received with the greatest cordiality on alighting from the train and a beautiful bouquet of spring flowers was presented to Miss Terry by Miss Rose Leclerq. The voyagers, in spite of fatigue, were in excellent health and spirits. Mr Irving expressed his fervent belief that an Englishman must visit America and meet its truly representative men and women before he can form any idea of the feeling which exists in the new country towards the old.'

Having expressed these cordial sentiments, Irving and Ellen Terry drove off together in a carriage. They were home. The American adulation was behind them, the prophets had come back to their own country.

But the actors' holiday from the Lyceum was short.

They had closed in New York on 26 April and the Lyceum opened on 31 May with the successful *Much Ado*. The reception of Ellen was 'equalled only by the deep murmur of pleasure, the prolonged outburst of cheering and the great waving of handkerchiefs which awaited the Benedick of the house when he stepped upon the stage'.

Irving appeared tired, but played Benedick with more than his former spirit and gaiety; the applause from the other side of the Atlantic had added élan to a performance which had not always received the acclaim of Ellen's Beatrice. At curtain fall Irving made one of his usual lengthy speeches, remarking what an inexpressible delight it was to be home, and then immediately announced that the season would be brief as the whole company would be off to America again in the autumn. It was not a tactful beginning to his new season. He added that he would be presenting 'the ancient comedy of *Twelfth Night*'.

This play was not a favourite with Victorian audiences. It was considered too fanciful, lacking in plot interest, and the humour was too coarse and too unkind. *Twelfth Night* had not been seen on the London stage for thirty-five years, since the days of Mr and Mrs Charles Kean. But backed up with American money the designers, headed by Hawes Craven, were given a free hand with the settings. They did not disappoint.

The sets were costly, rich, and romantic. The seacoast of Illyria unfolded on a rock-bound promontory in the light of a red sunset after the storm. The Duke Orsino reclined on a velvet couch, tied and tasselled in gold, and behind him in a dim mysterious alcove, dark with painted glass, minstrels played their soft melodies to the lovesick man. The noble palace of Olivia was splendid with columns, entablatures and sculptured friezes. Her garden was charming with clipped box and yew hedges, where she and her household basked all day on wide terraces bathed in perpetual sunshine. The kitchen fire, before which Sir Toby and his boon companions roared their catches, was warm and glowing to contrast with the ghostlike figure of Malvolio in his white nightshirt. But the last scene of all brought the play to a climax of adornment. The spreading portico of Olivia's house was flanked with branching palm trees beside a blue sea, the whole rendered more striking by the picturesque grouping of guards, pages, and ladies and gentlemen of the court.

There were sixteen of these elaborate sets to astonish the eyes, but the critics complained of the dropping of the songs in favour of the scenery, which clogged the action, particularly in the clown scenes between Sir Toby Belch and Sir Andrew Aguecheek. It was also remarked that 'The Wind and the Rain', sung at the end of the play, should be a *pathetic* epilogue; it was *not* a carol.

Ellen and Fred Terry played Viola and Sebastian, a good innovation much preferred to Kate Terry who had chosen to play both parts. Ellen and Fred played with the usual Terry verve and much in the spirit of the comedy. Miss Ellen Terry appeared in white hose, an elegant white tunic embroidered with gold which descended to the knees only, a short mantle, and a ruff of satin trimmed in like fashion. A coquettish cap completed an attire which, if hardly masculine, was sufficient to mark her assumption of the part of a youth of gentle breeding. To modern eyes her costume has much the look of an old-fashioned bathing girl wearing a sword.

Irving did not fare well with the critics. Malvolio is a notoriously difficult part, and audiences no longer considered madness a target for humour. He moved his audience to tears rather than laughter and turned comedy into tragedy, especially in the last scenes, where he was deeply tragic. His line at the end of the play, 'I'll be revenged on the whole pack of you', was delivered with the concentrated hate and ungovernable vehemance of a Shylock. Joseph Knight, on the other hand, thought Irving could probably claim to be the best Malvolio the stage had seen.

Twelfth Night was produced on one of the hottest July nights of the year. The pit and galleryites had been waiting in the dust and heat of Exeter Street since the morning. One paper reported censoriously that 'a man had even been seen to divest himself of coat and waistcoat – after a fashion which is confined, as a rule, to the patrons of the *melodrama* in the popular theatres of the suburbs.'

The reception by the stalls and boxes was friendly. The actors came to the footlights to receive their applause. Irving spoke, saying that he hoped they had liked his presentation of *Twelfth Night*. A few polite yes's went up from the ladies and gentlemen of the stalls. But there were loud cries of 'no' from pit and gallery. The long wait in Exeter Street and the hot night had not improved the temper of those in the cheap seats. Fresh from his American triumphs, Irving argued back:

'I cannot understand how a company of earnest comedians and amirable actors – having the three cardinal virtues – being sober, clean and perfect, and having exercised their abilities on one of the most difficult of Shakespeare's plays can have given you cause for dissatisfaction.'

He made a mistake, said Ellen; he should have smiled deprecatingly and accepted the customers' verdict. His guard had slipped and he had shown that he was furiously angry. His normal bow and acceptance of being the public's 'humble and obedient servant' would have been more appropriate. For once he had forgotten to play this role with his usual detachment. Ellen herself, in spite of the applause and the pleasure which her sprightly acting had given to public and critics, thought that she had not played Viola nearly as well as her sister Kate. Nor did she herself like the production, which she found dull and heavy. Henry's Malvolio was in her view fine and dignified, but she felt it had thrown the delicacy of the play out of balance.

Other disasters dogged the production. Ellen, studying her part down at a cottage near Hampton Court, had been stung by a horse-fly, and on the first night had to keep her arm in a sling. Every night the swelling grew worse until she had to play most of her scenes sitting in a chair. Bram Stoker's doctor brother came in to see the play, took one look at Ellen's hand and lanced it. She played that night, but collapsed later with blood poisoning and nearly lost her arm. The rumour went round that she was one of 'those actresses who feign illness and have straw laid down before their houses, while behind the drawn blinds they are having riotous supper parties, dancing the can-can and drinking champagne'. Irving, ever chivalrous, on hearing this slander wanted to write one of his usual scorchers to the press. But Ellen, more pliant and tactful, said it had not injured her in any way, and to answer would be undignified.

After the first few nights Ellen's part of Viola was taken over by another Terry, Marion. *Twelfth Night* ended after thirty-nine performances on 22 August; it had not been one of Irving's successes.

The following week, as a prelude to his Canadian and American tour, he played his old favourites *The Bells*, *Louis XI* and *Richelieu*, all plays he intended taking with him. Although in his farewell speech on the last night of *Richelieu* he announced that Ellen had been restored to health, she was still ill when the company sailed for Canada aboard the *Parisian* on 18 September. On this occasion Irving had arranged his own tour. He was no longer having his company bucketing about from one town to another at the whim of a manager, careless of the health and strength of his players.

He had decided on a quick return to America earlier in the year, and had written to his secretary, L. F. Austin, setting out his views:

'The seed we have sown, I mean to reap. Our work has been a revelation, and our success beyond all precedent. Our return tour will exceed this present one, I am certain, and I shall be my own manager – and have no middle man.'

As once he had determined to have his own theatre, so now he was determined to be completely his own master.

The tour began in Quebec and the company travelled to Montreal, London, Hamilton and Toronto. Ellen, still suffering from the after-effects of her illness, was allowed to stay behind in Montreal and catch up with the tour at Toronto. The rest of the tour, starting at Buffalo, with return visits to New York, Philadelphia, and Chicago, took in Pittsburg, Cleveland and Detroit. It lasted from 30 September 1884 to 4 April 1885, ending in New York as usual. Irving was lauded as before. He had eclipsed Edwin Booth in tragic acting.

On his second visit Irving was received more as an honorary American. Invited to give an address in the Saunders Memorial Theatre of Harvard University on 30 March 1885, he naturally chose as his subject 'The Art of Acting'. This time, unlike when he had his encounter with the pittites at the Lyceum, he pitched his lecture with delicate sensibility and awareness of the feelings of his audience:

'I know that on this stage', he said, 'you have enacted a Greek play with remarkable success. So, after all, it is not a body of mere tyros that I am addressing, but actors who have worn the sock and buskin, and declaimed the speeches which delighted audiences two thousand years ago.'

Irving's deep reading and feeling for the historical background of what he called his craft is sharply apparent in this lecture. Roscius, Betterton, Garrick and Macready were ever present in his mind. He seems to have felt himself to be a representative runner in a relay race:

'The older we grow the more acutely alive we are to the difficulties of our craft. I cannot give you a better illustration than a story of Macready. A dear friend of mine was with him when he played Hamlet for the last time, when the curtain had fallen, and the great actor was sadly thinking that the part he loved so much would never be his again. As he took off his velvet mantle and laid it aside, he muttered almost unconsciously the words of Horatio "Good-night, sweet Prince", and then turning to his friend said, "Ah, I am just beginning to realise the sweetness, the tenderness, the gentleness of this dear Hamlet." Believe me, the true artist never lingers fondly upon what he has done. He is ever thinking of what remains undone; ever striving towards an ideal it may never be his fortune to attain.'

It was Irving's own view. He countered the still current highbrow view that Shakespeare was better read than acted by quoting George Eliot, who said: 'In opposition to most people who love to read Shakespeare, I like to see his plays acted. His great tragedies thrill me, let them be acted how they may.' Irving emphasised the difficulties of naturalism on the stage and remarked how modern stage lighting had given the actor so many opportunities for development. In old pictures the actors were always seen standing downstage in a line. Why? Irving told a backstage story to underline his point.

Edmund Kean one night played Othello with more than his usual intensity. An admirer met him in the street the next day and was loud in his congratulations. 'I really thought you would have *choked* Iago, Mr Kean. You seemed so tremendously in earnest.' Kean looked at the man. 'In earnest! I should think so! Hang the fellow, he was trying to keep me out of focus!'

Irving was ever conscious of his lack of learning, ever humble when he was asked to lecture at universities. 'The only Alma Mater I ever knew', he would say, 'was the hard stage of a country theatre.' He was perhaps over-conscious of his lowly origins in an age of rich parvenus and snobs. Sir Squire Bancroft said that at the beginning of his career Irving had a strong smack of the country actor in his appearance, a suggestion of the type immortalised by Dickens. His insistence on the dignity of his profession sprang from this feeling. No amount of applause could entirely kill the past.

The second American tour proved to be as socially and financially profitable as the first. When it ended a huge public banquet of appreciation was given in his honour. Over a hundred names appeared on the invitation list. They included Henry Ward Beecher, Oliver Wendell Holmes, Edwin Booth, Lawrence Barrett, Mark Twain, and sundry assorted politicians, senators, and socialites. When sending Irving the invitation the distinguished hosts wrote that they hoped America would form part of Irving's theatrical season in the future.

They sailed in the *Arizona* and Ellen's son Gordon Craig was with them on the homeward journey. In a sudden fit of maternal homesickness Ellen had cabled: 'Bring out one of the children.' Craig said, 'It wasn't that she didn't care, only that she cared too much for both and couldn't decide which was to be left behind.' The homeward-bound picture of Irving, Ellen, the bearded Captain of the *Arizona*, and Irving's and Ellen's dogs, includes the grinning and precocious Gordon Craig.

But Irving had sailed back into another storm. For some time he had thought of making it possible to book pit and gallery seats. The appalling waits and the fights for the cheaper seats worried him. On many occasions he had sent out tea and bread and butter to the patiently waiting crowds. Would it not be better if instead of the discomfort and the fighting the pit and galleryites could book their seats in advance?

Bernard Shaw described the pit crush vividly:

'In my barbarous youth when one of the pleasures of theatre going was the fierce struggle at the pit door, I learned a lesson which I have never forgotten, namely that the secret of getting in was to wedge myself into the worst of the crush. When ribs and breastbone were on the verge of collapse, and the stout lady in front, after passionately calling on her escort to take her out – if he considered himself a man – had resigned herself to death, my hopes of a place in the front row ran high.'

Irving had decided to end this rib-crushing exercise. He spent £3,000 on making both pit and gallery more comfortable. He opened with his dear *Hamlet* on 2 May 1885. He was received with the usual roar of welcome. The bodies were taken up. The rites of war may have spoken loudly for Hamlet but the pit spoke loudly against him. The moment he mentioned the new arrangements for booking a roar of disapproval greeted him. This time he did not make the mistake of arguing, but said that time would decide the issue. 'So, gentlemen, with all my love, I do commend me to you and what so poor a man as Hamlet is may do, to express his love and friending to you, God willing, shall not lack!'

The new arrangements lasted a week. Irving was not put out. 'From more than one point of view, I was not sorry that it failed. We found that the dress circle and stalls people had gone to buy booked seats at a cheap rate. I believe ladies drove up in their broughams to the pit doors.'

In the row about the booking of seats Irving's Hamlet had been forgotten, but Clement Scott felt that he had rounded off and polished his original conception: 'America sends us back a better actor than the one who left our shores.'

Irving played himself in at the Lyceum with his usual repertoire of success, and then, on 28 May 1885, he revived Ellen's old triumph, *Olivia*, the dramatisation of *The Vicar of Wakefield*. This was one of Ellen's favourite parts, because, as she said, there was nothing which could touch the heart more than beauty and innocence led into folly. In her eighteenth-century clothes she glided on to the stage as sympathetic and charming as she had done seven years before. Her delicate gradations of mingled hopes and fears, her craving for news from the old home – everything she did touched the hearts of her audience.

Irving, however, failed to impress 'The Captious Critic' of the *Sporting and Dramatic News*: 'For most of the play he seemed to be the tender, unselfish, lovable Vicar, but now and then he seemed to step out from behind this mask and give the feeling of Dr Syntax rather than Dr Primrose.' Other faults were found by other critics. Dr Primrose was supposed to be celebrating his silver wedding. He should be a hale and hearty man of 50 not a white-haired old man of 70. There always has been a tendency on the part of actors to slip into a wheelchair for any character supposed to be over 50.

Even Ellen did not entirely please. One critic complained that she played every part in the same way. 'She has sympathetic individuality and a strange peculiar grace. But in the second scene she spent so much time putting Mr Irving to sleep that it almost had that same effect on me.'

Percy Fitzgerald paints a vivid picture of this production, which gives the effect of a sentimental picture of the eighteenth century (painted in the nineteenth century), a perfect watercolour of old farmyards, and farms with thatched roofs, and ideal peasant children smiling at stable doors with chickens pecking around their feet.

'The eye rests with infinite pleasure on this engaging figure of the Vicar with his powdered wig and rusted suit, the family singing at the spinet, Moses accompanying them with his flute, and the Vicar in his chair with his churchwarden pipe – and the cuckoo clock in the corner.'

A few writers found Ellen fidgety, flickering about the stage in a series of poses each in itself so charming that one could hardly account for the distrust she herself showed of it by instantly changing it for another. Be that as it may, the audience was dissolved in sentimental tears and took the betrayed Olivia, the dear old father, and the wicked Squire Thornhill to their hearts. So did the *Daily Telegraph* critic, who said that he had absolutely no hesitation in saying that the 'scene between father and daughter at the Dragon Inn, when the Vicar comes to seek the lamb that has strayed from the fold, is as fine an instance of true emotional acting as the modern playgoer has ever seen'.

Breezy Bill Terriss played Ellen's betrayer. Miss Winifred Emery played Sophia, Olivia's sister. Winifred Emery afterwards married Cyril Maude and became a star in her own right. She was a lady of disinterested observation, who on being asked her recollections of Ellen said: 'I could not stand so much playfulness.'

Olivia played until the season ended on 30 July and the upper crust departed to Cowes, Scotland, or their country estates.

The theatre was closed for holidays and redecoration. The reproductions of Bartolozzi's engravings and the charming little rococo reminders of Madame Vestris were considered old-fashioned and were to be swept away. While this was being carried out, Irving was planning his next production, which was to be a spectacular version of Goethe's *Faust*. No expense was to be spared and the settings were to be as romantic and Gothic as travel and thought could make them.

Germany was the home of both the romantic and the Gothic, so to Germany Irving must go. And not only Irving. He set out with Ellen and her children, Comyns Carr and his wife, Alice, who helped to design Ellen's costumes. Hawes Craven was also sent for to make detailed drawings on the spot of the old German timbered houses, the narrow streets, the ancient churches, the castles perched on crags over the Rhine, everything which had the right appeal for a generation drawn towards the picturesque.

The party made their headquarters in Nuremberg, but it was in Rothenburg, smaller and more obviously medieval, that Hawes Craven and Irving found their real inspiration. Henry, wearing his broad-brimmed holiday hat, cheerful and interested, filled endless trunks with china, relics, escutcheons, swords, and furniture. All the properties must be authentic. Everything interested him, from the sudden view of a narrow street full of shops to a fire devouring old wooden buildings. Each impression was to be turned into the real life of the theatre.

In public Irving behaved like a medieval king crying 'Largesse!' Gold coins filtered through his fingers as copper through the fingers of others. Ellen, accustomed to the frugality of a travelling theatre family, tried to restrain him – to no avail. When she told him it was vulgar, he said 'Do you think so?' and went on doing it. As soon as the news of his largesse was noised abroad, he was followed by crowds of beggars. The legend of the open-handed English milord died hard in the nineteenth century. On one occasion, when penetrating a dark alley with Comyns Carr and Ellen's son Teddie (then aged about 12), they were about to be set upon by a gang of toughs. Irving did not quail but turned on the would-be robbers one of the most terrifying of his gallery of evil masks. The gang, fearing some attack by a madman, melted into the shadows. Irving, Comyns Carr, and Teddie continued on their peaceful sightseeing way. To Irving, the whole episode was handled as he might have handled a mishap in the theatre.

Everything was to be thrown into making Wills's reworking of Goethe's *Faust* the most astonishing spectacle ever to have been seen on the stage.

An organ was installed for the cathedral scene, real electricity was connected to the foils in the duelling sequence so that they gave out devilish sparks, real steam hissed and bubbled as Mephistopheles appeared through the cloud. In the Brocken scene of the witches' sabbath, the 'diabolical crew' were trained to sway with strange possessed movements against a wild sky. The forgiveness awaiting the dead Margaret was transformed into a ladder of angels – the ladder being made with specially strengthened steel to take the angels' weight. The lower angels were young women, and to highlight the perspective illusion the angels became smaller and younger as they ascended into the dusty heaven of the 'flies'. The edict went forth: no angels may wear rings or bracelets. Their celestial status must be preserved.

Nothing was left to chance. The production itself combined, like a medieval painting, pictures on a human scale with diabolic visions of evil. The garden scenes with Margaret seen at the old well, red-brick walls, roses, and old trees; in the distance, the sombre towers of the city of Nuremberg suffused with a sad sunset charm, the old street, with a statue of the Madonna in a niche; Dr Faustus's book-lined study – everything conjured up in the spectator's mind the reality of old Germany. The spell was broken only by the sudden supernatural effects, appearances and diabolic visions.

Irving's feeling for the strange and macabre, his liking for Doré and Daumier, came to its full flowering with the production of *Faust*. The sense of evil was contrasted (as it was in his own mind) with the scenes of old-world rustic life, and over all hung Irving's favourite touch – the sense of impending doom.

When interviewed about his production Irving would not admit to its having cost £15,000, but the creators of spectaculars always refuse to count the price of their effects. A single peal of bells had cost £400.

One commentator wrote that Irving was an artist as well as an actor, and had more than once sacrificed himself as an actor for the artistic delight of mounting and adorning a dramatic theme which gave him no special opportunity for histrionic distinction. Not only did he sacrifice himself as an actor on these airy dreams, he was also spending the money so hard earned on the gruelling travelling across the United States. The cost of astonishing the bourgeois mind was considerable. Some newspaper critics were aware of this.

'Mr Irving has given a reality to stage illusion in the beauties of composition and colour. Those who are acquainted with the actor manager of the Lyceum Theatre know that his work has its spring in that absolute unselfishness of the true artist who does not count the cost of things, nor value his reward in money.'

If Mr Irving were to have successors it was said that he should have a national subsidy, or he would be consumed in his own artistic fervour.

The other cost to Irving was the nervous energy needed to control such a vast cast, which required subtle orchestration if the right effects were to be achieved. Alice Comyns Carr complained that when she saw Irving at rehearsals she realised that there were two different Irvings. The debonair holiday companion had been put off with his holiday hat, and in his place was a ruthless autocrat, 'rough in his handling of everything in the theatre – except Nell'.

No one was allowed to watch him at work, and he was ever ready with a flood of bitter satire if anyone accidentally strayed into his vision. This view of him contrasted with his kindness to his small-part actors, and the infinite patience with fools which Ellen had so often remarked upon. He was under a strain and had obviously no time to spare for artistic ladies who strayed into rehearsals to see how their arty dresses looked.

The backstage complications were immense, for it was the most expensive and complex of all the Lyceum productions. There were 400 ropes to be used by the scene shifters – and each rope was blessed with a name to avoid confusion. The list of properties and instructions to the carpenters was so long that it became a joke.

The rumours and news about *Faust* had created the usual stampede for tickets, which were so hard to get that a peer was said to have been seen waiting in the gallery queue.

The curtain went up to a brilliant audience which included the Prince and Princess of Wales and the Princess Louise (The Marchioness of Lorne). The Prince (in mourning for some relative) watched from behind the scenes. There were a few setbacks on the stage. The luscious visions of fleshly delights conjured up by Mephistopheles for Faust failed to appear; Irving's opponent in the fencing scene had forgotten his glove and was duly electrically shocked. Irving took this in his stride with a demonic laugh. The appearance of Mephistopheles, in a cloud of steam, was judged by some to be spoiled by the unmistakable hissing sounds of the steam engine. But the Brocken scene – vast, chilling, and strange with its atmosphere of dizzy heights shrouded in mists hovering above tortuous crevasses – was judged never to have been surpassed.

Irving seems to have played Mephistopheles with a sardonic

mockery worthy of a C. S. Lewis Devil. In Germany the Devil had always been played as a plump man of the world, the new idea of a slim, mocking Devil was Irving's own.

Edward Russell described the effect he produced:

'The conversation of Mephistopheles pierces to the thoughtful listener's very marrow. It is the smiling scorn the devil shows for all scruples which he knows will be overcome. His delivery of his words in a cynical tenor is most expressive. "I am myself an exemplary Christian." All the quintessence of profane belief is concentrated in his tone and accents.'

Russell also brings to life the feeling of the Brocken scene:

'The spectator is awed by the vast and noble rugged crags. The Evil One stands on the precipice from which his guest shrinks cowering back. Forms weird but squalid begin to congregate and gibber. At the word of the devil prince, all is mountain solitude. At another word all is witches' sabbath, and wild revel. Then Mephistopheles seated on a rock in front is fondled by two queer juvenile-seeming creatures for whom he appears to have, and they for him, an affection that curdles the beholder.'

Ellen, that eternal maiden, received the rewards of any betrayed maiden of the period; she was touching, and looked like an innocent girl in her teens. She was actually 38. She learned to spin to add authenticity to the spinning-wheel scene. In the bedroom scene she was again felt to look and act like a girl of 18. Was there a woman on the stage who could play so risky a scene with such exquisite unconsciousness?

One dissenting German voice was raised against the production – and Miss Terry. The production was highly displeasing, being impregnated with pessimism, and this critic was not at all impressed with what he called 'das famöse schlanke urbild der Intensityschule Miss Ellen Terry.' He obviously preferred his *mädeln* a little more substantial.

Ellen was not as enamoured of *Faust* as Irving. She remarked that many people found it claptrap, but admitted that Margaret was the part she liked better than any – outside Shakespeare. She said modestly that she played it beautifully – sometimes; and although the language was commonplace, the character of Margaret was 'all right – simple, touching and sublime'. Irving's Mephisto she found two-pence coloured. But he had his moments of real inspiration. One was when he wrote in the student's book: 'Ye shall be as Gods knowing good and evil.' He did not look at the book, and suddenly, as if by the power of his feeling, the evil spirit seemed to be present. Another strange moment was when Faust defied Mephisto, and he silenced Faust with four words: 'I am a Spirit!' 'Henry seemed to grow to a gigantic height. and to hover over the ground instead of walking on it – it was terrifying.'

There were casting problems. H. B. Conway was execrable on the first night as Faust and Irving sacked him, appropriately enough against a background of the Brocken scene. Conway was standing at the top of the mountain, as far away as he could get. His handsome face was red, and his eyes full of tears. Loveday came in, and announced baldly that George Alexander was to play Faust. It was Alexander's first real chance and he seized it with both hands. It was not entirely Conway's fault; he was a light comedy man. Demonic possession was not in his line.

Faust was cut up by many critics, condemned as a pantomime for adults, and shunned by the intelligentsia as a travesty of Goethe. Yet the Germans flocked to see it, and Goethe's fame rose with that of the Lyceum production. One hundred thousand translations of *Faust* were sold in the first months of the run. Crackers were marketed with Irving's picture on them and guaranteed to contain various devilish devices. There were Margaret shoes and Mephistopheles hats. The learned articles written about Goethe and this theatrical travesty of his thought were superseded by more burning topics, such as 'Could Faust marry Margaret?'

Nor was the scandal created by the plot without its uses. Mothers who allowed their daughters to hear the opera would not bring them to see Margaret being betrayed without music. Among the daughters forbidden by their mothers to sully their minds with Faust was Princess May, afterwards Queen Mary, consort of George V.

But in spite of its difficult beginnings, miscasting, and accidents – George Alexander and Irving were nearly killed by falling from a slide and narrowly missed being cast down to their death through a deep trap below – the play steamed and flashed on from strength to strength. It opened on 19 December 1885, and on 14 February Mesphistopheles sent Margaret a Valentine with a note:

White and red roses
Sweet and fresh posies
One bunch for Edy, angel of Mine,
One bunch for Nell, my dear Valentine.

On stage, Henry could be the personification of evil, off stage, he stood for the respectability of the stage and the upright figure of the English gentleman. On stage Ellen portrayed the noble-hearted, the betrayed, the innocent, and the pure. She was everyone's idea of perfect girlhood or perfect womanhood, according to the necessity of the part. Off stage, Henry's Nell was a different and more complicated woman. It could not have been an easy relationship.

Chapter 15

Mephisto (of the Grange)

In 1882, prowling around the outskirts of London, Irving had come upon an old derelict house in Brook Green, Hammersmith, then considered to be almost in the country. He transformed it into a quiet retreat with trees and arbours, a panelled hall, and a study with deep chairs and a large desk. Engravings picture him under the shadow of a tree in his garden with his St Bernard and his bulldog. It is difficult not to think that he planned this as a retreat for himself and Ellen for this was the year of *Romeo and Juliet* when, as Ellen said, 'Henry *felt* like Romeo'. He had bought a long lease of The Grange, Brook Green, and spent a great deal of money on it, yet he never lived there. It was said to be his summer retreat and was used for luncheons, dinner parties, and receptions. But it never became his home.

Yet in the spring of 1885 Ellen's husband Charles Kelly died. She was no longer a wife but a widow. It was possible at this crossroads that Irving could have persuaded his wife to divorce him. He had the financial wherewithal to dazzle Florence with rich settlements. Both he and Ellen were at the peak of their artistic and financial success. What caused them to hesitate from making a rounded whole of their professional and private lives?

The one acknowledged love of Ellen's, Godwin, the father of her spoiled children, died during the run of *Faust* in 1886. Other links with the past had been broken. Charles Reade, the man who had called her back from poverty and social ostracism to fame and prosperity, also died in the same year.

She had been Irving's partner and companion for nearly eight years. Ellen's son, Gordon Craig, said she had a passion for respectability, born of her early difficulties with her family. In her later years, when she looked back on her relationship with Irving, she said: 'We were terribly in love for a while. Then later on, when it didn't matter so much to me, he wanted us to go on, and so I did, because I was very, very fond of him, and he said he needed me.'

There had obviously been some turning-point in their relationship. It is always difficult to unravel connections between people of ambition who live in the public eye. The idolators of Irving like to paint him as a man of generosity, of strange charm, and of dedication. But he was also a man of a single purpose, a man who worked his actors till midnight and beyond, and then expected Ellen to act as hostess to his friends at the Beefsteak Club into the small hours of the morning. He lived much in public and lacked that tenderness and ability to retreat into private life which Ellen preserved. By the time she had become free and a widow, Irving had given her financial security – but she for her part had spent the years watching him. The swimmer at the side of the river had had time to reflect on the temperature of the water and had retreated.

She had had too much time to reflect on the fact that, married to Henry, at home or abroad she would never escape from the theatre. He took it with him everywhere. A sunset, a fire, the expression on a face – everything was turned in his mind to material for a play. She had lived with theatre since she was a small child, and now she retreated from the further prospect.

Graham Robertson, like Gordon Craig, draws a clear distinction between Ellen the actress and her apparent character once she was off stage. Irving's whole personality was the theatre. Only occasionally, with his old friend J. L. Toole, did he seem to spring to life again as if he stretched out his hand to touch a time of youth which had been passed on dusty stages and travelling from town to town. In struggling so hard and so long to become the actor he had lost the man, and it was a man of flesh and blood which Ellen sought.

She had spent too long acting and entertaining with Irving to imagine that she would find him a companion for 'larks' and the cosy, giggling companionship in which she indulged off stage. Irving's humour could be alternatively cutting or sardonic. He had none of the playfulness in which Ellen indulged and which perhaps he found irksome from time to time, though there was never a time when he did not indulge her, and was given in return that ungrudging admiration which was as necessary to him as breathing. Ellen also gave him the confidence born of the long years of training she had undergone as a child.

From 1882, the high point of their relationship, when Irving bought the Grange, their relationship seems to have become more everyday and matter of fact. Ellen often referred to him as her 'great comrade'. He was also her bread and butter, her lifeline, the supporter of her children and her household. He had produced carriages, servants and security for the child whose bed had been a mattress on the floor in theatrical digs, the baby who had been bundled into a shawl and taken to the theatre to sleep in the drawer of a dressing-table. Irving's gift to her was not a small one, and in her heart she knew this. In 1885, the year of *Faust*, Irving was already 47, in his day an age for achieving *gravitas*. The psychological moment for the throwing of caps over windmills was past.

When asked to lecture to the Philosophical Institution at Edinburgh in 1881 he had chosen as his subject 'The Stage As It Is'. 'The immortal part of the stage is its nobler part,' he said. 'Heaven forbid that I should seem to cover, even with a counterpane of courtesy, exhibitions of deliberate immorality. Happily this sort of thing is not common.'

Heroines must suffer and be seen to suffer for their sins. This view would naturally make personal relationships for prominent men awkward to manage, but on this he did not touch. He went on to say that he stood for justice for the art to which he was devoted. And then suddenly his own real feeling burst through the pompous phrases:

'How noble the privilege to work upon these finer feelings of universal humanity, how engrossing the fascination of steady eyes and sound sympathies, and beating hearts which an actor confronts . . . how rapturous the satisfaction of abandoning himself in such a presence and with such sympathisers to his author's grandest flights of thought and noblest bursts of emotional inspiration!'

He spoke from the heart. How beautiful to rouse the emotions of his audience and feel the waves of applause lapping round him like a warm sea! Better than the love of women, the cosiness of family life, or the pull of passion. For this everything can be abandoned, and one can live only for the moment when the gas is lit and the sea of faces awaits one in the darkened auditorium.

This was the elixir which Mephisto offered Faust. It was an elixir of which Ellen had not drunk and which she did not understand. Acting was work, and she considered herself a useful actress. She had never been stage-struck; she was like the smith who had been brought up to watch the sparks flying from the anvil as the hammer struck the metal. She knew why and how the sparks were struck, and there was no mystery in it. There was for Irving.

Like many men of his age Irving was a man's man, popular in the clubs to which he belonged. The cheerful companionship of brandy and cigars and old cronies round the table has little attraction for the average woman. It is a barrier between husband and wife, or lover and mistress.

Graham Robertson described Irving at supper in the Lyceum. Round the table were Squire Bancroft and his wife, Walter Pollock and his wife, Bram Stoker, and Ellen. But the picture of the others had faded from Robertson's mind. Only Irving's picture remained vivid:

'The bright candle-lit table among the shadows of the old Beefsteak Room – the beautiful ivory face of the host against the dark panelling – remains in my memory. Round that pale face which seemed to absorb and give out light, the rest of the scene grows vague and out of focus, save for another pale face on the wall beyond, the passionate face of Edmund Kean as Sir Giles Overreach.'

Strongly drawn to Kean's acting, and to his career, Irving had chosen Kean as one of the four great actors about whom he lectured in Oxford in June 1886. His lectures and speeches were often written for him by others, but into the lecture on the four actors he put much of himself. On Burbage he quoted Flecknoe: 'He had all the parts of an excellent orator, animating his words with speaking and speech with acting, never failing in his part when he had done speaking, but with his looks and gestures maintaining it still to the height.' It was a goal which Irving had set himself.

His sympathy with Betterton was for his lack of physical charms, and the fact that he had overcome a low grumbling voice to such an extent that he could enforce attention even from fops and orange girls. In the same way Irving had overcome his stammer, country accent, unpolished appearance, and awkward gait.

But it was to Kean that Irving devoted his most passionate oratory; like Kean he had suffered hardships, like Kean he felt he had that touch of genius in spite of his faults, and like Kean he hoped that although he was not a scholar he was, as he said of Kean, 'an actor who so closely studied with the inward eye of the artist the waves of emotion that might have agitated the minds of the beings whom he represented'.

Irving implored his learned listeners not to think of Kean as he became but to think of him as working with a concentrated energy for the one object which he sought to reach, the highest distinction in his calling, sparing no mental or physical labour to attain this end, an end which seemed to withdraw further and further from his grasp.

A few days after his lecture, Robert Browning sent Irving a present – the faded green silk purse with metal rings which had been found, empty in Kean's pocket after his death. It became one of the actor's treasures in his museum of treasures in Grafton Street.

When speaking of Garrick Irving agreed that the actor had yielded to the popular taste for pantomime and spectacle, but he added: 'We who live to please must please to live.' Irving was thinking of *Faust*, for with that production he had reached the height of prosperity. Oxford had honoured him; the undergraduates were said to be suffering from Irving mania, all wearing pince-nez and broad hats, while others sported silver engraved bracelets as a badge of their deep devotion to Miss Terry.

Apart from these academic junketings the usual Lyceum entertaining continued as lavishly as ever. On the ninety-ninth night of *Faust*, the Abbé Liszt was present and received an ovation from the audience. The orchestra played the Ungarischer Sturm-Marsch (*sic*), and in the Beefsteak Room Gunter's produced the maestro's favourite dish of lamb cutlets, mushrooms in butter, and lentil pudding. The hostess for the evening was, as always, Miss Terry.

Liszt was only one of a long line of celebrities who were drawn into the social net of the Lyceum Theatre. During the eighties and the nineties Irving's capacity for entertaining off stage matched his performances on stage. It was said that for a quarter of a century the Lyceum became part of the social history of London. Celebrities, visiting foreigners, statesmen, travellers, explorers, ambassadors, foreign princes, potentates, poets, novelists, historians, representatives of all the learned professions, industrialists, sportsmen, pretty ladies of fashion, less decorative philosophers and scientists, and Irving's old friends from his early days in the theatre – the cream of London's life all drifted through the Lyceum private entrance.

To crown these occasions came the Marlborough set, headed by the Prince of Wales himself. Younger members of the royal family were allowed to the Lyceum on occasions when Margaret was not being seduced by Faust. On the birthday of Princess May, afterwards the stately Queen Mary, the Duke and Duchess of Teck with the Princess and her three brothers were invited to supper after the show. The table was a mass of pink and white hawthorn (a delicate compliment to her name), with a birthday cake to match, and she was presented with a set of Shakespeare, bound in white vellum with book markers of blush rose silk.

The theatre staff and actors were treated in the same lavish and patriarchal way. At Christmas, when Victorian feelings of warmth and good cheer rose to a climax, Irving's goodwill was shown in practical ways. Every man and woman in the theatre (and there were five or six hundred of them) was presented with a goose, trimmings of sage and onion and apples, and a bottle of gin. The children currently playing were given a goose and a plum cake. In the green-room Christmas Eve was celebrated with punch and a huge Christmas cake. The punch bowl was as vast as Irving's productions, and amongst other ingredients a five-gallon keg of old whisky was used to fill it.

On Christmas Eve, 1882. he gave a Christmas Eve dinner to a party of twenty intimate friends – Ellen's family, Bram Stoker's family, and Loveday's family. They sat down to spiced beef, roast beef, turkey, and plum pudding, and when the flames of the pudding died away and the supper table was cleared, the porcelain was replaced by a roulette wheel and a silk bag containing five pounds' worth of new silver was put in front of each guest. When touring in America his Christmas entertaining was on the same scale. In 1884, in Pittsburg, his Christmas dinner guests numbered 100, and the whisky was served in pitchers the size of those used in a washbasin.

The intimate Beefsteak suppers were usually for thirty-six people, but the supper parties given so often on the stage for the 100th, 200th and 300th nights of Irving's successes were celebrated with princely pomp and up to 350 guests were bidden to these feasts.

Nor was The Grange, Brook Green – the home of romance which was never lived in – left out. Mephisto could conjure that also into life. When the Augustin Daly company came to London, Irving decided to invite the American company with Miss Ada Rehan and some of his own company to a cosy dinner party at The Grange. The three rooms on the first floor were converted into one. The partitions were levelled and the whole was elaborately decorated – just for one occasion.

When Irving was asked how his guests were going to get home late at night, he said grandly that cabs would be told to come at one o'clock. The cab drivers had all been paid in advance. The evening following this party, Irving gave another supper at the Lyceum for Miss Sarah Bernhardt to meet Miss Ada Rehan.

'These', said Austin Brereton, 'were indeed golden nights.' And a golden shower of sovereigns at the box office paid for them. The Lyceum was to Irving like Aladdin's lamp: he had only to rub it and entertainment could be provided for prince, prelate or pauper. There was no reason to think that the high point of prosperity reached by *Faust* could ever end.

The first run of the piece was interrupted in July 1886. There was to be a short holiday from Nuremberg and the Brocken. On 1 August 1886 a news item recorded:

'Mr Henry Irving and Miss Ellen Terry left Waterloo in a saloon carriage at 10.15 am yesterday for Southampton. The train was met there by Herr Keller, the German consul, the party was conveyed to the North German Lloyd's steamship *Fulda* on which special accommodation has been provided. The Captain set apart his cabin as a sitting room. Mr Irving informed a representative of the Press that he proposes on reaching America to go yachting with a friend on the East Coast and he expected to be back in England in five weeks' time.'

Mephisto was taking Margaret for a well-earned holiday. Did he perhaps hope to persuade her into marriage with the knowledge of financial security behind him? There is nothing so salutary as a long sea voyage for the fostering of tender feelings. The news item makes no mention of the children they normally took with them to give a family atmosphere to their journeys.

The run of the play resumed on 11 September 1886, and *Faust* ran without a break until the following spring. But both Irving and Ellen needed relief from the constant repetition of innocence and demonology. On Ash Wednesday, when all the London theatres closed, he gave a reading of *Hamlet*, interpreting all the parts and keeping the audience at the Birkbeck Institute riveted for three hours.

On 1 June 1887 he mounted a single performance of Byron's *Werner* as a benefit for an aged author of plays, Westland Marston. Scenery and costumes were specially designed and besides Irving and Ellen the cast included George Alexander, Martin Harvey and Winifred Emery. The production cost Irving over £1,000 and the receipts, also £1,000, went to Dr Marston. The aged author, with tears in his eyes, observed that fifty years before that afternoon he had written for Macready, and now he was finishing his career with the help of the greatest actor of his declining years. Irving never acted Werner again. It was simply a lavish present to an old servant of the theatre.

On 7 June of the same year he produced *The Amber Heart* as a present to Ellen, and gave her the sole rights in the play. It was a sentimental little piece by Alfred Calmour. Admirably mounted, it was also admirably lighted. 'Never before have the Lyceum tricks of light upon face and flowers been used to such conspicuous advantage,' said one commentator. Irving was using his soft gas lamps as a modern film producer uses camera and lights.

'Miss Ellen Terry was inspired as she has never been inspired before, and she struck the fount of melody so true that the whole house responded to its influence. This mystic, fairylike, deeply loving, basely wronged, half-spiritual, most human, Ellaline will remain in the long aftertime as one of the greatest of the artistic achievements of this incomparable artist.'

The story which caused this ecstatic outburst was of a lovely child – Ellen was 40 at the time – born possessed of a magic spell. So long as she wears her mother's amber heart about her neck the maiden will be free from the pangs and joys of love. Once the amulet is lost the innocent child will be exposed to the torture and grief of the absorbing passion. Mr Willard, as the old sage Coranto, warns the girl not to throw away her assets, but she heeds him not and is exposed to love's agony. Her happy childish heart is broken and 'yet the tears will not come'. Wisely she finds and puts the heart on again and is once more immune from tender feelings.

Not all the critics were equally pleased with this tear-jerker. Beerbohm Tree played the lover, Silvio, and the production seems to have been somewhat marred by Ellen's prompting of all the other actors, whose performances were dubbed 'muffled' – no doubt true if they had not learned their lines. But *The Amber Heart* was successful for Ellen and many years later, in her fifties, she was still playing the innocent virgin and enjoying the proceeds of Irving's kind present.

The year 1887 was not only the apotheosis of artistic and financial success for Irving but the fiftieth year of Queen Victoria's reign. His lavish expenditure on *Faust* came just at the right moment. A country of sound financial bottom could afford to spend lavishly on its entertainment, and *Faust* provided the right Gothic spectacle. Irving admitted to spending something in the region of £8,000 on these Gothic trimmings, but by the end of the season he was still taking over £1,000 a night.

It was at this high point that he began to think of his future. He was nearly 50, but his physical and mental powers were at their height. He consulted Lawson, later to become the first editor of the *Financial Times*. Lawson pointed out that there were weaknesses in the golden shower at the box office. The theatre was not a freehold, and Irving, unlike prudent financiers, was spending his *own* money on running expenses which rose continuously. Why not, said Lawson wisely, leave the complications of the business side to others? Turn the Lyceum into a company with a paid-up capital of some £200,000, or as an alternative sell half of himself and his prospects to a company for a fixed sum and profits. He would receive the benefits of his success without the ever-present danger of being unable to meet running expenses when fortune was perhaps not smiling so brightly? All the money he had poured into his theatre would be an asset. The rich beauty of its Italianesque pillars, the ornaments adapted from the Mazzini Palace and the Villa Madama, the richly decorated walls, the amber hangings lined with cerise, the plush arm rests, the frieze of cupids playing musical instruments, the circular ceiling with its medallions of assorted classical celebrities, even the proscenium arch with a number of boys emblematically personifying acting, music, and dancing – all could be turned to hard cash in Irving's bank.

Lawson had friends. Lord Rosebery could be asked to be chairman of the company, making an opening for an injection of Rothschild investment. It was a tempting prospect. The cities of the plain were stretched out before the thoughtful eyes of the man who had been glad to be given a set of warm woollen underwear. In his secretive way, Irving told no one of these plans. Bram Stoker was never aware of the proposals that were taking shape in that July of 1887.

It was time, suggested Lawson, to consider husbanding the harvest of *Faust*, putting the theatre's finances in a stable position and making his future secure. Irving considered the prospect of becoming the servant of a company, of selling half of himself to the Rothschilds and their gentlemen in the City. He rejected it. He was his own creation. The harvest was golden. Why share it?

When the 1887 season of *Faust* came to a close Irving made a happy and gracious speech. With so much success behind him he could afford to be gracious. He spoke humorously, almost complacently: 'It is not even possible to confess that *Faust* has been a failure; we produced it in '85 and as far as I know we shall be playing it in '88. This may be called the devil's own luck!' In Europe, in America, everyone everywhere wanted *Faust*.

It was decided that after a provincial tour in England the play would cross the Atlantic. He was going to take advantage of the floodtide of success. The provincial tour lasted from August to October, punctuated by the 'big feeds' and their long menus and even longer speeches.

The tour closed on 15 October, and the next day there took place in Stratford-upon-Avon another of those public ceremonies which were so often graced by the actor's presence and oratory, the presentation of a handsome drinking-fountain to the town, in memory of Shakespeare, by and to the greater glory of Mr G. W. Childs of Philadelphia. When Irving arrived at the station he was greeted as the hero of the hour; a procession headed by Sir Arthur Hodgson, the Mayor, preceded by the beadle and mace bearers, and the mayors of other neighbouring towns, aided by vicars, ministers of various churches, and even the Diplomatic Corps, represented by the

American Minister Mr Phelps – all aided this Anglo-American event. Irving, with an eye already on his American public, concluded his speech by saying that the ceremony had renewed hallowed associations with the mighty dead, and reminded two great nations of a bond which no calamity could dissolve.

The fountain still stands in Stratford. It is still large, but is no longer regarded as handsome. On market days it is surrounded by stalls and the bustle of buying and selling. Only a curious few ever read the inscription which was so solemnly commemorated in 1887.

Irving knew that *Faust* was to be the big draw of his third American tour and because of the heavy scenery, so essential to the spectacle, he cut the tour to four cities: five weeks in New York, two weeks in Philadelphia, four weeks in Chicago, four in Boston, and a final five weeks in New York.

When the play opened the American critics again unpacked their superlatives. Irving was hailed as having sacrificed his personal interest to true art. Ellen was beyond criticism. Tender and pathetic, she was the embodiment of purity and grace and evoked a storm of applause by kissing her lover's hand with an eloquent gesture of love, faith and sweet girlish submission. All this adulation of her innocence no doubt made Ellen hesitate even more to cross swords with the jealous Florence over the water, or to take a decisive step towards marriage.

Irving's performance as Mephistopheles caused William Winter to write a long essay on the art of this outstanding actor's performance in which he said: 'He fulfilled the conception of the poet in one essential and transcended it in another. . . . This fiend, towering to the loftiest summit of cold intellect is the embodiment of cruelty, malice, and scorn, pervaded and interfused with grim humour. That ideal Mr Irving made actual.'

There was no doubt, he concluded, that Irving wore the mantle of Macready. Why be niggardly in praise? Henry Irving was one of the greatest actors that ever lived. The only criticism which Winter allowed himself was that possibly the production of *Faust* was so magnificent that it might have tended to obscure and overwhelm the fine intellectual force, the beautiful delicacy and the consummate art with which he embodied Mephistopheles.

Ellen, playing Margaret night after night, still considered it a twopence coloured performance. But Irving had been trained and tempered in the theatre of the twopence coloured era. He convinced because he believed, like a preacher at a revivalist meeting.

At a supper party in England he re-created a mother with her child awaiting her husband's return. He did not change his dress; he used no props except a handkerchief to represent the child. By pure facial expression and gesture he roused his intimate audience to a series of emotions until, when finally the child slipped from the mother's arms through an open window, the women cried out in anguish and begged him to stop. As suddenly as it had been created the child disappeared and Irving put his handkerchief back into his pocket.

When Ellen dismissed Mephisto as twopence coloured, she was wrong. *Faust* was convincing because Irving believed it to be true.

Irving was unlucky again with his weather in America. *Faust* opened on 7 November 1887, during one of the worst blizzards New York had ever experienced.

The English actors fought their way like good King Wenceslas through ice and snow to the theatre, determined to act. The curtain went up late, but it went up to a very sparse audience. Many had paid, but few had risked being frozen. Then the blizzard subsided, and over $100,000 made the stoicism of the actors worthwhile.

The play was considered by the New York audience to be not only theatrical but very artistic. There was none of the highbrow carpings which had been heard from Goethe purists in London. The Goethe Society of New York asked Irving to address them, and *Faust* was as popular and successful as it had been in London.

The other American cities recorded different impressions of the sale of a soul to the Devil. It was said to have been particularly well received in Boston, where the old puritanical belief in a real Devil was still held. This strong Bostonian belief in a personal Devil brought in $4,582 in one evening. In Philadelphia, the crowds were even greater than in Boston, and there was a near riot of 'standees', who broke down a mahogany and glass door, eight feet high, to get a view of innocence and the Devil. In Chicago, said to be a city fearing neither God nor Devil, the reception was enthusiastic. The staging was voted superb; nothing approaching it had ever been seen in

America 'either in affluence of scenic fidelity, wonderfully skilful management of the lights, or in the harmony of colour, costume and scenery – all making a most imposing succession of splendid stage pictures whether of the streets and squares of old Nuremberg, or the dramatic culmination of the Brocken scene'. The report concluded: 'Standing room only.' Irving had good reason to be satisfied with his transatlantic reception.

The second run of *Faust* in New York was interrupted. Irving spent £1,000 to take *The Merchant of Venice* to West Point. Colonel Michie, the Professor of Mathematics at West Point, had become a friend of Irving during one of his previous tours and Irving as a friendly gesture offered to take Shakespeare to the cadets.

On Sunday, 11 March, the eastern seaboard suffered another great blizzard. Four feet of snow fell and the wind, blowing at a hundred miles an hour, had piled up huge drifts. New York was paralysed and its railways in a state of chaos, but the managers of two railway lines found a special train to enable Irving and the company to get through a week later, although without the scenery. The play was presented on 19 March in the Grant Hall, the cadets' mess room, with costumes and simple notices announcing 'A street in Venice' or 'Belmont'. The only decorations on the stage were the Union Jack and the Stars and Stripes joined together by a palm branch.

It was said that many of the cadets had never seen a play before, but at the end, in spite of it being a breach of discipline for a cadet to throw his cap in the air except at the word of command of a superior officer, caps *were* thrown up and cheers rang out. Ellen, giving one of her best and most charming performances as Portia, was in a transport of delight. Irving made one of his speeches, saying the joy bells were ringing in London because for the first time the British had captured West Point. He then presented to West Point a picture of Napoleon, done from life by Captain Marryat when he was a midshipman on the British warship *Bellerophon* which carried the conquered emperor to his exile and death in St Helena.

Colonel Michie seems to have been in as great a transport of delight over *The Merchant* as Ellen. He wrote to a friend: 'The cadets were overjoyed, enthusiastic, and full of gratitude. Irving's foresight is amazing to me. I am sure he alone could have appreciated the enormous benefit this act of his is bound to be in doing good both to England and America.'

On 26 March 1888 Irving sailed for England, £9,000 the richer for the three months he spent in America.

When the season opened again in London *Faust* was given once more, and in May 1888 Ellen was again touching all hearts with her *Amber Heart* in a double bill with *Robert Macaire*. This old play was the original Frederick Lemaître version. The French actor had turned a melodrama into a comedy drama. Irving played the foppish scoundrel Macaire to J. L. Toole's romping Jacques Strop.

But the public were no longer in a receptive mood for Irving's eccentric fooling. The play was very old, and the London season ended in July without showing a profit. Madame Bernhardt took over the theatre, and on 11 September Irving, in his usual way, set out to recoup his loss by a profitable tour of the provinces.

Ellen had decided to take a holiday. She had had enough of *Faust*, and Marion, her sister, took on the burden of Margaret's sufferings. The tour was a strenuous one, forty-three performances of *Faust*, eight of *Louis XI*, fourteen of *The Bells* and *Robert Macaire* and seven of *The Lyons Mail*. All this was interspersed with town hall receptions, suppers, dinners, and the laying of a foundation stone at the Theatre Royal, Bolton.

Ellen was perhaps wise to shrink from constant touring. She had been travelling for thirty years and she preferred to husband her strength. She was not made of whipcord and steel as Irving was said to be. Not for her the public occasions, the stone laying and the bazaar opening. Better a quiet retreat to the Tower Cottage at Winchelsea, with its roses round the door, and driving around the flowery meadows in her coster's cart or dancing on the lawn in bare feet and a white nightdress.

Occasionally, during Ellen's holidays, Irving came for weekends and he would sit 'in rather queer get-ups taking his ease in Nell's garden'. But while Ellen was free to dance and drive, Irving was already forming his plans for the next production, *Macbeth*, a play symbolic of ill luck.

Chapter 16

The Time and the Hour

Macbeth seems to have lingered in Ellen's mind as a critical point in the spiral of success at the Lyceum. She wrote: 'Perhaps Henry Irving and I might have gone on with Shakespeare to the end of the chapter if he had not been in such a hurry to produce *Macbeth*.' When Irving had played the part with the Batemans his notices had not been good, although the critics had not been entirely unsympathetic to his new reading of the part. But Irving felt that now, with experience and greater knowledge of his art, he could carry the play.

Ellen, at 41, was conscious of the passing of the years. She wanted to play Rosalind, Miranda, Cleopatra – Lady Macbeth could wait. In her memoirs she gave a list of the plays they ought to have done while still young enough: *As You Like It*, *The Tempest*, *Julius Caesar*, *King John*, *Anthony and Cleopatra*, *Richard II*. There were so many opportunities they could stretch out their hands to seize.

Irving, with his quirky nature and sometimes faulty judgement, had reasons against them all. In *The Tempest* he wanted to play not Prospero but Caliban. In *As You Like It*, not Jacques but Touchstone. In *Julius Caesar* Brutus was the part 'which needed acting'. 'Henry's imagination was sometimes his worst enemy,' wrote Ellen, who did not see herself as Lady Macbeth, a role described by Mrs Siddons as the grand fiendish part.

Irving was full of persuasion. Many years before, he had been given a book by Helen Faucit which described an entirely new aspect of Lady Macbeth. Mrs Siddons had seen the woman as a devoted wife who kills because of her eager and passionate sympathy with the great master wish of Macbeth's mind. But this, argued Ellen, was not at all the way Mrs Siddons had actually played it. He gave the book to Ellen who was at once struck by the fact that Mrs Siddons *had* made notes to indicate a human, feminine Lady Macbeth.

When she studied the part, with Mrs Siddon's notes, she noticed that the swoon after the murder of Duncan had been struck out as being *too terribly hypocritical*. This, said the great actress, was a *feigned* swoon. In the margin of the speech, 'Come you spirits that tend on mortal thoughts! Unsex me here', Mrs Siddons's note read: '*All this in a whisper*'. Ellen, quick to appreciate an effect, said, 'Of course, it ought to be in a whisper, but I couldn't do it, but the whisper is *right*!'

So the great war chariot of Irving's *Macbeth* began to roll slowly forward. Sullivan was called in to provide musical effects. Irving had no music himself, but with mime and hummings in his throat, exactly like Sheridan with Michael Kelly, Irving could make Sullivan and other composers he employed understand the effect he wanted, and he made them produce it. He would listen to a musician's idea and then say firmly, 'It's very fine – but for our purpose, it's no good at all.' On several occasions musicians went out of the theatre breathing fire and brimstone, only to return with the music rewritten to Irving's measure and admitting that dramatically he was right.

Against the background of towering battlements, gloomy Scottish castles, vast heaths and battlefields, Irving manipulated his equally vast crowds; like a painter he filled his huge living canvas with the clash of armed men. The rehearsals for *Macbeth* were exhausting to Irving and his performers, yet he brought his feeling for the use of huge crowds with dramatic effect to a pitch of perfection with this play.

While he would exhaust his small part players, Ellen he cherished and cajoled:

'I want to get these great multitudinous scenes over, and then we can attack *our* scenes. Your sensitiveness is so acute that you must suffer sometimes. You are not like anybody else – you see things with lightning quickness and unerring instinct sometimes. I feel confused when I'm thinking of one thing, and disturbed by another. But I do feel very sorry afterwards when I don't seem to heed what I so much value.'

It was the nearest he could get to an abject apology for overworking her.

Ellen said that at this time they were able to be of the right use to each other. 'Henry could never have worked with a very strong woman. I might have deteriorated in partnership with a weaker man whose ends were less fine, whose motives were less pure. I had the taste and artistic knowledge that his upbringing had not developed in him. For years he did things to please me. Later on I gave up asking him. . . .' When she wrote that it was much later on, but at the time of *Macbeth* he was still doing things to please her.

He was an early master of public relations and had asked Comyns Carr to write a pamphlet setting out the new interpretation of Macbeth. He was to be portrayed as guilty from the outset. The idea of murder was already in his mind when he saw the witches, who were the emanation of his own thoughts. This was the reading he had put into the part when he had first played it, and he had not changed his mind. This time he was determined his view would be accepted.

The public excitement about the new Lyceum offering was at its usual fever pitch. Some press comments were in a faintly sneering tone: 'The enthusiasm and interest in these Lyceum first nights has been working up year by year. It has even become customary for the papers to give extraordinary and it must be said ludicrous sketches of the state of things.' Even the queue in the street was counted. There were ten gentlemen and four ladies at seven o'clock in the morning. The ladies in sombre black, such as befits a tragedy, munched at sandwiches; three of the gentlemen smoked their pipes; another conned an acting edition of the play; another was reading critic Carr's pamphlet.

When the curtain went up the enthusiasm of the flower and chivalry in the stalls and boxes was equal to that of the pit queue who had been 'squatting on their haunches in the street'. The noble and titled, the U.S. Ambassador and Mrs Phelps, Sir Arthur Sullivan, D'Oyley Carte, Mr and Mrs Oscar Wilde, Genevieve Ward, and Mr and Mrs Pinero were amongst the distinguished audience. The seal of approval of the Terry family had been given to Ellen for some years now, and the centre box was occupied by Mr and Mrs Arthur Lewis, she so well remembered as the lovely Kate Terry. Her brood of four daughters were all dressed alike, in white, with white wreaths of flowers in their hair. Other Terrys included Ellen's mother, and her sisters Marion and Florence Terry.

The curtain fell to the usual Lyceum applause; Irving made his usual Lyceum speech, thanking his usual audience for their support. One well-wisher called out: 'You deserve it, sir!' 'I am glad to hear you say so,' replied Irving crisply. He once told an interviewer that he always felt a little depressed by the first-night audience, and was happier when the play had settled down. But he successfully hid his real feelings from audience and friends.

The curtain fell and he was ready for what was described as the 'friendly foray behind the scenes, where you find Mr Irving with an overcoat thrown over his costume beset by a throng of enthusiasts, shaking hands with everyone, listening to a chorus of praise, and looking delighted to see everyone. It is a curious Bohemian picture which Henri Murger would have described lovingly.'

All was as usual after *Macbeth*. Ellen did not appear, 'but from time to time the merry laughter which pealed down a certain staircase in the wings showed to Mr Irving's guests that the lady was being looked after, doubtless by the bevy of fair girls herebefore referred to'. The Terrys had become socially very acceptable and were enjoying the fact.

The ordeal was over. There was nothing to do but to await the decision of the critics. They were much as expected – disappointment that Irving had not reconsidered his views of 1875. Was there any reason why *Macbeth* should not at least *look* like a man of physical valour? The Victorians wanted a man of chivalry and courage and Macbeth to many of them was obviously an Empire builder led astray by listening to bad advice from a parcel of witches who had lured him from his regimental duty.

But some critics were sympathetic. Even his old adversary William Archer wrote: 'For my part I have no quarrel with Mr Irving's conception of Macbeth. During the greater part of the action, Macbeth is in a state of nervous agitation varying from subdued tremor to blue funk – he says so himself, and he should know.' Most critics, however, objected to the craven Macbeth, and one added that Macbeth should show no touch of Mephistopheles. 'But though our heartstrings are untouched, this wild, haggard man's anguish does grip us by the throat' – no doubt a medical difference of some importance.

Ellen remembered Irving most distinctly in the last Act after the battle, when he looked like 'a great famished wolf . . . weak with the fatigue of a giant exhausted . . . spent as one whose exertions have been ten times as great as those of commoner men of rougher fibre and coarser strength'.

Her comment would have been as valid for Irving's own personal forces, equally spent in the service of his theatre. His passion for realism was carried to an extreme in *Macbeth*, for he wore authentic armour. A friend visiting him backstage remarked to Collinson, his dresser, that he supposed the armour to be papier mâché. Collinson said laconically: 'Pick it up'. The man could hardly lift it, so great was its weight. Careless of his health, Irving piled burden on burden in order to get the exact effect he saw in his mind's eye. No physical effort must be spared and no expense grudged.

For Ellen Mrs Comyns Carr had created a series of magnificent costumes. The grandest of these was the 'beetle wing' dress in which she was painted by Sargent, copied from a dress which Jenny Jerome had worn. Ellen was excited by her dresses and wrote to Edy, her daughter, in Germany: 'I wish you could see my dresses. They are superb, especially the first one: green beetles on it, and such a cloak! The whole thing is Rossetti – rich stained glass effects.' Her red hair fell from under a purple veil, and her startling green dress, iridiscent with the wings of beetles, shimmered like emeralds. Over it was flung a huge wine-coloured cloak with gold embroideries. Oscar Wilde remarked after the first night: 'Judging from the banquet, Lady Macbeth seems to be an economical housekeeper and evidently patronises local industries for her husband's clothes and servants' liveries, but she takes care to do all her *own* shopping in Byzantium.'

Her clothes may have dazzled the eye, but her performance was felt to be out of key with the play. There was no precedent for this gentle, affectionate Lady Macbeth, displaying a supreme wifely devotion to her sinister-looking lord with his wry moustache and reddish hue. When the ghastly moment came, there was something shocking in the suggestion of cold-blooded murder from such delicate lips as hers. The speech beginning 'Yet I do fear thy nature' was delivered as if speaking of some too generous-minded person who did not sufficiently study his own interests, and she urged him on to crime in accents of mingled tenderness and reproach. A long way from a Siddons performance, although in the sleep-walking scene

Ellen held the house in a state of painful stillness from which it recovered with an effort as if it had been hypnotised.

The spectacular effects were commended, and the musical setting of Sir Arthur Sullivan was praised, although Irving's fondness for gloom caused some to strain their eyes and ears to catch what was going on. Gloom may indicate mystery, but this was not helped by the beams of limelight that followed the principal performers around.

A fortnight or so later, Irving was taken ill and for ten days Hermann Vezin, who had acted with Ellen at the Court Theatre, took over. Irving was 51 and perhaps had begun to feel the weight of his years and the double responsibility of managing the theatre and acting the leading parts.

But by the end of January he was back in his armour and working as hard as ever.

In April 1889 Irving closed the theatre for three performances. The prince of players was to give a command performance for the Prince of Wales and Queen Victoria at Sandringham. The Queen had been a great playgoer in her youth and early married life, and had been criticised by some puritanical people for patronising such a godless form of entertainment. In the past she had enjoyed visiting the Haymarket under Buckstone, but after Albert's death she had put away such pleasant diversions with her retreat into widowhood. Now the Prince of Wales had invited Irving to Sandringham, and she was to see Mr Irving himself in that gripping play *The Bells*, and the famous Miss Terry playing Portia. A special programme was printed on white satin with a silk-corded edge headed 'V.R. Theatre Royal, Sandringham'. Irving had small scenery specially built with a proscenium arch to fit the room where the play was to be given.

No money changed hands between royal patrons and players. The following day, Irving was interviewed by the *Sunday Times* about the great occasion:

'I called upon Mr Irving yesterday and invited a conversation about his visit to Sandringham. I found him in the midst of breakfast at his quiet chambers in Grafton Street. Fussie, the clever English terrier is sitting by the actor's side, watchful for its share of the frugal meal.'

The *Sunday Times* man said it was rather late for breakfast. Irving explained that he had only reached home at six o'clock in the morning, after leaving Sandringham between two and three in the morning. He described his drive through the forests and the countryside on his way to Sandringham. After the performance he and Miss Terry had dined with the royal family. They had had a delightful time. 'The Prince of Wales gave me – from her Majesty – these links – beautiful are they not? The diamonds you see form her Majesty's monogram. The honour conferred upon myself and the Lyceum Company is one which we *all* share, we actors of the time. It reflects all round.'

The reporter then let himself go with a few flights of fancy: 'As I said good-bye, Irving flung his library window wide open letting in the first real spring sunshine. The perfume of the itinerant flower stalls off Piccadilly seemed to fill the sunny air of the animated street like a benediction.'

The public accepted Macbeth and his charming if sentimental Lady Macbeth and the play ran for six months, taking nearly £50,000 – the longest run of any *Macbeth*. Irving's cut version of the play sold equally well. Ellen's fears proved groundless. Sheer spectacle had proved triumphant with the public as it always did at the Lyceum.

During the late eighties, when Irving was 50 and Ellen over 40, the problems of their children began to push themselves to the fore. Irving's boys had been brought up conventionally by a conventional mother to consider their father a ridiculous mountebank. But he was a mountebank who paid the bills for their education and he was a mountebank with an international reputation.

In 1887 his sons, Harry and Laurence, were 17 and 16. Their father had been assiduously kept away from them, no doubt for fear that his raffish companions might contaminate Florence's sons. But once they were grown up the decisions were becoming more open to the boys themselves. Irving represented patronage for their future. Or perhaps they had come to a time of life when Florence's story of the marriage did not seem to be as simple as when they were children. The sufferings of a *femme seule* incline to pall over the years.

Both Irving's sons had been educated at Marlborough, and now was the moment to decide on the next step. The eldest son Harry wrote to Irving saying he wanted to go on the stage. It was the last thing which Irving, like most actors, wanted for his children. He warned of the hardships. In his early days, he had sometimes played eighteen parts in a week and been forced to sit up all night with a wet towel round his head trying to master the words. His name would be a handicap to his son, not a help. Unless Harry put in hard study he would be simply a nine days' wonder. There was nothing 'to weigh against the hard exacting work of a lifetime'. Everything depended on satisfying and pleasing the public, a demanding master.

Irving was ever conscious of the knife edge of success. At the pinnacle there was farther to fall. His boys, looking at him from the outside, had no idea of the inner worries, or the hardships and dedication demanded by his work. His wishes were for Harry to go to Oxford and Laurence into the Diplomatic Service. Later, if they were still set on a theatrical career, a knowledge and understanding of English and foreign literature would deepen and widen their chances. He regretted the lacunae in his education. Ellen on several occasions remarked how Henry embarrassed her by talking art to artists, and music to musicians. If self-help could produce the whole cultured man, Irving was that man. But the inner insecurities persisted; deep down a parvenu is always a parvenu.

The boys took his advice for a while. Harry went to New College, Oxford, and Laurence studied modern languages in preparation for a diplomatic career.

Ellen's children, though never estranged from her as Irving's had been, had the opposite disadvantage; they had been spoiled. That plump rosy cherub Teddie had failed at prep school and had been taken away from Bradfield. Ellen, like Irving, wanted to protect her children from the drudgery and hard work of her own stage career. She had never had a childhood, she had been a wage-earner from the age of eight. Her children, like Irving's, were going to have a different life; they were going to be protected; there was going to be no horrible theatre for them.

Edith, her daughter had, like Ted, played small parts about the theatre. She had been one of the smaller angels in *Faust*. She had been trained in Germany as a muscian, but rheumatism in her hands prevented her from following this career and she too began to act.

Ted wrote that 1889 was the beginning of his awakening to the full reason for life. It was the theatre and nothing else. The same year he joined the company at the Lyceum and Henry Irving and his theatre became his real master and his real school. His mother's efforts to keep him out of the theatre were to be quite useless, as Irving's were with his own. All their four children were drawn in different ways and by different paths to acting, and to arts connected with the stage.

Gordon Craig, like many spoiled children, was extremely critical of his mother's action. 'If at six years old, when I walked on to the stage at the Court Theatre, I had been kept there, I should have swum without study.' By the time he was 17 he would have had ten years' experience and have been as accustomed to the 'cold water' of an audience as was his mother. As it was, he complained, he had to begin to learn very late.

Ted complained of his mother's double look and actressy behaviour, but his own character bore many affinities with his mother's, and all his life he managed to find ladies to lean on and to support him in the dilettante existence he chose to lead. But in 1889 he was at the beginning, everything seemed full of promise, and Irving was to find him an important part in his new production, *The Dead Heart*.

If the new school of critics and dramatists had been as active in 1889 as they were to become a few years later, they would have voted *The Dead Heart* to be deader than a doornail. It was an old drama first put on by Benjamin Webster at the Adelphi in 1859, a drama of the French revolution, enlivened by the cockney of J. L. Toole in his younger days and Kate Kelly as Cerisette. The plot was exactly the same as that of Dickens's *Tale of Two Cities*, and had been written by a man called Watts Phillips, and the suggestion was made that the author had stolen the story. Miss Emma Watts Phillips wrote to the press in defence of her dead brother:

'I, as Watts Phillips sister, know the idea of the plot of *The Dead Heart* was drawn out some while before it was put in form for Mr. Webster's perusal. Also that the manuscript was long in that manager's hands as Mr. Irving states, before the play was produced. Those who are old enough to have been acquainted with Mr. Webster will know that it was *not* rare with him to purchase dramas, and then for a time place them on the shelf.'

She went on to say that her dead brother as a young dramatist had to fight for his rights, even though it was against the great novelist Dickens, and this had caused much ill feeling.

It is often said an idea is in the air. But, as Sheridan remarked, Shakespeare just happened to hit on it first. Plays lying about in managers' offices are likely to be read, or referred to in the presence of great novelists temporarily short of ideas. There is, after all, no copyright in ideas; they may be in the air, but they may also be in managers' offices, and consequently fair game.

When *The Dead Heart* was produced by Irving Dickens was dead, but the controversy had not died down and the actor stoutly defended the reputation of the playwright.

The Victorians were fascinated by the French Revolution. Secure as they felt themselves to be behind the bastions of democracy, it was easy for them to wipe their eyes over the spectacle of the innocent victims of Madame Guillotine. Irving was a child of his times: 'I'm full of the French Revolution and could pass an examination. In our play at the taking of the Bastille we must have a starving crowd, hungry, eager, cadaverous faces, and the contrast to the red and fat crowd (the blood gorged ones) would be striking.'

Henry was also fascinated with the idea of his part. First he would look wonderfully handsome in his yellow coat, with dark wavy hair, leading the dance of the students in the Parisian pleasure-garden; then he would be rescued from the Bastille as a doleful creature, with matted hair, unkempt beard and wandering eye, blinking like an owl in the light and beating his brain in his frenzy to get back his memory as the blacksmith files away the murderous chains. Finally, noble and self-sacrificing, he would be seen in the early morning light beside the guillotine.

Irving admitted to having 'improved' the play. He had cut out the humour. *The Dead Heart* was a melodrama pure and simple. He had a few difficulties to overcome with Ellen, who later wrote: 'Here was I in the very noonday of life, fresh from Lady Macbeth and still young enough to play Rosalind, suddenly called upon to play a rather uninteresting *mother* in *The Dead Heart*.' This was going to call for all Henry's tact and persuasion but he set to manfully. He had been copying out his part in an account book, 'a little more handy to put in one's pocket. It is really very short, but difficult to act, though, and so is yours. I like this "piling up" sort of acting, and I am sure you will when you play the part.' He added that it was restful. But Ellen was not deceived: 'Crafty old Henry – all this was to put me in conceit with my part!'

Apart from prancing around in yellow satin as a jolly student and dying nobly in the pale moonlit dawn, Irving also had a duel with Bancroft as the wicked Abbé Latour. This received some advance publicity from Monsieur Bertrand, the French fencing master who had trained Irving and Bancroft for the scene. The Frenchman's fencing school was a splendid salon, heavily decorated with arms, pictures, sculptures, and emblems of the art of swordsmanship. Bertrand, obviously not one to let down his guard, said of Irving's duel with Bancroft: 'Ce n'est pas une convention – c'est une réalité!'

Unlike the duel, the plot was far from a reality. Apart from the disputed Sydney Carton sacrifice, there were touches of Dumas and every tragedy of revenge after twenty years. The frivolous Catherine Duval – Ellen in muslin flounces and furbelows – is trapped by the wicked Abbé into being found in the room of the Comte de St Valery. Landry (Irving) is thrown into gaol by the inevitable *lettre de cachet*, and after staggering out at the fall of the Bastille he rises with the Revolution. But Catherine, having stupidly married an aristocrat, finds herself on the wrong side. Will the relentless Landry save her son from the guillotine? Can she waken a heart so dead?

'Give me back my son,' pleads the widowed Catherine to Landry. 'If you have not forgotten all, if there yet lingers in this voice which first whispered in your ear "I love you" but one sweet echo of the past, let it plead for mercy now! I cannot live without my son – kill him and you kill me!' In practice Ellen was more concerned with her part being killed by Irving's duels, his whiskered prisoner blinking in the light, and his noble self-sacrifice.

But Irving had a trump card up his sleeve – the young Comte de St Valery could be played by Gordon Craig. Ellen's over-maternal heart melted. Her son was going to show how clever he was, looking splendidly handsome, first as the white-wigged aristo and then as the dishevelled prisoner condemned to die. The critics were kind to him: Mr Gordon Craig was the handsome son of a beautiful mother, whom he much resembled. He had made a small part stand out in intellect and picturesqueness.

Irving had placated Ellen with a career for her son, and triumph for herself. She earned acclaim for pathos, and with good notices for moving the audience to genuine emotions she was able to forget the humiliation of playing a grey-haired old mother when she felt she should have been playing Rosalind. Irving seized all his own chances with both hands, and ended, as Burne-Jones wrote, 'Nobility itself – I had never seen his face so beatified before.'

All that, and the maddened mob storming the Bastille with flags waving, women cheering, men shrieking, cannons roaring and prison gates falling with a crash – it was hardly surprising that *The Dead Heart* ran for six months and was included in Irving's repertory, playing in all for nearly 200 performances.

When the play closed, Irving promised for the next season a production of *Ravenswood*, adapted by Herman Merivale from Scott's *The Bride of Lammermoor*. It was a promise he would have done better not to fulfil. The *Scots Observer* remarked that his adaptation was a curious mixture of recklessness and timidity. Another critic remarked: 'In Edgar Mr Irving has a character after his own heart – romantic, picturesque, impressive and full of influence. He is the dominant figure in every one of the important scenes.' The reason for the production was self-evident. Actors often consider plays where they are never off stage to be splendid pieces of writing; the audience can take a different view.

The first night was enlivened by a fracas in the stalls. Willie Wilde, Oscar's brother, was engaged in a heated altercation with a nameless American gentleman who had commented loudly and unfavourably on the play. The American was reproved by Joseph Hatton, who was called a snobbish blackguard for his pains. Hatton's reply was swift – he crushed the American's opera hat down on his head. The combatants were restrained and pacified by Mr Samuel French, the eminent publisher of acting editions.

After the show there was the usual party with Ellen in her white bridal gown, youthful and handsome, passing from group to group with 'a merry word and a pleasant smile', while Irving received his friends still dressed in the sable velvet costume of Ravenswood, with a russet brown cloak thrown over his shoulder. Ellen commented laconically on the play: 'I had to lose my poor wits (as in Ophelia), and with hardly a word to say I was able to make an effect. The love scene at the well I did nicely. My "Ravenswood" riding dress set a fashion for ladies' coats for quite a long time.'

A fashion in ladies' coats was not quite the target Irving was aiming for. Nor did Ellen's light-hearted attitude towards the play always please him. At one dramatic moment, at the Wolf's Crag, Lucy is seized with hysterical laughter in her scene with Cabel Balderstone; off stage Irving came up to her, very much annoyed.

'Why did you alter the laugh? It put me out altogether, I was waiting for you to finish.'

'I laughed as usual.'

'No you didn't. You always say ha-ha seventeen times – you only said it fourteen times tonight.'

Ellen remarked later, '*I* knew nothing about those seventeen ha-ha's, it was pure luck my getting the same number every night. But now I am sure to get it wrong – I shall see Henry standing there counting!'

Graham Robertson described the close of the last Act, when the craggy coast disappeared and the stage 'strewn with the dead body of William Terriss, and other objects of interest, miraculously cleared itself, and when the shadow lifted, the final tableau was revealed, the incoming tide rippling over the Kelpie's Flow under a sky full of the glory of the dawn'. All this illusion was created simply by Irving's genius with gas lighting.

Ellen suggested to Robertson that they should watch the transformation scene from behind a rock. But as Terriss, the dead body, skidded along on a sliding plank, the corpse giggled, and said: 'Look out – *your* rock's going next!' The two delinquents crawled off stage, it was a race between them and the rock. 'Thank goodness', said Ellen, 'Henry went straight up to his room.' Henry did not like 'larks' on the stage; there was to be no giggling in his temple of art.

In spite of Kelpie's Flow, the great hall at Ravenswood, and the dell in the spring coppice with the Mermaiden's Well bubbling up in a sea of bluebells, the play was a failure and only ran eighty-nine nights.

The nineties were already beginning. Haunted heroes were no longer as admired as they once had been. The long shadows of a change of taste were beginning to fall. The voices demanding a different drama were beginning to be raised.

Chapter 17

The Serpent in the Forest

Ellen's son described the stage at the Lyceum as a sunlit clearing, a glade in the forest. Into this glade came Irving like the enchanter about to conjure his characters out of the air, a Prospero to whom all spells were possible. But already by 1892 a serpent, who was later to become an enchanter himself, was coiled about a tree in the forest glade.

Ellen had written to Bernard Shaw in 1892 when he was still 'Corno di Bassetto', writing about music, and asked him to help a young friend of hers, Elvira Gambogi. Ellen was 44; she had been acting for Irving for nearly fourteen years. She was restless.

Irving, at the top of the tree, was content; he chose the plays, his actors acted them, the public paid, and he could see no reason to change anything. Unlike Prospero, his charm had not been o'erthrown. He was directing his great orchestra and the music to him was as sweet as ever. He had beaten down many of the critics who had attacked him in the beginning. He had raised the stage to respectability, and even eminence.

The year 1892, when Ellen began her letters to Shaw, was also the year of *Henry VIII*, the most spectacular of all Irving's productions. It had fourteen scenes, all richly embellished with the costly architecture and furnishings of the Tudor period. Everything was grandly to scale. A vaulted roof of the palace of Bridewell, council chambers, streets, royal apartments, romantic gardens, the King's Stairs at Westminster – nothing was lacking in this dream of old London. Irving had studied the play carefully and had decided that it was a pageant or it was nothing. 'Shakespeare', he said, 'I am sure had the same idea, and it was in trying to carry it out that he burned down the Globe Theatre by letting off a cannon.'

Into his rich settings Irving crammed ever richer pageants, handling his huge cast with an unerring touch. The masquerade in the Hall at York Palace would, it was said, have needed half a dozen ballets to emulate it. The Queen tried by the Cardinals, the sad Queen at her embroidery with her singing maids round her, the fall of Wolsey – every act unfolded itself with more and more magnificence. The white-haired Queen Katherine died with an elaborate accompanying vision of angels with 'lilies and rustling wings floating all about the room, and ceilings'. Having landed, the angels present the dying queen with a chaplet of flowers.

Queen Ann Boleyn's coronation took place against further tapestries of period faces seen at lattice windows, garlands of roses twined from house to house, trumpet-blowing soldiers in armour, priests, bishops, and the Lord Mayor of London (complete with mace), until finally with another flourish of trumpets Ann (Violet Vanbrugh) was seen under a rich pallium carried shoulder high above the crowd.

The clothes were as expensive as the settings. Seymour Lucas had personally guaranteed the correctness of every ruff, head-dress, sword-belt and shoe. Nor had Henry forgotten his own costume, which was to be richer than all; the silk of his Cardinal's robe was to be specially dyed by the dyers appointed to the Cardinal's College in Rome. Some pernickety critic complained it was too grand, and the colour wrong. Irving replied that he had a respectful desire to represent the Cardinal clothed as he was in life and his robes were *most* expensive. The same could be said of Irving's productions. But he had a reply: 'When you are getting into the skin of a character, you need not neglect his wardrobe.'

The production costs were nearly £12,000. The actors and the supers drew £20,000 in wages and salaries for the seven months' season. Added to this were the running costs of the theatre, not to forget the lavish entertaining which Gunter's were only too happy to conjure up at the drop of a cheque.

Irving dominated all this grandeur with his swishing silk robes and a new reading of Wolsey. 'In Mr Henry Irving's Wolsey we see nothing of the toady or parvenu, the farewell to all his greatness is that of a keenly sensitive man, disappointed in his friends,' wrote Clement Scott.

Irving lived every minute of the part. When the Duke and Duchess of Devonshire gave a huge fancy-dress ball at Devonshire House, it was not Henry Irving but Cardinal Wolsey who elected to be a guest. Ellen wrote: 'I was told by one who was present at this ball that as the Cardinal swept up the staircase, his long train held magnificently over his arm, a sudden wave of reality seemed to sweep upstairs with him and reduce to pettiest make-believe all the aristocratic masquerade that surrounded him.' But make-believe was his reality.

The *Saturday Review*, not yet dominated by G.B.S., appreciated his grandeur and praised his reading unreservedly. Irving had that rare gift of impressing the spectator with the idea that he was thinking less of himself than of the man he represented. He played the last scene for sympathy: 'When the curtain at last slowly descended on the retreating form of that humbled and sorrowing man, the deeply moved audience insisted on its being lifted again and again.'

Ellen, obviously not charmed at being reduced to a white-haired lady at 44, remarked: 'It was a magnificent production, but not very interesting to me.' She played the Queen with all the stops pulled out to draw as many tears as Irving. Except for her white hair, her Queen was no care-worn matron. Scott said that it was inconceivable that such a king, even bluff King Hal, should have dreamed of divorcing so dainty a queen.

The theatre was packed during the whole of the lavish run. Money, nearly £60,000 of it, flowed into the box office, and as quickly melted into the thin air. The season ended in a loss. If the production had not been very interesting to Ellen, it had been even less interesting to Irving's bank manager.

Against the background of *Henry VIII* and his white-haired Queen, just as the season was nearing its close, came the first of the letters from Shaw. With the same glib Celtic tongue as her own father, G.B.S. told Ellen that she was wasting her talents. Ben Terry had said there should be 'none of these second fiddle parts, like Ophelia, for you, Duchess.' G.B.S. contrasted the futile plays in which she acted, like *The Amber Heart* and *Nance Oldfield*, with the *Lady from the Sea*. He had seen an indifferent girl playing Ibsen, and then:

'Act Two was another visit to another theatre. There I found the woman who OUGHT to have played the Lady from the Sea, the woman with all the nameless charm, all the skill, all the force in the world, all the genius – playing, guess what? A charade, the whole artistic weight of which would not have taxed the strength of the top joint of her little finger.'

The charade was *Nance Oldfield*, a play which Ellen had bought for herself and had played with *The Corsican Brothers* in a double bill a few months before. It was a piece of eighteenth-century pastiche by Charles Reade. There was, said one critic, no historical foundation for this tale of Alexander Oldworthy's infatuation for Mrs Anne Oldfield – 'But what does it matter when we have Ellen Terry in her pale blue and white gown with dainty knots of ribbons and her lace handkerchief, looking for all the world as if she had stepped out of one of Sir Joshua Reynolds' canvases?'

The plot was the same as that of *The Belle's Stratagem*, Mrs Oldfield pretending to be a slattern to disillusion a young man who had fallen in love with her. 'Miss Terry sails between the Scylla of weakness and the Charybdis of buffoonery, sliding gaily off the back of a sofa without the least shadow of offence.' Such a rompish performance would have shocked Mrs Oldfield, the original of Cibber's Lady Betty Modish, for she was a woman of much grandeur and style.

The production of *Nance Oldfield* was one of Irving's indulgences to Ellen, and as with *The Amber Heart* she went on to play it into her late middle age for hundreds of performances. She said that although she must have acted Nance Oldfield hundreds of times she never had an Alexander Oldworthy so good as her own son. On the first night neither of them knew their lines, and they had their parts written out, and pinned all over the furniture. Henry's reaction to this lack of professionalism is not recorded.

Shaw disapproved of Ellen's Amber Hearts and Nance Oldfields, but secretly Ellen loved them and warmed to the cooing of the audience. Yet she was also listening with half an ear to the voice of the tempter in the forest calling her to higher flights of artistry. Shaw later said (writing of himself in the royal third person): 'With this letter G.B.S. unmasks the battery which he kept trained on Ellen Terry and the Irving management at the Lyceum until its end.' Shaw may have had his batteries trained on the Lyceum management, but he also had his gaze set on his own advancement.

While Irving was basking in his own eminence, presiding at dinners, opening bazaars, giving readings, touring, speechmaking, receiving an honorary degree from Dublin University, and planning stupendous productions of *King Lear* and *Becket*, Shaw had begun to write plays and to make plans. He was gathering allies and fellow attackers.

William Archer was one of the original authors of *The Fashionable Tragedian*, the pamphlet which had scurrilously attacked and mocked Irving. While he occasionally threw Irving a crumb of critical comfort, he was not, in the long term, an admirer. But Irving had his defenders, one of whom had written to the magazine *The Players* attacking the attackers:

'The success of the New School is the result of very personal machinery of tireless and indefatigable log-rolling. Mr Archer advertises Mr Bernard Shaw; Mr Bernard Shaw takes off his cap in public to Mr A. B. Walkley and Mr A. B. Walkley excepts Mr William Archer from the general condemnation of critics as illiterate persons.'

There seems to have been civil war among the critics, for the letter continues that George Moore had accused Clement Scott of drinking free brandies and sodas in theatre bars, and Mr Archer had implied that Scott was scarcely sane. The new critics had attacked the idea of an actor-manager, but, said the letter writer, no one would go to the Lyceum to see Irving playing a running footman. On the other hand, he added that Irving had brought some of this on himself. He was a speechmaking actor – on a par with a crowing hen and a whistling woman. He had recently been on a provincial circuit in a blaze of oratory with invitations to aldermanic feeds and municipal muffin-worries. There were faults on both sides, and Irving's rhetoric was not to the taste of the younger generation. Irving was beginning to be associated with bishops and princes of the Church, reproved the writer, and it would *not* be a surprise if he appeared at a public gathering in lawn sleeves.

Now, however, he was to leave his sacerdotal character and play Lear. It was to be produced in November of 1892. *King Lear* was not a popular play with the Victorian audience and he had much prejudice to contend with. The weather did not help; London produced one of its thickest pea-soup fogs for the occasion. One critic said that he refused to write about the play. He had groped his way home at one o'clock in the morning in a choking and blinding fog. 'My mind is a sheer chaos of vague impressions.' Tomorrow he would have a column at his disposal and he hoped that 'chaos will have become cosmos'.

The tragedy unfolded before a series of vast imaginative sets. The illustrations from the souvenir programme of the play give an idea of a production in which the scenery dwarfed the figures of the actors. Lear denounces Goneril in a huge crumbling Roman hall, and the pillars of deserted temples have full-grown trees sprouting between them. These sets give the impression of a primitive king trying to hold his kingdom together in the wreck of a civilisation. The outside scenes show a Saxon hovel with smoking torches, and the heath has a cromlech amid the shattered oaks.

Irving had also brought all his Celtic imagination to bear on the character of the King: 'There can be no doubt about what he is, this weird and gaunt old man. He is a Priest-King, a Druid, ancient in mystery, the monarch from whom Merlin obtained his crabbed text. In his saffron robes he has pored over mystic lore until the wall which divides ghosts from shadow-casting men has grown as glass.'

Clement Scott was moved to deep emotion by Ellen and Irving:

'The picture that will most delight is the Lear of reconciliation, the foolish, fond old man with the beloved Cordelia, ever now in his arms, the gold of her sunny hair contrasted with the snow of his.'

And what a beautiful touch it was when the doting father brushed away his daughter's tears and tasted the salt drops. Ellen was mollified by the fact that she was said to look younger as Cordelia than when she played Beatrice.

Gordon Craig, who played Oswald, gives a picture of Irving at the rehearsals of *King Lear*:

'A few of us were aware how remarkable were Irving's rehearsal performances of the characters he was *not* down in the programme to play. On many they were entirely lost . . . when he was showing Haviland the way to play the fool in King Lear, with the words "Let me hire him too – here's my coxcomb", in slithering far-off tones, he feathered on to the stage – sideways – doffed an imaginary cap and floated two steps till he alighted on the edge of a table, smiled once, and then blew out the smile.'

Dissenting voices were raised against Irving's Lear. 'Twenty Five Years A First Nighter' said he had made a note on the corner of his programme that Irving had pronounced the word 'sterility' as if it were spelt 'stair-ril-la-ta-a'. When he thought of the painstaking study which the greatest French actors bestowed on their diction he despaired of the future of the English stage. Another critic took exception to Lear's unpatriotic conduct in taking aid from foreigners in circumstances of domestic stress.

In January Irving became ill with what was called the 'grippe', one of the first of the 'flu epidemics. He had no understudy, for he had always taken his good health for granted. He said to Stoker: 'Can't play tonight, better close the theatre.' But W. J. Holloway, an old actor, trained to emergencies, came to the rescue. He went home and studied the part in one day. The audience gave him full-throated praise for a plucky effort, and his comrades on the stage gave him a hearty cheer. A few days later Irving was back.

Undeterred by illness, a month later, in February, Irving had brought Tennyson's *Becket* on to the stage. It was another Lyceum spectacle of vast cost and extreme complexity of production. Tennyson had written this verse play many years before, and Irving had had it by him since 1879. Stoker said that he took it regularly on tour with him, and brooded over it. *Becket* had been written for the study not the stage, and indeed many critics took the view that none of Tennyson's plays should have appeared except in a library.

In 1890 Irving had got as far as going to see Tennyson, then living near Haslemere. The Laureate had been sickened by all the publicity surrounding his home on the Isle of Wight, where sightseers had smashed the windows of his workroom and picked the walls clean of carvings and left nothing but bare bricks. But in 1892 the poet was back at Farringford, ill and fretful, and Stoker went to see him to ask if Irving could alter the play. 'Irving may do whatever he pleases with it,' said the ailing Tennyson. Then, attracted by his own work, the old poet began to intone some of the speeches out loud, with some pleasure, breaking off to say, 'Henry Irving paid me a great compliment when he said I would have made a fine actor.' But soon after Stoker's visit Tennyson was ill again and said to his doctor sadly, 'I suppose I shall never see *Becket*, but I can trust Irving, he will do me justice.'

He did the poet more than justice. He created an entertainment out of an undramatic poem. *Becket* was tricked out with the usual vast halls, bluebell woods for Rosamund's bower, and Gothic cathedral scenes. But Irving as Becket dominated the play and lived within it. His strange personality, his developed dignity, his strong feeling of the sharp knife-edge of triumph and failure in life, everything was poured into *Becket*. And his dedication to the theatre was transmuted into Becket's single-minded devotion to Holy Mother Church.

Becket was to be one of Irving's greatest successes. It was produced on 6 February 1893, and it remained in his repertory to the end of his life. Even William Archer, strenuously campaigning for the New Drama with his friends Walkley and Shaw, could not forbear to cheer.

It would be difficult for Irving to fail in an ascetic, sacerdotal character. His cast of countenance and his manner were prelatical in the highest degree. Nature destined him for a prince of the Church. Even his diction was praised. In an age of cheap printing and cheap paper, thousands of words were poured out in praise of *Becket*. The holy blissful martyr brought holy blissful returns to the box office.

Irving took his part with the greatest seriousness: 'Becket is a noble and human part, and I will say that I do not see how any one could act it and feel it thoroughly without being a better man for it. It is full of some of the noblest thoughts and elements of introspection that may come to us in this life of ours.'

Irving's aunt had wanted him to be a minister. As it turned out, some of his greatest successes had come from playing princes of the Church: the crafty Richelieu, the ambitious Wolsey, and the noble soldier-priest Becket. Lawn sleeves may have eluded him in life, but on the stage he unhesitatingly awarded himself cardinals' hats and bishops' mitres.

Ellen had the small part of Fair Rosamund. In her autobiography she hardly refers to *Becket*. Henry had scooped all the notices with his nobility; Ellen was relegated to last paragraphs, and the usual adjectives – charming and touching – decorated her Fair Rosamund's bower. Irving spent a great deal of money for her on jewelled robes, gold circlets, and rich crosses and rosaries to tone with her nun's robe. But actresses have never found that charming costumes atone for small parts.

The play was received with rapture 'marked with a sincerity of feeling seldom seen in the theatre'. 'God Bless You' and 'Happy

Birthday' – Irving was 55 on the first night – brought down the curtain in a warm bath of sentiment and congratulation.

The holy martyr was to be further crowned. The Lyceum programme carried the announcement: 'Her Majesty the Queen having commanded a performance of *Becket* to be given at Windsor Castle on Saturday March 18th, the theatre will be closed on that evening.'

Irving, in his usual princely way, paid all the expenses for this royal one-night stand. One hundred and eighty actors and staff were taken by special train to Windsor. Hawes Craven and Harker painted special scenery for the Waterloo Chamber. The audience included the Empress Frederick, the Prince of Wales, Prince Christian of Denmark, Prince and Princess Henry of Battenberg, and the Marquess of Lorne. In the middle of this galaxy of princely relations sat the Queen herself in her black dress and white cap. For Irving it was the ultimate accolade.

The run of *Becket* seemed very successful. But financially it bore many resemblances to Mr Micawber's recipe for disaster. Receipts: £75,372 14s 9d. Expenses: £79,627 14s 1d. It was the floodtide of fame, but the financial tide was ebbing. And there were only a few months to wait before the forest glade acquired its serpent and Shaw became a theatre critic.

All was to be recouped, however, on the other side of the Atlantic, there was no need to worry. The expenses could be justified. This time the US tour was going to begin in California, the home of sunshine and of gold. The curtain went up on Irving's fourth American tour at the Grand Opera House, San Francisco, where the enthusiasm of the people was equalled by the receipts.

Fourteen performances were given. Ellen opened the programme with *Nance Oldfield*, and Irving played *The Bells*. *Becket* was seen for the first time in America; and the West Coast enjoyed all the old repertory favourites: *The Merchant of Venice*, *Olivia*, and that old tear-jerker, *Charles I*.

San Francisco threw its hospitable doors wide to the actor. The grandest dinner was planned by the Bohemian Club. This had been started in 1872 by half a dozen distinguished San Francisco journalists who felt the need of a congenial gathering place away from the boisterous atmosphere of saloons. By the time of Irving's arrival the club had become much grander. It had adopted an owl as the symbol of someone working at night, and the club's motto, 'Weaving

Spiders Come Not Here', was a mild warning that the club was not to be used as a branch of the Stock Exchange. They had two kinds of entertainment – High Jinks and Low Jinks. Irving, representative of all that was loftiest in entertainment, rated High Jinks.

The official description of Irving's visit in the Annals of the Bohemian Club paints a curious picture of his reception:

'Irving arrived at the portals of the Club at seven o'clock in the charge of Mr Robertson and Mr Graham. As they ascended the steps, bells of every sort and description from the mellow chime of the Cathedral bell to the boarding house dinner bell rang out in wild alarm gathering in volume until the party reached the library floor, where it ended in one grand tumult. This subtle allusion to one of his famous plays brought a smile to the lips of the deafened actor.'

The bells having died down, the orchestra started up what was called a gastronomic march. The dining-room had been turned into a flower-decked banqueting hall:

'The decorations, which were designed by Mr Jouillin were all of a golden tint to represent Henry VIII's Field of the Cloth of Gold. There were yellow silk draperies, on which were massed yellow poppies, sun flowers, and marigolds. There were piles of fruit overflowing from baskets hidden in ferns, oranges, yellow plums, grape fruit and golden nectarines, while a bust of Shakespeare draped with the Star Spangled Banner and the Union Jack gave an international accent to the color scheme.'

The 'big feed' began and was concluded with the usual long speeches. Miss Terry (not present on this masculine occasion) was toasted and a huge basket of flowers was sent to her. General Foote read a sonnet to the actor, and then the ceremony of initiation began. Irving was to be made a Bohemian.

'Presently there was a knock at the door and Cardinal Wolsey appeared to conduct the astonished Mr Irving to the Jinks Room. This latter apartment was in gloom, except for the stage where stood an altar containing a huge bowl of punch filled with leaping flames, in the ghostly light of which could be discerned several owls perched about it in solemn expectancy.'

Irving in his character of neophyte was seated near the stage alone; the High Priest of Bohemia approached him, and round him in a semicircle stood eight Bohemians, representing the characters he had most frequently portrayed. They came slowly forward (to the sound of horror music) and addressed the actor:

'You who have pictured the modern world,' they said solemnly, and then intoned the various characteristics which they represented:

Louis XI	– My vile hypocrisy
Macbeth	– My blood-stained soul
Becket	– My barbarous martyrdom
Hamlet	– My disordered brain
Wolsey	– My arrogant ambition
Shylock	– My vengeful hate
Mephistopheles	– Me the Fiend Incarnate

They then spoke in chorus: 'You who have sounded all our secret depths, behold us now in this Bohemian World. List! List! Oh, List!' Up went the lights, the orchestra broke into that popular dance tune, 'Ta-ra-ra Boom-de-ay', and Irving found himself surrounded by his friends.

Not to be outdone Irving asked all the Bohemians to supper at the Maison Riche, 'the affair being most informal and delightful'. He seems always to have been at his friendliest and most expansive in America. Perhaps he felt he did not have to keep up so solemn and dignified an appearance so far from home.

In San Francisco, as usual, he patronised the local theatre – the Chinese Theatre. The audience, hundreds of them, entirely male, sat there with wooden, blank and silent faces. But Irving said he had never enjoyed a theatre more; it was quaint, primitive and immensely funny. After the show he inquired why the actors were eating behind the scenes. 'Actor no go for walkee because him velly bad man; all people say him velly bad man.' Actors would have things thrown at them in the street. Irving looked at the theatre manager and his interpreter. 'Surely you *yourselves* like actors?' The two Chinamen shook their heads in unison. 'We no likee actors – velly bad people – no actor good man – quite impossible.'

Fortunately for Irving the audiences at the Opera House were not of the same opinion. At the farewell performance, they cheered so loudly that 'the mighty sound of their voices was heard far out in the street. They stamped their feet, and this huge audience was moved beyond its control. As he left the theatre a mob (consisting of ladies and gentlemen) howled itself hoarse.'

Irving took nearly $6,000 for each performance in San Francisco. After San Francisco there were two nights in Portland, Oregon, one night in Tacoma, one night in Seattle, three days in Minneapolis, three days at St Paul, five weeks in Chicago, eight weeks in New York and four weeks in Boston. It was a gruelling programme for a man who had been acting for close on forty years with few breaks or holidays.

American reporters were constantly astonished at the trouble which Irving took to keep them out of the theatre. Backstage was sacred and not to be invaded by interviewers. But on his tour one reporter had an ingenious plan for getting into Boston's Tremont Theatre. Charles C. Percival answered an advertisement for forty-seven supers over five foot eight who were required for *Becket*. The reporter was, as he said himself, young and strong, and out of the one hundred men who applied he was chosen to be a knight in one scene and what he called a 'shouter' in another. He was told that his role was to look fiercely at Irving and threaten him with a sword. They were ushered on to the stage and waited in their proper positions. The reporter wrote:

'I still kept my eyes open for the main chance, a glimpse of Irving. Soon a tall, gaunt figure in dark clothes enveloped in a black overcoat surmounted by a tall, black silk hat with a wide rim, and attended by a queer looking dog with a small head and a barrel-shaped body and a stub tail strode on to the stage.'

The ugly dog was the much cherished Fussie.

'Irving had a pleasant word for everyone and the rehearsal was soon over. Evening came and we were all directed to a dressing room nearly under the stage, and here after some preparation during which the make-up man affixed me to a huge pair of fierce moustachios and an imperial, I was handed a sword and spear. The armor was heavy and I experienced some difficulty in getting around. But the curtain rose and I made my debut as an actor by standing in the rear in a group of other knights. When the proper moment came we looked as fierce as we could and shouted "Sign", laying our hands on our swords. We could hear the audience applaud, and I felt as if my future dramatic success was assured.

'All of Irving's company are of an English type and uniformly polite. But my dreams of witnessing the performance vanished, for the rest of the evening I did the duty of a shout from an adjoining room close to the stage. Ellen Terry was met by a maid with wraps at the end of each act who also removed the perspiration from her face.'

When the curtain came down between the acts the reporter was amused to see Irving handing back his pectoral cross and taking his pince-nez from his dresser. Apart from the English politeness, the reporter noticed that Irving was very considerate to his employees and inspected the quarters of the supers, and, finding them somewhat littered and dirty, ordered the whole room to be washed and cleaned before the next performance. But at the end of the week, the amateur knight was very glad to take off his heavy armour and return to his desk. To prove that his story was true the ingenious newspaperman printed in his column the 'Super's Ticket', which gave him entrée to the stage door, with the number of performances he had attended carefully ticked.

At the Tremont Theatre a special Harvard Night was arranged and the local newspaper published a drawing of Ellen Terry giving her rompish performance as Nance Oldfield.

All the cities of America acclaimed Irving equally. His intense professionalism and expertise were appreciated. Even his assistant Bram Stoker and his treasurer C. E. Howson were commended as entertaining men. 'These Englishmen have an unaffected manner, lacking in airs,' said the Boston *Journal*. What the Americans particularly commended was the fact that Irving had been the sole architect of his own fortune and had emerged from obscurity to fame and from poverty to wealth. He was one of themselves.

The Boston *Sunday Herald* painted a vignette of the socialites arriving to see an Irving performance. A white-suited footman descends from his seat on the box, opens the door, while a gentleman in evening clothes assists his wife to alight. Over the lady's brown hair is thrown a lace scarf, and her diamonds glisten in the lights as she strolls through the theatre lobby. First nights in Boston were as grand as those in London.

This fourth tour of America had been as phenomenally successful as the first, and the progress of Irving was written about and pictured all along his route. A drawing – 'En route with Henry Irving The Great Actor and Miss Ellen Terry, Fresh from New Triumphs' – shows the arrival of his special train. Irving is seen in the foreground with a frogged, fur-collared, long coat and soft travelling hat, with his barrel-shaped dog at his heels, and Ellen alights from the train looking like a contemporary fashion plate with a buttoned coat and jaunty toque.

His organisation was also intensely admired. 'It is made up of ninety-three persons all told, about one third of which belong to the fair sex. A full train of palace cars is required to transport them, and in addition to this, there are ten baggage cars of scenery and properties.'

For a final two weeks the baggage cars rumbled into New York, where the tour ended on St Patrick's Day, 1894: 'Henry Irving brought his phenomenal engagement at Abbey's new theatre on the corner of Broadway and 38th Street to a close on Saturday night with one of those brief but gracious speeches for which he is noted.' The newspapers searched the dictionary for superlatives, whether for the acting, the organisation, or the loyalty of the company. A eulogy of Miss Terry, and a short poem describing her mouth as rosebuds filled with snow, ended the panegyric.

A farewell dinner was given at Delmonico's on 19 March, and on the 21st Henry Irving, Miss Terry and the Lyceum Company left New York on the *Majestic*.

It had all been warming to the heart and lucrative for the bank balance.

Chapter 18

G.B.S. Advancing

In 1895 Edmund Yates, the theatre critic of the influential *Saturday Review*, died, and in January 1895 Shaw was invited by Frank Harris to take his place.

It was a watershed. At last Shaw had the sharp weapons in his hand to try to bring down the accepted ideas of Irving's Lyceum. Years later he wrote grandiloquently in the third person explaining his actions. He admitted that it was a siege laid to the theatre of the nineteenth century by an author who had to cut his own way into it at the point of a pen. Until then, he said, Shakespeare had been conventionally ranked as a giant among psychologists and philosophers, but Ibsen dwarfed him so absurdly in those aspects that it became impossible for the moment to take him seriously as an intellectual force.

Shaw's judgement has lost much ground in the last thirty or forty years. Shakespeare, with his blood, torture, and men living on knife-edges, has more *rapport* with the Hitler and post-Hitler ages. The nineteenth-century writer, like Shaw, protected as he was from the sharp facts of the cruelty of man to man by centuries of slow political progress, and by the British Navy, had no idea that this progress was to prove only a small interlude. The age of the gun, the kidnapping, the hostage, and the terror bomb was still a few years in the future. Reading Shaw, one is amused and amazed. Amused at the sparkling champagne of his comedy, but amazed that the political ideas on which he prided himself proved to be so much dust blown before the winds of barbarism.

Although, like the Pope, G.B.S. has been voted infallible, the diamond-glitter of his criticisms shows flaws. The soft brogue of his native tongue caused him to take *The Colleen Bawn* seriously. *The Importance of Being Earnest* he dismissed as humour adulterated by stock mechanical fun. Attacking censorship, he scoffed at the idea that if the stage were freed managers would immediately produce licentious plays and actresses would stop clothing themselves decently. A cheerful, optimistic view of human nature proved wrong. Even his fury against Sir Henry and Sardoodledum was coloured with angry regret that Ellen and Henry were not acting in his plays. More than eighty years after it was written, *The Importance* wakes an audience into life and laughter; ripeness is all, and proves that Shaw, Ibsen and Wilde can bloom in the same garden, but not always in the way in which G.B.S. imagined.

But in 1895 Shaw was the iconoclast, the new man. He was the attacker and the besieged citadel was the Lyceum Theatre. His first spears were aimed at King Arthur's Great Hall at Camelot.

The play, *King Arthur*, was written by J. Comyns Carr. He was one of those semi-Bohemian characters who abounded in Irving's time. He left stockbroking for the Bar, then drifted into journalism to become an art critic, a friend of Burne-Jones, Alma Tadema and Dante Gabriel Rossetti. Subsequently he took to tinkering about with writing plays and became a friend of Irving's. Irving gave Carr an old play by W. G. Wills on the subject of King Arthur. Comyns Carr wrote: 'At first the project took the form of an offer on Irving's part that I should revise, and in part re-write Wills's slovenly essay.' He turned down the idea and decided to get away from Tennyson: 'I had long known and loved the Arthurian legends as they are enshrined in Sir Thomas Malory's exquisite romance.'

Comyns Carr set to work with a will. He wrote reams of verse and in an inspired moment suggested Burne-Jones to design the costumes and the settings. He even went down to Burne-Jones's house, The Grange, and while the painter was at work in his studio, a captive audience of one, he read the entire play to him. Carr recorded that the painter was delighted with the play, was deeply versed in all the Arthurian lore, and in his painting returned again and again to that great cycle of romance.

The romance of King Arthur became a Lyceum reality. The Magic Mere, the Holy Grail, the Whitehorn Wood, the Black Barge, the Tower above Camelot, and the Passing of Arthur, all took shape in the mind of Burne-Jones and were translated into solid scenery by the Lyceum scene-painters. At Buscot Park, in Buckinghamshire, the briar rose paintings in the dining-room, intricate with flowers, knights, and ladies, give an impression of how Burne-Jones designed his sets for *King Arthur*.

Comyns Carr wrote a long programme note explaining his ideas about the dawn of time, and what Arthur bethought him when addressed by Merlin. The critics were bethinking themselves of Tennyson, and they heartily disliked King Arthur in his suit of black armour, and a Merlin who looked like one of the witches in *Macbeth*.

An additional horror, much commented on, was that the actors were actually wearing their own hair; cut according to a Bond Street style, nothing could have been more unsuitable for the Knights of the Round Table. Added to this, Comyns Carr had played down the nobility and concentrated on the adultery:

> 'Some sin there was – though unrecorded here,
> Some stain that smirched her seeming purity,
> Which Lancelot, all too noble, could not urge
> Else were it not in nature to refuse
> So sweet a gift.'

Other critics were asking themselves the pertinent question: Is this Poetry? And they were answering in a very shaky affirmative.

Irving was found to be full of pathos as the trusting husband with a false friend. His King Arthur was found to be both human and idyllic. Ellen reaped her usual harvest of kind notices; she had given a charming impersonation invested with perfect grace and womanliness. She was the perfect Guinevere, clad in white samite, mystic, wonderful; all her dresses were dreams. But the Queen's maying in her Whitehorn Wood, the misty lake, and the dreams of Camelot were totally demolished by Shaw.

Irving had made a brave step forward, wrote Shaw. He had resolved to get rid of the author, and put in his place his dear old friend Comyns Carr, an encyclopaedic gentleman. 'For in poetry Mr Comyns Carr is frankly a jobber and nothing else.' Shaw imagined that Irving had said to Carr:

'Write what trash you like, and I will play the real King Arthur over the head of your stuff. And the end of it was that Mr Comyns Carr was too much for Mr Irving. When King Arthur, having broken down in an attempt to hit Lancelot with his sword, left Guinevere grovelling on the floor with her head within an inch of his toes, and stood plainly conveying to the numerous bystanders that this was the proper position for a female who had forgotten herself so far as to prefer another man to him, one's gorge rose.'

Shaw rode out, with his lance at the ready, in defence of the wronged Ellen: 'That vision of a fine figure of a woman, torn with sobs and remorse, stretched at the feet of a nobly superior and deeply wronged lord of creation, is no doubt still as popular with the men whose sentimental vanity it flatters as it was in the days of the *Idylls Of The King*.' Breaking his lance for Ellen, Shaw saw her as the actress who was grovelling at the feet of the actor manager. An actress who should be acting in the plays of one Bernard Shaw, 'What a theatre for a woman of genius to be attached to! Schoolgirl charades like *Nance Oldfield*, blank verse by Wills and Comyns Carr, with intervals of hashed Shakespeare!'

But even Shaw could not fault the settings, which in his view brought a feeling of fifteenth-century Italy on to the stage. With Burne-Jones to design, and Harker and Hawes Craven to paint the settings, and one hand on Malory and Tennyson from his bookshelves, Irving seemed to have put his other hand on a ready-made success.

The year of King Arthur and the Knights was also the year Irving became Sir Henry. In May 1895 it was announced that he was to be knighted, the first actor ever to achieve this now somewhat diminished glory. Bram Stoker had been consulted about the possibility of Irving accepting a knighthood during Gladstone's administration in 1883, but Irving had refused. Gladstone was his friend; he sat in the wings in a special box near the stage because he was deaf. Irving's official reason for refusing the honour was that he felt an actor should not be knighted while actively pursuing his calling. But in the twelve years since 1883 many things had changed, other arts had benefited by official recognition. And now, perhaps, Irving felt himself to be beyond criticism, an actor who could accept an honour with grace and dignity.

He received the accolade at Windsor Castle on 18 July 1895. He wrote:

'I went to Windsor with twelve others. The room in which The Queen received us was a small one, and I had to walk but a few steps forward and kneel. The Queen extended her hand, which I kissed, and her Majesty touched me on each shoulder with the sword and said "Rise Sir Henry", and I rose. Then departing from her usual custom, she added "It gives me great pleasure, sir." I bowed and then withdrew from the room with my face to her Majesty. Walking backwards is unusual for me and I felt constantly as if I would bump into someone.'

Irving saw it as an accolade for his whole profession. He had received it from the hands of the Queen of his country and the Empress of a vast Empire. It honoured every man and woman on the stage. It had been a long road from Sunderland to Windsor, from the trumpery feathered hat and property sword to the light touch of the Queen's real sword on his shoulder, and her firm voice in his ear.

The next day the Lyceum Theatre staged a celebration of its own, one of those sentimental theatrical occasions when fulsome compliments are exchanged and enmities and jealousies forgotten. An address of congratulation was drawn up in a volume enclosed in a casket of gold and crystal. It was designed by Johnstone Forbes-Robertson, and signed by four thousand of Irving's fellow actors and actresses. Squire Bancroft read the address, which was written by Pinero. The panegyric concluded: 'From generation to generation, the English actor will be reminded that his position in the public regard is founded in no small degree upon the pre-eminence of your career, and upon the nobility, dignity, and sweetness of your private character.'

The cheers died down, Irving overcame his emotion and made a feeling reply: No more honours could come to him, and he felt this knighthood as a pledge to work with more strenuous endeavour for the well-being of his calling and his art. He then smiled, and used the old actor's phrase 'Won't you come round?' as a joke. But to the assembled worshipping audience it was not a joke. Hundreds left their seats and thronged on to the stage to look with awe upon the casket, which was inspected like some holy relic unveiled upon an altar.

In March 1895 Irving had been ill again and was out of the cast. Perhaps he was feeling both the weight of his own years and King

Arthur's armour. When the season opened again in May he substituted a triple bill: Pinero's old curtain raiser, *Bygones*, *Don Quixote*, a one-act dramatisation of his favourite childhood book, and Conan Doyle's *A Story of Waterloo*. This last had crept on to the stage at Bristol the previous autumn to loud applause from the public. When the play opened in London even the critic A. B. Walkley admitted that he was quite surprised to find himself 'fairly blubbering at the Lyceum the other night. The play presents one of those signs of mortality in human affairs which do come home to the mind and touch it.'

Walkley gave a quick vignette of Irving in this play about a veteran of Waterloo: 'The delight of the old man over his new pipe, his constant repetition of his own anecdote "The riggiment's proud o' ye", says the Regent, "and I'm proud of the riggiment, says I, and a damned good answer too, says the Regent, and burst out a laffin".'

Another of the old man's constant repetitions was, 'That wouldn't a' done for the Dook.' It didn't do for Shaw, either, and afforded him an excellent opportunity for attack: 'A squeak is heard behind the scenes: it is the childish treble that once rang like a trumpet on the powder waggon at Waterloo. Enter Mr Irving, in a dirty white wig, toothless, blear-eyed, shaky at the knees, stooping at the shoulders, incredibly aged and very poor – but respectable.'

The play ended, much to Shaw's dissatisfaction, with the old man suddenly springing up to attention: 'The Guards want powder, and by God, the Guards shall have it!' With these words Corporal Brewster fell back, dead in his chair. No doubt to the relief of G.B.S., who was not more appreciative of Irving's *Don Quixote*, although here he did throw the actor a crumb of comfort: 'Abortive as *Don Quixote* is, there are moments when Wills vanishes and we have Cervantes as the author, and Irving as the actor – no cheap combination.'

Shaw's dislike of Irving's productions was tempered by his desire to use him and Ellen for his plays. His account of his dealings with Irving over his plays depicts the actor as a foolish, pompous, unintelligent man. But now that he had the weapons of attack in his hand G.B.S. was no longer concerned with the sensibilities of mere actors.

According to Shaw, the ploy used by the actor-manager was to buy options on plays written by critics which were never to be produced, and translations of plays which would never be heard on the stage.

In this way the critics, happy to receive £100, could be silenced. Irving bought up the plays not to perform them, 'but to prevent any possible rival getting hold of them. His direct bribery was frank and lordly; it was the kind known as Chicken and Champagne. His first nights ended with a banquet on the stage to which it was a social distinction to be invited.'

Shaw was smugly pleased that he always accepted the invitation – and never went. But Irving's banquets were more part of his actor's nature than attempts to bribe critics. They were the proof, like his knighthood, that at last he had escaped from the poverty and distress of his beginnings. They were his justification. By giving them he had living proof that he was Sir Henry Irving, a leader of art and society. It was a simple, childish demonstration of grandeur which Shaw would never understand. Shaw was the Jaeger-clad, vegetable eating, non-drinking leader of the new school. Grandeur was the unacceptable face of the old theatre which he so despised.

The tug of war between Ellen and Irving and Shaw began in earnest when Shaw heard that Ellen was to play in *Madame Sans Gêne*, a play about a washerwoman and Napoleon which had been a vehicle for the French actress Réjane. Shaw wrote to Ellen: 'To my great exasperation I heard that you are going to play in *Madame Sans Gêne*. And I have just finished a beautiful little one act play for Napoleon and a Strange Lady who will be murdered by someone else whilst you are nonsensically pretending to play a washerwoman.' The beautiful little play was *The Man of Destiny*, which Shaw himself later described as 'hardly more than a bravura piece to display the virtuosity of the two principal performers'.

According to Ellen's son, Shaw had derived all his very voluminous stage directions from watching Irving and Ellen acting. They were so explicit and obvious that they left little to an actor's imagination. The long and flattering description of the Strange Lady was certainly a portrait done from the stalls.

Ellen was torn between Shaw's flattery and the security which Irving had always given her. It is the eternal choice for the actor between the secure and the ephemeral. Shaw kindly described bright new jewels of plays. Supposing they should turn out to be worthless beads after all? Although she was prepared to risk her position at the Lyceum, she did push the play, keeping Shaw hoping for a production and yet knowing that it was too small a piece for that theatre. Later

Shaw wrote – at some length – about Irving's methods of putting him off, and of how he had treated Irving as a 'baby'. But in the end, perhaps Ellen's few sentences tell the truth: 'For reasons of his own Henry never produced Mr Shaw's play, and there was a good deal of fuss made about it at the time, but Mr Shaw was not so well known as he is now and the so-called "rejection" was probably of use to him as an advertisement.'

In September 1896 Irving sailed once more with his company to America. The New World was again to be used to redress the finances of the old. He put up at the Plaza, and then went holidaying to the Adirondacks. From Montreal to Richmond, Charleston, and New Orleans – everywhere he was again received as the player-prince. He gave the old money-spinning favourites, *Faust*, *The Merchant of Venice*, *King Arthur* and *Waterloo*. *King Arthur* was new to America and seen to be full of beauty, charm, harmony, and taste – the very atmosphere of the England of good King Arthur – and dear old Corporal Brewster drew the usual sentimental tears.

This tour lasted from September 1895 to May 1896, and, apart from various one-act plays, Irving took twelve different plays touring across the continent. The harvest was over half a million dollars, but, as usual with Irving, when the expenses were deducted the profit was small.

By that time, from all his strenuous touring and travelling in the British provinces and America, his profits only came to some eight thousand pounds, a small return for his exertions.

He had always overpaid his actors, and their salaries on the American tour alone came to £53,000. Ellen was paid £300 a week when in America and £200 in the provinces. Like the touring actor he essentially was, Irving lived only from town to town and from performance to performance. He overpaid his actors because he had known what it was to be underpaid. He once remarked that a man never recovered from not having enough to eat when he was younger.

Now, with his coffers not greatly replenished, he sailed back to the colder waters of England. His next production was to be *Cymbeline*. Before the first night Shaw was already writing long letters to Ellen explaining exactly how she should play her part. His attacks on Shakespeare were another piece of self-advertisement. But when Hector Bolitho, one of Shaw's biographers, taxed him with this he said: 'What a horrid libel! I never thought about drawing attention to myself because I could not help doing it every time I put pen to paper. Besides my own Shakespearean output was then unwritten. I had nothing to speak of to draw attention to.' Bolitho retorted: 'Except yourself.'

Shaw's combined attacks on Shakespeare and Irving were bringing him more and more to the fore. His cooing, wooing letters to Ellen were another attempt to breach the enemy's defences. She had sent him an acting version of *Cymbeline*, and he replied, in a letter full of seeming surprise, that Ellen's notes on the play showed her to be no mere piece of charm, but a woman who gave good value for money as an actress. It was, after all, the métier to which she had been trained as a child, and should have been no matter for surprise to anybody. When he came to write about her performance as Imogen, the critic Shaw especially commended her reading of the summons to this 'same blessed Milford', a reading style which the correspondent Shaw had himself suggested.

Whether from kindness or from truth, Shaw was astonished by Irving as Iachimo: 'I knew Shakespeare's play inside out before last Tuesday, but this Iachimo was quite fresh and novel to me.' He had to admit that he had watched it with delight, it was a true impersonation, unbroken in its life-current from end to end, varied on the surface with comedy and sustained in the beauty of its execution.

Irving's acting versions of Shakespeare came in for less praise. Shaw said that in a true republic of art 'Sir Henry Irving would ere this have expiated his acting versions on the scaffold. He does not merely cut plays: he disembowels them.'

There were other unflattering views. An unknown writer in a magazine called *Pick me Up* wrote that the new production at the Lyceum was the result of the joint effort of Sir Henry Irving and Mr William Shakespeare, Shakespeare in the writer's mind clearly coming a bad second. As Iachimo Irving looked like Daniel in the Lion's Den in the prints given away in Sunday schools; Miss Terry was warned against lying on her back – not a healthy practice after a liberal supper. 'Iachimo creeps out of his box and walks round to take some minute observations of the lady's appearance – in a very décolletée nightdress so that he can go back to his friends to brag about things that haven't been and circumstances that never were.' Although it was all very daintily done, if it had been a modern play, he wrote, the London County Council would have had something to say about this. Some of Shakespeare's scenes in *Cymbeline* came as a sharp surprise to the writer, who suggested that they would be more suitable for the Empire Promenade where the expensive light ladies plied their trade.

The battle scenes were impressive, the scenery of a rare and singular majesty, but somehow the headless gentleman failed to attract and the play was only acted for seventy-two nights.

On 25 November Irving acted *The Bells* on the twenty-fifth anniversary of its first performance, and was presented with an enormous medieval silver bell when the curtain fell. On the twenty-first anniversary of *The Bells*, Irving had been given a statuette of himself as Mathias. Now he was loaded down with the bell itself. He thought back on his long career and spoke again with kindness of 'Colonel' Bateman who had given him his first chance.

Twenty-five years! Twenty-five years of applause, of success, largesse and behaving *en prince*. What was he thinking as he stood there holding the immense bell? Of all the audiences in England, in America, of clapping hands, of speeches and of celebrations? Twenty-five years of toil, of getting and spending, and twenty-five years of being 'The Governor', the supreme commander of his motley army. It had been a long twenty-five years. He was two years away from his sixtieth birthday and had been acting for forty years. His staff, his small-part actors, his servants and acquaintances – all found him the soul of generosity and kindness. Yet Ellen Terry said of him that he seemed to be able to do without love, without a home life, and without close relationships. She wondered whether anyone ever knew him.

Bram Stoker was his closest friend and adviser, yet when writing from the Plaza in New York to Hawkins, who ran the magazine *The Theatre*, Irving said: 'You are quite wrong about Bram Stoker' – adding that he was a very genial man, but knew as much about the theatre as the man in the moon. It was not a sentence which would have pleased Stoker, who had given his whole life to Irving and the Lyceum.

The man he always clung to in real friendship was J. L. Toole, the comedian, the man who could set the theatre in a roar merely by pulling a funny face. With Toole he could think and feel as he did when he was young, when everything was a beautiful dream, and nothing had yet been achieved.

Irving's sons had drifted into the theatre. But when Ben Webster asked if he had seen the notice in the papers that Harry was to play Hamlet, Irving said: 'Harr-y? Hm. Ham-let? Sill-y.' In Chicago Irving had produced a one-act play by his son Laurence, *Godefroi and Yolande*, with Ellen playing a leprosy-stricken Yolande in a bright red wig. But Irving can hardly be said to have promoted the careers of his sons with any degree of compassion or energy, at least at the beginning. It was as if his own young struggles had made him immune from understanding them. They had started at the top. They had no idea of the meaning of struggle and achievement.

In his clubs, at his dinners, what a good fellow he was! And yet when he went back to his home, which looked like a dressing-room, or his dressing-room which was his home, did he perhaps look in the mirror and see no one there – only the reflections of Hamlet, Romeo, Claude Melnotte, and the twopence coloured people of his youth?

In Ellen's memoirs the enthusiasm and excitement are felt right up to the production of *Macbeth* – the clothes, the production, the paintings by Mr Sargent of herself in her beetle-wing dress. And then little by little the enthusiasm evaporates. The public Henry was gradually taking over the man. In that same November, when Henry was celebrating twenty-five years of *The Bells*, Ellen was writing to Shaw about Florence Irving: 'Henry married her, he knew he didn't love, thought he ought to, and he had better have killed her straight off.' He had perhaps killed instead his own capacity to feel.

Ellen may have been foolish in many ways but she showed much common sense when she said: 'It is happy not to be clever.' Both Irving and Shaw were clever in their different ways, clever and self-centred. Clever enough to see how men and women could be managed, but, like the Snow Queen, lacking a heart. Shaw spoke of Ellen having many enduring friendships, some transient fancies, and five domestic partnerships 'of which two were not legalised, though they would have been if the English marriage law had been decently reasonable.' These were the partnerships with Godwin and Irving. But the moment for marrying Irving had passed. Ellen's sentimentality and Irving's sardonic humour had failed to grow together; the vine still clung to the trellis, but only from self-interest; and the trellis supported the vine, for its decorative value. Besides, they were both middle-aged people now, and their children were marrying.

Irving's son, Harry, had married the young actress Dorothea Baird, who had played Trilby. The report of the wedding noted that Sir Henry was not present at the ceremony. He had sent a blue enamel and diamond watch, and a cheque. Lady Irving kindly gave a piano; as far as Henry was concerned she had played herself out long ago.

Ellen's son Teddie had also married, not entirely to Ellen's satisfaction. She liked her chicks to be always with her. When she was interviewed shortly after the marriage, the lady correspondent recorded that, 'Miss Terry was very sad at losing her son, in spite of her affection for his wife, and she has a great dread of the day that may take her daughter from her.' Shaw was wise when he suggested Candida as the perfect part for Ellen. She was always more mother than lover.

Irving's friend, biographer, and hagiographer, Austin Brereton says: 'Saturday 19th December is an ominous date in the life story of Henry Irving.'

It was the day on which he revived *Richard III*. It had been one of his greatest creations under the economical Mrs Bateman. Now, with a better cast and twenty years' experience, he was poised for an outstanding success in one of his favourite parts. Ellen was allegedly ill. She had rejected the second fiddle part of the Lady Ann and gone on holiday to Germany. Irving was to bear the burden of his first-night nerves, and the five hundred guests to supper, without her tactful presence.

The official accounts of the opening of *Richard III* tend to gloss over the night's doings. His notices were good. J. F. Nisbet of *The Times* found him sinister, sardonic, weird and grimly humorous. Even the francophile Henry James found him 'sinister-sardonic flowered over as vividly as may be with the elegant-grotesque.'

After the show he greeted his guests as usual, and then, according to the official accounts, sat up late smoking cigars with Professor James Dewar and friends at the Garrick Club. Dewar walked with Irving to Grafton Street, and at dawn went home. Irving had a bath, and then fell down the stairs, rupturing the ligaments of his knee. Only Shaw penetrated the truth, and then, perhaps, by accident:

'As to Sir Henry Irving's performance, I am not prepared to judge it, in point of execution, by what he did on the first night. He was best in the Court scenes. In the heavy single-handed scenes which Cibber loved he was not, as it seemed to be, answering his helm satisfactorily; and he was occasionally a little out of temper with his own nervous condition.'

Many years afterwards, when speaking of his negotiations over *The Man of Destiny*, Shaw said: 'Nothing more happened until the unlucky first, and only night, of his revival of *Richard III*, when he did one or two odd things on the stage, and then fell downstairs and disabled himself by hurting his knee.' Shaw said that he had written a faithful but extremely stupid notice saying that Irving was not answering his helm, but that he ought to have seen that what was the matter was that he had drunk a little too much. G.B.S., who lunched on a cheese sandwich and ginger beer, could not perhaps be expected to note the symptoms. But his notice added to the injury by referring to Kean's habit of lying down on a sofa 'when he was too tired or drunk to keep his feet during the final scenes'. In the 1930s Shaw wrote that he was not a man of insinuations and stabs in the back; if he had thought Irving was drunk he would have said so unequivocally. But in public print about a national hero?

When Shaw's notice appeared Irving was already laid up and unable to act. Ellen was in Germany and the Lyceum was in a state of anger with Shaw.

Ellen had once made a small joke about Irving saying pompously in a speech that his actors were clean, sober, and perfect. *Richard III* was, unfortunately, neither sober nor perfect on that memorable first night. Harry Irving did not share the general indignation, and said that it served the old man right, and would teach him to keep sober the next time. It was a sardonic comment worthy of his father.

Irving never forgot Shaw's review, and it was the end of any hopes that he would ever produce a play by Shaw, even had he intended to do so. Ellen tried to play the mediator between critic and actor: 'Henry has been much vexed lately by what he calls your attacks upon him in the *Saturday Review*. For the life of me I cannot realise how it feels, the *pain* for a thing of the kind.' But then Ellen usually received honeyed reports. Irving had been understandably angered by Shaw's critique of the stop-gap production of *Olivia*, with Ellen and Vezin, which had been put on after the débâcle of *Richard III*. Shaw had written that it was a *relief* to see a play at the Lyceum without Irving.

Even Ellen had lost her sunny outlook in the generally dispiriting atmosphere at the theatre. The loss on the season had been £10,000. She wrote to Shaw: 'This last week I've had real courage to consent to live, being out of love with life! The first time! Nobody sees, except my dresser at the theatre, and I don't speak to her of how I feel. It would make her ill.'

Shaw was cock-a-hoop, happily anticipating a new row with Irving, that symbol of the boring pomposity of the Victorian theatre. To Ellen, Henry was a man who had been her love. They had to act together in *Madame Sans Gêne* to try to redress the balance of Henry's mistakes. 'I didn't bother him about details, for we both had to play our parts decently before a good many hundred, but my heart was beating all the while. Don't quarrel with H! That would add to my unhappiness. I kiss you on the tip of your innocent nose.' Shaw, suddenly repentant, wrote back: 'Don't be anxious, I'll behave nicely.'

Eventually Irving wrote to Shaw, making no excuses for rejecting Shaw's play, *The Man of Destiny*. He wrote simply asking Shaw to leave him alone.

Perhaps, in his heart of hearts, Irving was coming to realise that he was fighting a rearguard action. He was fighting gamely, but with each attack he had retreated a few paces. The attackers were full of heart and full of fight, feeling that all their successes were before them.

Chapter 19

Enter Mrs Aria

The alleyways and souks of human relationships are made more mazelike by the evasions, the half-truths, and the ability of men and women to look on the sunlit side of their own actions. Henry Irving and Ellen were no different in this respect from the general run of humanity.

How did this profitable emotional and professional duet finally split? Ellen's story was that Henry had left her for Mrs Aria. She wished to appear as someone who had poured out her talents, her love, and her womanhood for the benefit of a man who was innately cold and incapable of returning the richness of the love she had given him. Irving said nothing. They destroyed their letters to one another; only a few notes, couched in loving terms, remain to testify to their long years together.

Irving died long before Ellen. He died before the tight emotional corset of his age had been unloosed. So his side of the story remains obscure. Ellen lived on to the franker 1920s and was able to speak freely to a younger woman, Marguerite Steen.

Ellen's charm, however, stretches out from beyond the grave and her biographers deny that the Irving–Terry association was more than a professional partnership. Yet if she was as totally feminine and charming as contemporary critics claim, it would be churlish to believe that Henry had resisted those charms.

Ellen had been brought up in the hard school of touring from the age of eight. When it came to her taste in men she had a split personality. Her feelings as an actress and an artist drew her towards men of talent: Watts, the painter; Godwin, the architect; and Irving the actor. These men were all steps in the furtherance of her career.

They gave her education, and help with her profession. But as a creature of moods and of varying feminine needs her body drew her towards the over-masculinity of her second and third husbands, and her 'close friend', Frank Cooper, none of them particularly intelligent men. She was drawn to Shaw the playwright on an intellectual level, but it was too late for him to be of use to her; and she had become afraid to leave the shelter of the Lyceum.

Ellen was over 50 when the golden partnership split up, and when Henry left her for Eliza Aria perhaps her sunny charm had finally cloyed. Charm is a curious commodity and those who have it find it impossible not to use it for their own ends. When it is allied to histrionic ability and the need for the concealment of a long relationship, perhaps it wears thin. Both Ellen and Henry had been subjected to the adulation of their public for many years. Henry remained detached and sceptical. But was Ellen as worship-proof as her 'great comrade'?

Who was Mrs Aria? She is referred to contemptuously as a Jewish journalist, but from her autobiography, untruthfully named *My Sentimental Self*, she appears a wholly practical, intelligent woman. Allowing for the old-fashioned style of her writing, there gleams through her gossip a woman with a sharp wit.

She had been married young to a good Jewish boy. Her comments on this bring her character into sharp focus: 'Nothing in David Aria's life became him so well as his leaving me for South Africa five years after I had driven with him from the Synagogue to hear his first rapture expressed in: "I wonder what won the Lincoln Handicap?" My David danced and gambled before the Ark.'

He had suffered, said Mrs Aria, from the fatal belief that he knew which horse would come in first. When his financial crash came, David Aria's idea was, according to his wife, 'that we should sell the house and its contents, and live in apartments while he looked for another opening for his talents. I knew what *that* meant. I had a cousin who had been looking for an opening for twenty years – and living upon the family all the time.'

Through her brother James she had many connections with the theatre and journalism. He wrote libretti for musical comedies like *The Gaiety Girl*, *Floradora*, and *The Geisha*. He took as his nom de plume 'Owen Hall', for he admitted that he had never been out of debt since he left prep school, but this did not worry him. 'I know that my Receiver liveth,' he would say.

If Ellen and Henry were coy about their relationship, Mrs Aria is no less reticent. She begins a chapter on Henry Irving: 'I do not know to what beneficent fairy I owed my first introduction to Henry Irving.' It is to be suspected that Mrs Aria, being the gossip writer and journalist she was, had been throwing out lines for this encounter for some time, and that she was her own beneficent fairy.

She flattered him, mentioning the impossibility of getting seats to see him in *Waterloo*. He asked her where she lived, and she coyly told him: 'In Brunswick Place, next door to the French Convent, where the sisters wearing beautiful blue veils walk up and down in a garden.' 'Um', said Henry, 'I am sure you do not wish it had been a monastery.' The party broke up; Henry was warmly embraced by most of the ladies. Mrs Aria said she watched 'the progress of kissing-time to catch his whimsical glance, just a spark to light me to comprehension of that keen humour which was so delightfully his. The morning after brought me evidence of his remembrance in a note containing two stalls for *Waterloo* – "Nothing much to see, but a pleasure to know you will be present."'

The first step had been taken. A few months later, when Irving was down in Norfolk working on *Peter the Great* with his son Laurence, Mrs Aria happened by a curious coincidence to be staying at Cromer and sent him a telegram asking him to tea. The thought uppermost in her mind was: 'Shall I have the power to amuse him?' She had quickly and accurately judged her main attraction for him.

The photograph of Mrs Aria shows a plump lady upholstered in nineteenth-century dress, holding the long necklace of the period and gazing sentimentally at the picture of her sister, Julia Frankau, the novelist writing under the pen-name of 'Frank Danby'. Julia, on hearing that Eliza had finally become hostess to Henry, sent a telegram of congratulations: 'Grapple him to your soul with hoops of steel.' This dramatically expressed telegram, with its quotation from *Hamlet*, does not give the impression that it was a chance meeting.

The picture which Eliza Aria paints of Irving is a man of monosyllabic conversation, occasional caustic wit, and a fascination with the subject of murder. There are only two brief references to Ellen Terry in Eliza's book; and in Ellen's *Story of My Life* none at all to Eliza Aria. The rivalry of the ladies, like the physical facts of their relationship with Irving, were carefully concealed. If the claws of the ladies were sharp, they were enclosed in hand-made velvet gloves. Even with pens in their hands they kept firmly to the cosy gossipy roles which convention demanded they should play.

Whether Ellen tired of Irving or Irving of Ellen, it is impossible to judge. They had been lovers, partners, and co-partners since the seventies. That seems certain. She was no longer in her first youth, and had been dallying with the iconoclastic ideas of Shaw for some time. Perhaps Irving, seeing the shadows of the theatre to come, shied away from them. He wanted reassurance, he wanted companionship, and he wanted someone who made him laugh. Eliza had a sharp humour, and – best of all – she was not part of his past.

The pages of her book are full of vignettes, such as driving with Irving in an open carriage to see the blossoming hawthorn – to Richmond, to Epping Forest, or to Barnet, for in the 1890s these were leafy retreats from the smoke of London. From Eliza Aria's pages comes a picture of Irving sitting in his carriage with his son, discussing tales of awful crimes, the more ingenious, artful and bloody the better. 'Father and son would sit opposite each other, Harry upright, Irving deep down in the corner of the carriage,' she wrote. Father and son discussed with Eliza why the worst of men always seemed to have devoted women whose loyalty stood firm from murder to the scaffold. They turned to Eliza for an explanation: 'Women do not love men for what they are, but for what they think they are, or hope they may become to them exclusively. We make and fit your haloes,' said Eliza firmly.

Mrs Aria had met Irving some time during the Jubilee Year of 1897. She does not give an exact date, but during that summer Irving did give several performances of the play she mentions, *A Story of Waterloo* and the Jubilee itself was celebrated at the Lyceum by two special performances of that play and *The Bells*.

There was a matinee for the Indian and Colonial troops. Two thousand soldiers massed at Chelsea barracks, and the streets were cleared as they marched towards the Lyceum to the quick step of the Guard's Fife and Drum Band, with the crowds thronging the streets, cheering them all the way. Bram Stoker, remembering the beauty of the past, was moved by the great occasion, as much a celebration of Irving and the Lyceum as of Queen Victoria:

'Every colour and ethnological variety from coal black through yellow and brown to the light type of Anglo-Saxon reared in the new realms beyond the seas – section after section they marched into the theatre all coming in by the great entrance without once stopping or even marking time. No such audience could have been had for this military piece. It sounded the note of the unity of the Empire which was then in celebration. All were already tuned to it. The scene at the end was indescribable – a veritable ecstasy of loyal passion.'

After the performance, in his princely way, Irving threw open the saloons to entertain the troops. Fortunately his hospitality was not abused. Only two drummer boys got drunk.

Two days later, it was the turn of the Colonial Premiers and the Indian Princes; the theatre was filled with all the grandeur, the sparkle and glory of a country at the peak of its power and wealth. The curtain was lowered when the last words of the play were spoken, and within a very few minutes the stage became a banqueting hall with soft music, flowers, and an immense flower-decked supper table to greet Irving's five hundred distinguished guests. An invitation to the Lyceum was as much a seal of greatness as a visit to Buckingham Palace.

The entertaining was as lavish as ever, but the receipts at the box office were less impressive. This year, 1897, saw the production of *Madame Sans Gêne*, with Ellen doing a romp as a washerwoman turned grand lady, a performance not universally popular. Some critics remarked that they would have been content with a little less 'fun', and added that Miss Terry was merely playing at being vulgar, whereas Réjane was brilliantly vulgar. Comyns Carr, Irving's tame playwright, was censured for using phrases like 'that shuts your mouth' and 'stir your stumps'. These expressions may have been risqué in French. In English, they were downright gross.

Padded out to look like Napoleon, Irving played a very small part. His huge costume and fleshings were thickly lined to make him seem short and fat. His desk was huge to make him seem small, and all the men surrounding him on stage were above his height, and even the stage set had oversize pillars. His performance was praised. Even Shaw, having used up most of his space defending Ellen's so-called 'vulgarity', was compelled to admit that Irving seized every opportunity to show what an old stage hand can do with an empty part.

'The result is that he produced the illusion of the Emperor behind the part.'

Jules Claretie found the Lyceum production faultless, and another French critic, Augustin Filon, was equally complimentary about Irving: 'We have before us one of those rare careers which are so perfectly ordered towards the accomplishment of some end by a resolute and inflexible will that there is to be found in them no single wasted minute or ill-directed endeavour.' Filon had seized the essential truth behind the man, and noted one of Irving's sayings: 'The learning how to do a thing is the doing of it.'

In the cast, playing the hero, was Frank Cooper, one of those actors who were constantly commended as 'manly'. Shaw took a different view and called him a misfit, and spoke of his too burly Richmond in *Richard III*. He imagined Cooper saying to the Almighty: 'Look on my forces with a gracious eye – or you will have me to reckon with afterwards!' Shaw emphasised that the last line was not actually spoken by Mr Cooper. He was not giving any quarter to Irving, the Lyceum, or supporting players like Frank Cooper.

There was no reason for Shaw to know that cracks were already appearing in the financial fabric. Though Howson was supposed to be the 'Treasurer', only Bram Stoker and Irving knew the real facts of the losses in 1897; Irving's accident was the main cause of the loss of £10,000. But it was necessary for the theatre to appear in the flourishing state it had been in in the past. A bold front, lavish entertaining, and grand public appearances were essential.

On 29 May, in Jubilee Year, Irving read scenes from Tennyson's *Becket* in the chapter house of Canterbury Cathedral, in order to raise funds for the restoration of the chapter house. It was a marathon performance, lasting three hours. Just as the story of Becket's martyrdom was 'advancing step by step to the dreadfulness of doom' there was heard in the distance the real voices of the real choristers singing Evensong – the very effect Irving had used on stage translated into reality. The Mayor of Canterbury proposed a vote of thanks to the actor and pocketed £215 for his fund; Irving, as usual, paid all the expenses.

When the Lyceum closed for the holidays, Irving met his son and Mrs Aria at Sheringham in Norfolk. A few weeks' rest, and in September he began a fourteen-week tour which, to some extent, covered his losses.

In the last week of the tour, at the beginning of December, he lost his dog Fussie. Mrs Aria, Irving's new 'comrade', had little time for the faithful Fussie. She wrote: 'Fussie, the terrier I disliked because my soup would grow cold in its bowl while his appetite was coaxed, was our invariable follower, although retrieving sticks and stones did not improve his cough, nor ease his slight limp. Irving was devoted to the little beast and would never have another dog after he died. Laurence always declared that Fussie crept away and committed suicide through a hole in the scenery because his father spoke crossly to him during rehearsal. Fussie had been given to Henry by Ellen, who wrote: 'Fussie had his affections alienated by a course of chops, tomatoes, strawberries, biscuits soaked in champagne, and a beautiful fur rug of his very own presented by the Baroness Burdett-Coutts.'

'It was at Manchester Fussie met his death. A carpenter had thown down his coat with a ham sandwich in the pocket over an open trap on the stage. Fussie, nosing and nudging after the sandwich, fell through and was killed instantly. When they brought up the dog after the performance – every man took his hat off, but Henry was not told till the end of the play.'

Henry in fact took the news so quietly that Ellen was frightened, and asked Laurence, his son, who was on the tour with them, to go round to the hotel with her and see if Henry was all right. When they arrived in Irving's room, they found him sitting eating his supper with 'poor dead Fussie, who would never eat supper any more, curled up on his rug on the sofa. Henry was talking to the dog exactly as if it were alive. The next day he took Fussie back in the train with him to London, covered in a coat.'

The dog was buried in Hyde Park, but Henry had the head stuffed and kept it in his rooms at Grafton Street, not entirely to Mrs Aria's satisfaction. 'I hope he rests in peace, but he was stuffed outside all canine recognition,' she said realistically.

After Fussie died, Ellen felt that Henry was really alone and while he never spoke about the dog's death it was easy for her to know how he felt.

'The first time Henry went to the Lyceum after Fussie's death', she related, 'everyone was anxious and distressed. Then an odd thing happened. The wardrobe cat, who had never been near the room in Fussie's lifetime, came down and sat on Fussie's cushion.' Walter, Irving's dresser, looked anxiously at the cat. Suddenly Irving said gruffly that he had better go out and get the cat some meat. From that moment the cat always sat in Irving's dressing-room.

Ellen, who always liked to be surrounded by birds and dogs, took Irving's sorrow about Fussie seriously. But Fussie, like Ellen, was part of the rich years which seemed to have disappeared into the past so quickly.

Five days after the death of Fussie, William Terriss – Breezy Bill, the extrovert hero who had played so many parts with Irving and Ellen, the actor who took life and the theatre lightly, who could make even Irving laugh at his delinquencies and lack of reverence for the theatre – was stabbed to death at the stage door of the Adelphi. He had left the Lyceum and for some time had been playing noble heroes to his mistress Jessie Millward's pure heroines in melodramas, with great commercial success.

Shaw wrote *The Devil's Disciple* with Terriss in mind, and went round to Jessie Millward's flat to read it to him. Terriss listened in deep perplexity and fell asleep, being revived later with strong cups of tea, and decided not to do it; if a play couldn't keep him awake, it was no good to his Adelphi audience. When the play was produced with some success in America, Terriss sent for Shaw to discuss it, but before he could keep the appointment Terriss was stabbed by a lunatic. The Adelphi, in its old aspect as a temple of melodrama, may be said melodramatically to have perished with him.

When the tragedy happened, Irving was at the theatre with Eliza. A note was sent round to his box. He gave the messenger five shillings, but did not open the letter, saying, 'I never open letters in public.' But the commissionaire was insistent: 'There is bad news, mum, make him read it.' One of Irving's friends had found out where he was and sent round the note so that his first hearing of the news would not be the melancholy voices of the newsboys calling out: 'Murder of William Terriss!'

Irving's character showed at its best when Terriss was killed. He was no hypocrite, in spite of the respectable persona behind which he conducted his affairs – and *affaires*. Terriss had died in Jessie's arms and Jessie must be consoled. A few days later Irving went round to her flat. 'My dear', he said, 'I have just come from Bedford Park – I was asked to convey to the Terriss family a message of condolence from the Queen.'

The wife had been visited, so Irving's official duty was done. He had then gone round immediately to Jessie, the one person who had mattered in Terriss's life: 'Is there anything I can do for you?' 'Yes', said Jessie Millward, 'I should like you to be with me at the funeral.' Without hesitation Irving replied: 'Of course, my dear.'

On the morning of the funeral he called round, bringing his bunch of violets. Irving, Seymour Hicks, and Jessie Millward drove to Brompton Cemetery together. The murder and the publicity surrounding it had attracted a huge crowd. Some said there were more than ten thousand people. One newspaper reported:

'Miss Millward, clothed in deepest black and leaning on the arm of Sir Henry Irving, was the most conspicuous figure at the funeral of William Terriss at Brompton Cemetery today. She was one of the dead actor's oldest and closest friends, and her parting kiss was the last thing he felt before he lost consciousness. She has neither slept nor cried, and has hardly eaten or spoken. Her friends are afraid she may lose her reason. Among the immense number of floral tributes hers was the most regarded, a cushion of white chrysanthemums bearing in purple violets the words "To my dear Comrade".'

It was generally thought that Miss Millward, without her great comrade, would not continue her career. And some thought Sir Henry looked pale and care-worn in the raw December air. He was dressed in deepest black and looked slightly bent as he supported Miss Millward, whom he escorted home. Irving had been greatly affected by the tragic death of Terriss. He had supported him during his first tour in America and was one of his best friends. He looked older and wearier than ever before. Many said that he had aged ten years.

But work had to go on. He was rehearsing his son Laurence's play, *Peter the Great*, which was to open on 1 January. But, in spite of his financial troubles and the burden of directing, he found time to go round every night to see Jessie. He suggested that she should go abroad, and then return to the stage – and to work. Work was his banner and his inspiration. It must be so for others. She shook her head: 'I can never return to the stage.' Irving looked at her with compassion and said simply: 'You *must*, it is your work, and in work lies relief.'

Terriss was killed by a man called Prince, whom he had once employed as a super and subsequently helped with money when he was unemployed. It was a murder for personal publicity, for Prince had been heard muttering that soon his name would be on everyone's lips. He was sent to Broadmoor, where he subsequently conducted the asylum band with professional élan. This bore out Irving's sarcastic remarks to Eliza about the murder: 'They will find some excuse to get him off – mad or something. Terriss was an actor, his murderer will not be executed.' His deep feeling for the loss of his friend was still rooted in resentment at the general prejudice against his beautiful art. Not even his knighthood had been enough compensation.

He did not easily forget the murder. At a dinner for the Actors' Benevolent Fund he said: 'Since that terrible crime was committed certain individuals, who seem to possess all the murderer's points of vanity and ill will, endeavour to levy a sort of blackmail under threats. Only the other day it was said to our secretary by a disappointed applicant that Terriss's murderer was not the *only* one who carried a knife. . . .'

A fortnight after the murder of Terriss Irving opened in *Peter the Great*. The play was received with respect tinged with touches of horror. The theme of Tsar Peter condemning his own son to death was not felt to be something which could happen at Windsor.

The play was long drawn out and even brutal. It was said that there was unnecessary emphasis on the horrible. The torture scene, with the agonising cries of the victims, would not add to the popularity of the piece. Taste had changed in England since the seventeenth century, when D'Urfey's impaled victims and headless trunks were savoured. The *St James's Budget* remarked that the atmosphere of the piece was redolent with the cruelty and savagery of a barbaric age in which men's lives were at the mercy of a despot's whim. Under the proud protection of the British Navy humanity had naturally moved away from such old unhappy far-off ferocities.

Irving's acting was praised, his Peter the Great was described as a weird, fantastic, impressive composition, 'a creature who perpetrates his cruelties with a Petruchio-like boisterousness and grim jocularity'.

Ellen Terry was felt to be very poorly served by the small part of Catherine: it was thin, unimportant, and drawn on the lines of Madame Sans Gêne.

Shaw was not invited to the first night, but someone – probably Ellen – had sent him the play. He wrote a brilliant historical essay of nearly two thousand words, praising the play as modern and realistic, and not disagreeing with Laurence Irving's divergences from history. He ended by remarking: 'What the representation at the Lyceum is like, Heaven and my fellow critics know; I do not. Sir Henry Irving has not invited me to witness it.' Shaw considered this to be an appeal for him to stay away. But there was no need for such modesty on Mr *Laurence* Irving's part. 'I take it that Sir Henry is modest on his own.'

The mounting of the piece was spectacular and expensive, the scene of the gardens of St Elmo, with Vesuvius suddenly breaking into flames, being especially commended.

Playing the part of the Tsarevich's mistress was Miss Ethel Barrymore. If the play did not get good notices Miss Barrymore's costumes had heavy coverage in *The Lady*, which became quite ecstatic with descriptions of froggings, velvets, satins, braids and silver buttons. The brilliant function was, of course, saddened by the absence of Fussie, 'whose tragic death took place three weeks ago – as has already been recorded', said *The Lady* truthfully.

For the first time Mrs Aria was invited to the supper after a first night. 'You don't know my boy, Harry,' said Irving to Mrs Aria, who looked up from her Gunter's chicken sandwich to see 'that wonderful pair standing together, the father's hand on the son's arm'. Apart from the wonderful pair, what particularly impressed her was the twelve-foot linen cloth embroidered in golden squares enclosing the name of every character which Irving had ever played. Looking at it, Eliza wondered how many loving feminine hands had contributed to its making.

Ellen does not appear to have met Mrs Aria on this occasion, because on 18 February she wrote to Shaw: 'Who is Mrs A? I only know she is a journalist and "a friend" of H.I.'s. I never set eyes on her, and she has no idea *I* know of her. (This is fun, and it would be better fun, if I knew something about *her*.) If you know her personally don't "give away" that I know of her existence.'

On 6 February 1898 Irving was 60. *Peter the Great* had only proved a *succés d'estime* on the appeal of its being a joint effort of father and son. Even a Command Performance for Queen Alexandra had failed to give a fillip to the audiences. Eliza reassured Irving that it was liked. 'Liked, yes, they like it – but they don't come,' retorted Irving grimly.

The comparative failure of *Peter the Great* was overshadowed by a much harder blow. Stoker told the story:

'At ten minutes past five on the morning of Friday February 18th there was a knock at the door of my house in Chelsea. It was a cab driver with a letter. The Lyceum Storage, Bear Lane, Southwark was on fire. The fourwheeler was waiting, and we drove there as fast as the horse would go through the dim dank morning which was bitterly cold. Bear Lane was in chaos. There was so much stuff in storage that nothing could be done till the fire had burned itself out.'

Stoker stood in the grey morning watching the years of Irving's work drift away in smoke. This was his capital, his stock-in-trade for profitable tours in the future, going up in flames. The firemen were merely there to prevent the fire spreading. Two hundred and sixty scenes, many of great expense and elaboration, two thousand pieces of scenery, expensive large props – the settings for forty-four plays – all was disappearing into the chill February air. Stoker remarked that the cost price was about £30,000, but this was the least part of the loss. Nothing could ever repay the time, the labour, or the artistic experience which had created these settings. It was a devastating blow to the repertory side of Irving's management. With this scenery in store he could put on plays which had already been studied and rehearsed. The scenery also represented Irving's savings.

The fire was so fierce that it burned the structure of the railway arches to a depth of three bricks and turned the coping stones to powder. But not only had it burned the railway arches, it had deprived Irving of his future. Had it not happened he could have continued to play his old repertoire in the provinces, in America, and in London for many years. The newspaper reporters seized their opportunity; there is nothing like a fire for a quick theatrical effect.

'Materials being parched and dried by many long runs by the hot fires of the footlights were no sooner alight than they vanished in curling clouds of black smoke,' wrote one happy reporter. The faithful Stoker, gazing in horror at the vast destruction, was seized upon and interviewed: 'What has gone, Mr Stoker?'

Stoker did a quick calculation: '£20,000 of scenery, and big properties.'

'Of what plays?'

'From memory – *Charles I, Olivia, Macbeth, Much Ado, Cymbeline, Richard III, The Corsican Brothers, Romeo and Juliet, Louis XI, King Lear, Othello* —'

At this point Mr Stoker was reported as having lost his breath. 'What have you in the theatre?' he was next asked.

'Only *The Bells*, *Waterloo*, *The Merchant of Venice* and *Peter the Great*.'

But Stoker put up a bold front. The costumes had not gone; serious as the loss might be, it would not entail shutting the theatre. The scenery could easily be reconstructed, and the plays would reappear, better than ever, he said bravely.

'What does Sir Henry say?'

'He bears it calmly.'

The reporter then let himself go in a final burst of fine writing: 'And passing out I heard the sound of *The Bells*, the Wild Bells, ringing madly in the murky air.'

Irving's sour comment on the disaster was aimed at the New Drama. Perhaps the fire had been caused by a spark of that moral indignation shown by people who wanted plays without scenery. It is curious that on the same day as the disaster, when Ellen was writing to G.B.S. about Mrs A. in her sprightly girlish way, she made no mention of the fire.

Irving carried doggedly on. His next project was *The Medicine Man*, which he had commissioned from Robert Hichens and H. D. Traill. Ellen hated the play. She wrote to Shaw saying: 'It "lunatics" me to watch Henry at these rehearsals. Hours and hours of loving care on this twaddle! He just adores his absurd part.' She was enjoying a few days' rest from her part of Sylvia, which was detestable, she said. Dorothea Irving (Baird) or her sister Marion should have played it; they would do it sincerely. She was going to send the play to Shaw – right or wrong, and he could read it as her adviser. She despaired of doing anything with her part. If the thing were successful, 'I believe I'll give it all up, sell my possessions, try to get back some of the money I've lent, and live on £3 a week as I did in the days gone by with Edward.' Ellen was banging her wooden spoon in a rare old tantrum.

The 'thing' was not a success.

The theme stemmed from the story of a lion tamer, Van Amburgh, who professed to be able to quell the most ferocious animals, animal or human, by the power of his eye alone. Although it lasted for over three hours, there was only enough in it to make a half-hour sketch.

Shaw, carefully primed by Ellen, echoed her letter: 'Sir Henry Irving was perfectly delighted with his part, but Miss Terry took her bow as if to say: "Don't blame me, *I* didn't write it."'

The season, it need hardly be stressed, closed with a loss. Only Stoker and Henry knew the full extent of the total losses. The whole theatre was run like a gigantic secret service operation. Stoker wrote: 'There was strict reticence on financial matters. Not one official of the theatre, outside myself, knew the whole of the incomings and outgoings. Not even that official (Howson) designated 'Treasurer' knew anything of the high finance of the undertaking. The Box Office keeper made entry of daily receipts.' But even he did not know the total takings in ready money. Howson was allowed to pay some salaries; others were paid by Irving or by Stoker. Each department – carpenters, property men, wardrobe, gas men, electricians, supers, chorus, and orchestra – was operated separately. Perhaps Irving did not want to know himself the full extent of his expenditure or his losses.

When *The Medicine Man* closed Irving went off on holiday to Cromer with Mrs Aria. Ellen was touring the provinces with the 'manly' Frank Cooper in *Othello* and *The Lady of Lyons*. She wrote to Shaw: 'The only reason for my doing it is that I've nothing in the way of any interesting part to look forward to for the next three years (which will I suppose see the end of me) and these two, Desdemona and Pauline, are easy as I've done them before.'

The small parts which Henry had thown to Ellen like bones were not to her liking, and he was touring on his own. In October he reached Edinburgh, the city where he had enjoyed his first tentative successes. On the Sunday after the engagement he took a day off and went to see Lord Rosebery at his country home. He got wet, and having no clothes to change into, as his luggage had been forwarded to Glasgow, he travelled from Edinburgh to Glasgow in an unheated railway carriage in his wet clothes and soaking shoes.

On 13 October 1898 he was playing to a full house and great applause in Glasgow in *Madame Sans Gêne*. Just before the second act, when Napoleon makes his first entrance, Irving sent for Bram Stoker. Stoker found Irving sitting in his dressing-room, already dressed for his part, but his face was drawn with pain.

'I think there must be something wrong with me. Every breath is like a sword stab. I don't think I ought to be suffering like this without seeing someone.'

'Shall I dismiss the audience?'

'No! I shall be able to get through all right, but when I have seen a doctor – we may have to make some change tomorrow.'

The doctor arrived during the last act, and diagnosed pneumonia and pleurisy, a serious illness before the days of antibiotics. Two special nurses were engaged. There was nothing to do except to wait for the crisis.

When Walter, his dresser, visited him in hospital, he was shocked to see a once powerful man mortally stricken, thin and drawn, with a stubbly white beard. As he came out of the sick room Walter was in tears, and said to Stoker: 'He is like Corporal Brewster.' Stoker stole quietly into the room. He remembered the moment vividly: 'He looked like a picture of the dying Falstaff drawn by Mistress Quickly, "His nose was as sharp as a pen".' Long years spent listening to simulated emotions could give Irving's two faithful friends only theatrical similes when their deepest emotions were aroused. They had no words of their own.

The crisis passed, and by 7 December Irving was well enough to go back to Grafton Street, but for the rest of his life he found it difficult to walk upstairs without an enormous and painful effort.

Ellen's comment on Henry's illness was written to G.B.S.: 'Henry slowly, surely, makes progress towards normal naughtiness.' It was hard for her to believe that the man who had dominated and ruled her life for so long could succumb to a simple illness. Next week, surely, he would be as tiresome as ever.

She was on tour and thinking of going to see him, but was too ill to travel to Glasgow as she had intended: 'You see I must keep on! We had very good houses at Manchester.' She added that Bradford had been disappointing.

Irving went down to Bournemouth to recuperate. Friends rallied round. Pinero wrote to ask if he could help with rehearsals of any new production: 'It would be a pure labour of love for me to fag for you.' Irving wrote back a letter full of gratitude, saying that he had decided not to produce anything new; he was going to travel, to realise, and not to speculate.

But he was turned aside from these sensible ideas. The astute Comyns Carr and his two brothers, one of whom just happened to be a solicitor, and the other a financier, approached Irving. What a good idea it would be if Irving transferred his lease, his furniture and fittings, to a company. Irving need only act on one hundred nights in the year at the Lyceum.

There were strings. Irving had to shoulder most of expenses as well as giving the company a quarter of his profits, even when he was on lucrative American tours. The dice were loaded against him: he was to give himself, his theatre, and his life's work for an immediate £26,000.

Stoker tried to persuade Irving not to sign, but by the time Stoker came back from arranging an American tour Irving had been totally 'sold to the company store', and the terms were even more unfavourable than they had seemed at first sight.

When Comyns Carr wrote his inevitable book of reminiscences, *Some Eminent Victorians*, Irving appeared in it and not always in a favourable light. But Comyns Carr's financial dealings, and the taking over of Irving at a knock-down price, are played down. Reading between the lines it seems certain that Irving made a bad bargain, and Carr's reticence on the subject would seem to prove it. Buying up the life's work of a sick man at a bargain price does not look very attractive in print. To counterbalance this, Carr slipped in stories of Irving's conceit and rancour against supposed enemies, and mentioned 'his trick of waiting for his foe'.

Once Irving had made up his mind he was immovable. For more than twenty years he had been his own master, and in his weakened state he felt he had no alternative but to sign. Possibly his state was worse than he had admitted to Stoker. He had borrowed money from friends, and in addition doctors were advising him to move house. The darkness, the lack of sunlight, and the strain of climbing the stairs in Grafton Street were not good for him.

Mrs Aria helped him to move into a flat in Stratton Street, Piccadilly. She seems to have had a free hand with the decorations. He made no stipulations, except that there should be plenty of crimson, a good theatre colour, in the rooms. Some of his books and bric-à-brac were sold to meet immediate expenses.

Mrs Aria was pleased with her work:

'When completed the flat had a lordly air, the crimson walls interrupted by a stained-glass window with a sill bearing fine bronzes amid vases of majolica, while the soft pink drawing-room was definitely French, in the pattern of its brocade, and its carved gilt frames, and the large dining-room endowed with magnificent specimens of blue and gold Chinese embroideries amongst its straight close rows of pictures – amongst them a fine study by Clint of the weird, wild face of Edmund Kean.'

Looking at Kean's face, Irving said that it is an actor's fate to be judged by delusive echoes. 'Some fifty years hence some old fool will be saying, there never was an actor like Henry Irving.'

Neither Ellen nor Mrs Aria seems to have realised how ill the man was. He kept up his indomitable front and spoke with the defiance of the undefeated. In private he used five hundred handkerchiefs a week for his lung had remained infected. But Stoker noticed a certain shrinkage within himself. The whole landscape had diminished – and the horizon had become limited. He loved to talk shop, but there was no longer so much to discuss; the decisions had gone to others. The illumination had gone, the brilliant gaslight burned with a lower flame, and the man had grown smaller with his horizons.

Stoker said of him: 'He was a man with all a man's weaknesses and mutabilities as well as a man's strong qualities. Had he not had in his own nature all the qualities of natural man how could he have portrayed such forces whose fidelity to natural type became famous?'

He had played frail old men on the stage. In real life the part did not suit him. And he refused to play it.

Chapter 20

Envoi

'I've grown old while I dreamed'
Les Vrilles de la Vigne – Colette

He had lost his theatre to what Ellen called a 'cheap and nasty Company'. It was no longer Henry Irving at the Lyceum, but he had to go on. He had no resources except his will, and the talent he had started with so many years before. In front of him still were years of acting and touring in special trains at strange hours.

After his illness he made two six-month tours of America, in hard winters, through snows ten feet deep, with railway engines blowing up, shattered into scrap iron, and all the hardships which he had endured when he was younger and well. On his crossing to the United States in the autumn of 1899, still frail in health, the ship was struck by a hurricane and the seas rose higher than the mast, the wind reaching a force of a hundred miles an hour. Irving, attracted by the drama of the storm, went out and stood on the bridge.

At sixty-one he had travelled over 50,000 miles and had crossed the Atlantic eighteen times. His had been a long and arduous life of work, and it still stretched in front of him.

He produced *Robespierre*, another piece of what Shaw called Sardoodledum, with vast crowd scenes on the old lavish scale. The critics, conscious of Sir Henry's return to health, were as kind as they could be but the piece suffered from a 'Tale of Two Cities' sameness, and although Irving acted with artistic skill he failed to move, and Miss Terry was seen in yet another part not worthy of her. Miss Terry had in fact been complaining to Mr Shaw about her small parts for some time. She had had enough of trusting to Henry's good faith.

Robespierre failed to please London. Miss Terry and Mr Irving were less of a team than they had been when they set out for that arduous tour of the United States in October, 1899. She had spent a good deal of time writing to G.B.S. about *Captain Brassbound's Conversion,* and before sailing from England had given what was called a 'copyright' performance of the play.

Henry had retreated more into himself than usual and she was uncertain of any future plans. Perhaps on the boat he would tell her. 'He is worried now and I can't bear to push him,' she wrote. She turned to more cheerful things. 'We all enjoyed doing your play immensely. H.I. never came near the place! Horrid of him.' Shaw was still taking what he called a grim delight in attacking Irving.

But neither Shaw nor Ellen seems to have realised that they were no longer dealing with the old Irving. The face, the bearing were the same, but he had begun to feel the loss cf control over his theatre. His failing health was something in which he could not believe, and for a while his will still triumphed.

Ellen wanted to leave the company, but Irving was already proposing yet another tour in America. Unfortunately 'this beastly *Robespierre* is what they call a boom over here, and we can carry it on for a long time,' she wrote. She longed to retire to her little farm, at Smallhythe in Kent, but the security was a lure to her, and Henry was set on another tour of America.

They arrived back in England in May 1900 and in the autumn were touring the provinces. Ellen wrote to Shaw: 'I feel so certain that Henry just hates me!' She could only guess this for he was exactly the same as he was when she was so certain that he loved her. But they had not really met for years except in front of other people. It was all her own fault: 'It is *I* am changed – not he.'

They were both acting their parts on and off the stage. Henry the indomitable, and Ellen the charming. The masks were the same but the faces behind them were older, though perhaps not any wiser.

He spent his holidays with Mrs Aria who paints a different picture of him. He was always the courageous philosopher, a careless trusting Bohemian, but never a fool or a weakling. All the stories of his extreme melancholy caused by the death of his dog, the loss of his scenery and his illness were rubbish. When travelling with Eliza he wore his soft drab holiday hat, 'a rascal with a half inch square deliberately jagged away for ventilation'.

They holidayed in Norfolk, in Derbyshire and in Cornwall. They made shorter expeditions and they went to Stratford, where crowds of Americans ran after him constantly stopping him and asking for autographs. He never minded giving them, for he loved America and the Americans, always acknowledging their affection for him and feeling gratitude for the success they gave him.

When he travelled he still travelled like royalty. Eliza said their departure from a station in London was always impressive. Irving was preceded up the platform by the station-master, carrying his top hat; two porters led the convoy. Mrs Aria followed with her daughter, her companion, her maid, and Walter, Irving's dresser. Irving looked sardonically at the numerous trunks and packages which were being escorted by his secretary and a baggage man from the Lyceum. 'Might be a touring company,' he said.

In Cornwall, where he passed his childhood, he found his perfect holiday spot: King Arthur's Castle Hotel, a Victorian Gothic building standing incongruously perched on a cliff spoiling the rocky coastline near Tintagel. But here the air was strong and cold, air in which it was easier to breathe – air which blew straight across the Atlantic.

The hotel itself had that grandiose appearance, outside and in, which Irving preferred. The lofty rooms were richly furnished like his stage sets, and outside the sea stretched away to the horizon. It was here he had decided to retire in a few years' time to write his memoirs. But money had to be made and saved before he could achieve that desirable end. There was more work to be done, more touring to make up the losses to the company which now owned him.

By December 1900 even Ellen had begun to realise that Henry's indomitable façade was deceptive: 'Henry is very ill. He is splendid but he must give in, and he knows it.' She had decided to carry on the tour. 'He is very good now and lets me do everything for him.' She was happy when he had a cross, irritable day, for then she knew he was feeling better. She was clearly still very fond of him.

Even so, he could not let go. In the spring of 1901 he produced *Coriolanus*. Once he had decided on a course of conduct he would take no advice, and would never change his plans. When he said 'Let there be *Coriolanus*', then there was *Coriolanus*. It was produced in the spring of 1901 from designs made by Alma Tadema twenty years before. The notices were polite, but the play was not liked, and in the autumn Irving set out to tour America yet again with Ellen. Only the most tenuous links still held them together.

It was to be their last tour of America as a partnership, and it lasted twenty-nine weeks, until the spring of 1902.

Ellen's belief in the healing qualities of touring America was well justified, for she was being paid £300 a week. They played in over twenty American cities and were as lavishly entertained as ever. Two days before he sailed for England Irving travelled to Princeton to give a lecture on 'Shakespeare and Bacon'. He wore his scarlet robes as an honorary academic and was received with a storm of applause. The old drawing power still held.

Ellen and Irving sailed from New York on 21 March 1902. When she reached England, Ellen left the cast and the 'cheap and nasty' Lyceum Theatre Company, as she had called it. Irving was putting on *Faust*. Ellen at 55 felt herself too old to play the virginal Margaret, and Shaw wrote sarcastically asking whether she was to play the part of the old servant.

The last of Irving's receptions at the Lyceum was in 1902. It was to have been given for the coronation of King Edward VII. But, although the King was ill and the coronation postponed, the curtain went up on Irving's reception just the same. It was said to have been much finer and grander than that given at the India Office.

There were endless rows of tubs of flowers and palms, a Union Jack forming a centrepiece made from thousands of coloured lights, a great crown flaming over a sea of guests, Premiers from all the great colonies, peers and their bejewelled peeresses, statesmen, ecclesiastics, soldiers, artists, men of science, and, most spectacular of all the Indian princes wearing over half a million pounds' worth of jewels – followed closely by men from Scotland Yard.

Everyone was moving and smiling against a backcloth of crimson velvet, and on the crimson-covered stage, in the centre of the crowd, stood Irving. It was his last appearance as host at the Lyceum. Two weeks later the Lyceum closed its doors.

On 19 July 1902 Irving played Shylock to Ellen's Portia for the last time and the curtain fell on their long partnership. The London

County Council had driven the last nail into the coffin of the Lyceum Theatre Company; they had demanded structural alterations against fire risks. Funds were exhausted.

The fine dreams of the Company ended in angry scenes with heckling from shareholders who had lost money. The pocket is ever the most sensitive part of man's anatomy. The directors tried to put the blame on Irving. But Stoker sprang to his defence.

Irving had, it was true, been paid £26,500 in cash, he said, and he had repaid the company £29,000 by his work. He had given up not only his lease of the theatre, but two years of heavy work, and had personally lost nearly £3,000. Shareholders who had come to execrate Irving remained to cheer.

Irving threw his share certificates into the fire.

It was not the Company alone which had ruined Irving. The New Theatre had advanced. With the coming of the Edwardian theatre came a new spirit. The noble, suffering, and pure heroines so long portrayed by Ellen were *démodées*. Shaw was beginning to see his plays staged. The feeling of the age was becoming more light-hearted. It was now the day of the urbane man of the world, the errant husband, or the peccant diplomat with scarlet ribbons across his impeccable evening dress. New hands were seizing the reins of management and the public wanted wit not spectacle. The old romantic theatre was dying.

As Sir George Alexander said, 'I invented the man of forty', and Eliza Aria echoed his sentiment. So long as any comedy showed her Alexander with a broad red ribbon across his evening waistcoat, 'I shall go and hear him once a week.'

The Lyceum lights were put out. And Ellen had finally parted from Irving. He wrote to her: 'The place is now given up to the rats – all light cut off, and only Barry (the stage-door keeper) and a foreman left. Everything of mine I've moved away, including the cat!'

The rumour was that Ellen had left the sinking ship, but she felt that she had done Henry a real service by refusing to play in his last production, *Dante*. 'It cost me £12,000, the sum I was offered to accompany him to America after its production at Drury Lane,' she said. Henry had not treated her badly. Nor had she treated him badly. 'Our separation could not be avoided.' They had played in twenty-seven pieces, and in most of them she had portrayed the young and beautiful heroine. *Macbeth* and *Henry VIII*, in which she could still have played, had disappeared in the fire. There was only *The Merchant of Venice* left for her.

Dante, which was produced in 1903, was translated from the French of MM. Sardou and Moreau by Irving's son Laurence. Irving had to shoulder all the expenses because the Company had cheerfully bowed out. *The Times* remarked that a special circle of Hell ought to be reserved for the authors. There was much scenery and many mechanical effects, and brilliant triumphs of stage management, and Sir Henry, of course, born to look like Dante. 'But he wanders through the play as a perambulating commentator.'

The play was Irving's last new production. His old hold on the public managed to make a moderate success of it; but he insisted that it was 'triumphant', a word which was now constantly on his lips, as if it were a charm to beckon back success.

In the autumn of 1903 he was in America yet again, without Ellen now, and appeared for the last time at the Harlem Opera House, New York on 25 March 1904 as *Louis XI*. He was being urged on all sides to try new playwrights and to produce new plays. But when he could take £4,000 in a week's touring with the old repertoire why take risks? He had now decided to retire after fifty years of acting, and two years of touring would give him a modest competence. He had been offered several thousand pounds for his memoirs. He would write them in his sitting-room in King Arthur's Castle Hotel, with the windows open to the Atlantic, in the country where his life had begun.

But during the first of these tours in the spring of 1905, at Wolverhampton, he collapsed. Ellen went to see him. She got up early and scoured the streets to find a good florist; there were going to be no white flowers for Henry. She must have daffodils. She remembered the day in 1892 when she had come back to the Lyceum after the death of her mother, and found her dressing-room filled with daffodils, as Henry said, 'to make it look like sunshine'.

The careful Ellen first went to see Henry's doctor. The heart was dangerously weak, and he must not work so hard. Ellen said: 'He will though, and he's stronger than anyone.' She remembered their last tour together, when his cough was rending him and he could hardly stand from weakness, but acted so brilliantly and strongly that it would have been easy to believe in 'the triumph of mind over matter, in Christian Science in fact'.

Henry was sitting up in bed, looking like some beautiful grey tree Ellen remembered having seen in Savannah, and his old dressing-gown hung on his frail body like grey draperies. The two old actors looked at each other, much moved, and unable to speak at first.

'What a wonderful life you've had, haven't you?' asked Ellen.

'Oh, yes – a wonderful life – of work,' he replied.

'What have you got out of it all? You and I are getting on, as they say. Do you ever think, as I do sometimes, what you have got out of life?'

Their eyes met. Like Tchekov's actor in *Swan Song*, they looked into the pit of innumerable theatres – the black hole which had swallowed up forty years of their lives. They looked into the darkness and saw it all, down to the smallest detail. Yet 'Where there's art, where there is genius, there is neither old age, nor loneliness, nor sickness, and death itself is robbed of half its terror.' They both knew it, in different ways.

Ellen spoke again, asking him what he had got out of life. He stroked his chin and smiled: 'Let me see, a good cigar, a good glass of wine, and good friends.' He kissed Ellen's hand.

'And the end – how would you like that to come?'

He repeated her question, and then snapped his fingers and said, with perfect timing: 'Like that!' Ellen stayed with him for three hours, and then she left.

The doctor had told him that he must never play *The Bells* again, for his death as Mathias was real to him, so real that his eyes would disappear, his face grow grey and his limbs cold.

He recovered and acted for another season in London, playing *Becket* at Drury Lane on 10 June 1905. He made his usual polite speech and went back to his dressing-room, but the audience would not leave the theatre and went on shouting and applauding. The safety curtain was raised, the audience sang 'Auld Lang Syne', and he appeared and said a final goodbye.

It was his farewell to London. He went off on holiday with Mrs Aria to Yorkshire.

It was very cold that summer and the winds sweeping across the heather made Eliza shiver. She made a joke of it: 'You like your country *frappé*.' Irving said the cold was good for him, but a young doctor in their hotel remarked that Sir Henry looked ill. He should go to Egypt and take some rest in the sun.

It was not to be considered, the work had to go on.

Just before his tour began at Sheffield, Eliza and Irving, with his son Harry, went to see George Alexander in *The Prodigal Son* at Drury Lane. Eliza remembered sitting in the carriage, watching the two men under the pale light of the theatre entrance, two tall spare men wearing their correct tall silk hats at the same elegant angle and smoking their cigars. It was to be her last picture of them together.

On 12 October he played *The Bells*, which Stoker dreaded. He sat down in a listless way and had not begun to dress for his part when Stoker went in to him. His fatigue was not for one part, but for hundreds of parts, and for a lifetime. But he was determined to play Mathias to prove himself. His will had been the controlling power from the beginning of his career. He was real only when he was unreal, and in pretence was his life and truth. His farewell tour meant his fortune, his escape from poverty. He would carry it through. The following night he played *Becket* and seemed better and stronger.

His first words on the stage had been: 'Here's to our enterprise.' The enterprise had been long. And now, as Becket, his last words rounded it off: 'Into Thy hands, oh Lord, into Thy Hands.'

He chatted to Stoker and then suddenly shook him unexpectedly by the hand saying, 'Muffle up your throat, old chap, it is bitterly cold. Good night and God Bless you!' He went out into the street, a touring actor walking towards his hotel after a lifetime of performances.

Stoker was having supper when he was sent for. Sir Henry was ill, he had fainted in the hall of the Midland Hotel. There were twenty men grouped round him. He lay full length on the floor, dead. He showed none of the usual ungracefulness of death. He had died dramatically and gracefully, as an actor should.

The following day the streets were thronged with waiting crowds as the coffin was driven to the railway station. All heads were uncovered, and only an occasional sob broke the silence. The actor who had so often been cheered on his way now left in silence.

The body lay in state in the house of Baroness Burdett-Coutts. She had made her dining-room into a *chapelle ardente,* full of flowers.

Now began the negotiations about the funeral. Surely Westminster Abbey was the correct place for so great a man. But here Lady

Irving, the long neglected Florence, stepped in. She had been totally ignored in the actor's will. He had left his remaining property to his two sons, and to Mrs Aria.

Florence approached Shaw; he could surely prevent the insult to her of an Abbey funeral. Shaw intimated that the widow of a famous actor might expect to receive a state pension. What would it profit her to expose Mrs Aria and lose her pension? Lady Irving settled for the Abbey funeral, and the pension.

Mrs Aria did not send a wreath. But she had an enormous pall made of thousands of laurel leaves. It was so large that it covered the coffin and draped to the ground on either side. She was very proud of that pall, specially designed, which had taken a dozen florists some two days to make.

The sun burst through the Abbey windows and turned the laurel pall to gold as the coffin was carried in and as the fourteen pall-bearers walked up the aisle to the sound of the Dead March in Saul. It was just the effect that Irving would have planned for himself.

Ellen said that she missed Henry's face at his own funeral. It seemed to her as if he were directing the whole ceremony, and she could hear him saying, 'Get on, get on!' in the parts of the service that dragged.

His effects were sold at Christie, Manson and Woods including the green purse with the metal rings which had been found empty on the body of Edmund Kean. Irving's purse at the end was as empty as Kean's – a *peau de chagrin* through which had disappeared over two million pounds. Even his death was exploited by the sheet music publishers by a hymn on the cover of which appeared his photograph, flanked by lilies crowned with the words 'Into Thy Hands!'

Acres of print commemorated his death, not to the pleasure of Lady Irving, who made her solicitor write a sharp little letter to the press. Headed 'The Late Sir Henry Irving', it ran: 'Now that the excitement of Sir Henry Irving's funeral is over, it may not be amiss to inquire how it is that in the midst of all this enthusiastic display no mention that I have seen has been made of his wife.' After a brief résumé of her marriage and separation, the letter concluded: 'It may interest many of your readers to know that Lady Irving is in excellent health, notwithstanding the shock and excitement of the last few days.'

Shaw had a few last words. He sent back his ticket for the funeral with a note: 'Literature, alas, has no place at his death as it had no place in his life.' G.B.S. also wrote to a Viennese paper saying that Irving was only interested in himself as an imaginary figure in an imaginary setting and lived as in a dream. This was translated as: 'He was a narrow-minded egotist, devoid of culture, and living on the dream of his own greatness.'

Ellen wrote to reprove Shaw. He had never written the words when Henry was well, at work, and fighting. 'Did he have faults? Yes! But of course *we* have none. I feel badly. I'm sorry because I didn't do enough whilst I could – just a little longer.'

Everyone had behaved as usual. Lady Irving had been self-important. Shaw had stung to the last. Ellen had dropped a tear of regret for the days that had been so lovely and full of promise. Mrs Aria had made a splendid pall, and then she constructed what she called her 'Treasure Corner', consisting of Henry's Chinese curtain, a model of his hand, the lace collar worn by Edmund Kean, a bust of Irving, several portraits of him, and on an easel Henry's holiday hat and the handkerchief he used the last time he played *The Bells*.

Eliza had bought up a few souvenirs at the Christie sale, and when she looked at herself in his great carved mirror she liked to remember him as he was – tall, elegant, and quizzical. 'I would not have my eagle bereft of a single feather,' she said.

Ellen's pretty cottage still stands in the countryside of Kent. In summer the windows open on to a landscape blowing with wild-flowers. Her upstairs sitting-room is gay with blue and white china, and her books and pictures are all lovingly arrayed.

But Henry Irving, the travelling actor, had travelled on, leaving no home behind him.

Bibliography

ARCHER, WILLIAM

About the Theatre, London, 1885.

English Dramatists.

Henry Irving, Actor and Manager.

Masks and Faces.

Old Drama and New, London, 1923.

Study and Stage, London, 1899.

Theatrical World of 1893–97, London, 1898.

ARCHER, WILLIAM, and LOW, ROBERT M., Pamphlet, London, 1877.

ARIA, ELIZA

My Sentimental Self, London, 1922.

Clothes, London, 1906.

ASKEW, ALICE AND CLAUDE, The Actor Manager (a novel), London, n.d.

BEERBOHM, MAX, *Around Theatres*, London, 1953.

BENSON, FRANK, *My Memories*, London.

BERRY, CLAUDE, *Portrait of Cornwall.*

BOHEMIAN CLUB, SAN FRANCISCO. *History of the Bohemian Club*, San Francisco, 1973.

BOOTH, J. B., *The Days We Knew*, London, 1943.

BRERETON, AUSTIN, *Life of Henry Irving* (2 vols), London, 1908.

COLEMAN, JOHN

Fifty Years of an Actor's Life.

Players and Playwrights I have Known.

COMYNS CARR, J., *Some Eminent Victorians*, London, 1908.

COMYNS CARR, MRS J., Reminiscences, London.

COOK, DUTTON

A Book of the Play, London, 1876.

Hours With the Players (2 vols), London, 1881.

Nights at the Play, London, 1883.

On the Stage (2 vols), London, 1883.

CRAIG, EDWARD GORDON

Ellen Terry and her Secret Self, London, 1932.

Henry Irving, London, 1930.

On the Art of the Theatre, London, 1957.

The Theatre Advancing, London, 1921.

DALY, FREDERIC (L. F. AUSTIN), *Henry Irving in England and America*, London, 1884.

DARTON, HARVEY, *Vincent Crummles, his Theatre and his Times*, London, 1926.

DOBBS, BRIAN, *Drury Lane*, London, 1972.

DORAN, DR, *Their Majesties' Servants*, London, 1868.

FARSON, DANIEL, *The Man Who Wrote Dracula*, London, 1975.

FINDLATER, RICHARD, *The Player Kings*, London, 1971.

FITZGERALD, PERCY, *Henry Irving, a Record of Twenty Years at the Lyceum*, London, 1893.

FRISWELL, LAURA HAIN, *A Memoir of J. H. Friswell.*

GIELGUD, JOHN, *Early Stages*, London, 1939.

GIELGUD, KATE TERRY, *Autobiography.*

GLASSTONE, VICTOR, *Victorian and Edwardian Theatres, an Architectural Survey.*

HATTON, JOSEPH, *Henry Irving's Impressions of America*, London, 1884.

HIATT, CHARLES, *Henry Irving, a Record and a Review*, London, 1899.

IRVING, HENRY

English Actors, a Discourse, Oxford, 1886.

Essay on Shakespeare and Bacon in the Preface to *Hamlet* in the Stage Shakespeare Series, London, n.d.

Four Addresses on the Drama, London, 1893.

IRVING, LAURENCE, *Henry Irving, the Actor and his World*, London, 1951.

KELLY, MICHAEL, *Solo recital* (ed. Trewin and Van Thal), 1972.

KNIGHT, JOSEPH, *Theatrical Notes, 1874–1879.*

LAYARD, GEORGE, *Life, Letters and Diaries of Shirley Brooks.*

LEWES, G. H., *On Actors and the Art of Acting*, London, 1875.

MACFALL, HALDANE, *Sir Henry Irving*, London, 1906.

MACKENZIE, COMPTON, *Echoes*, London, n.d.

MAKER, LAWRENCE, *Cob and Moorstone.*

MANVELL, ROGER, *Ellen Terry*, London, 1968.

MAUDE, PAMELA, *Worlds Away*, London, 1964.

MENPES, MORTIMER, *Henry Irving.*

NASH, GEORGE, *Edward Gordon Craig*, HMSO, London, 1967.

NEWTON, CHANCE, *Cues and Curtain Calls.*

NICOLL, ALLARDYCE, *History of English Drama*, Vols III and IV, Cambridge, 1955; Vol. V, Cambridge, 1957.

PASCOE, CHARLES E., *The Dramatic List* (originally printed 1880), a Record of the Performances of Living Actors and Actresses of the British Stage. Reprinted New York, 1926.

PEARCE, CHARLES, E., *Mme Vestris and her Times*, London, 1930.

PEARSON, HESKETH
Bernard Shaw, his Life and Personality, London, 1942.
Life of Oscar Wilde.
POLLOCK, SIR FREDERICK, Ed., McReady's *Reminiscences* (2 vols), London.
POLLOCK, WALTER HERRIES, *Impressions of Henry Irving*, London.
POPE, W. MCQUEEN
Drury Lane, London, n.d.
Ladies First, London, 1952.
ROBINS, ELIZABETH, *Both Sides of the Curtain*, London, 1940.
ROWE, JOHN, *Cornwall in the Age of the Industrial Revolution.*
ROWELL, GEORGE, *The Victorian Theatre.*
ROWSE, A. L.
Cornish Anthology.
A Cornish Childhood.
West Country Stories.
RUSSELL, W. CLARK, *Representative Actors*, London, n.d.
SCOTT, CLEMENT, *From The Bells to King Arthur*, London, 1897.
SHAW, G. BERNARD
Complete Plays, London, 1931.
Our Theatres in the Nineties, London, 1932.
Prefaces to the Plays, London, 1938.
SMILES, SAMUEL, *Self Help*, London, 1859.
STEEN, MARGUERITE, *A Pride of Terries*, London, 1962.
STIRLING, EDWARD, *Old Drury Lane* (2 vols), London, 1881.
SUTTON, GRAHAM, *Fish and Actors*, London, 1924.
TERRY, ELLEN
Four Lectures on Shakespeare (Ed. Christopher St John), memoirs with biographical notes and additional biographical chapters, Eds Edith Craig and C. St John, London, 1933.
The Story of My Life, London, n.d.
Ellen Terry and Bernard Shaw, a correspondence edited by C. St John, London, 1932.
THOMPSON, W. HARDING, *Cornwall*, a Survey of Its Coasts, Moors and Valleys with suggestions for its preservation, London, 1930.
TURNER MICHAEL, *Parlour Poetry*, London, 1967.
VANBRUGH, IRENE, *To Tell My Story*, London.
VANDENHOFF, GEORGE, *Dramatic Reminiscences.*
WARD, GENEVIEVE, *Both Sides of the Curtain*, London, 1918.
WARDEN, GERTRUDE, *Stage Love and Real Love*, n.d.

WATSON, ERNEST BRADLEE, *Sheridan to Robertson.*

WILLIAMS, CLIFFORD JOHN, *Madame Vestris*, a Theatrical Biography.

WILLIAMS, HARCOURT, *Irving as Romeo*, 1946.

WILLS, F., *W. G. Wills, Dramatist and Painter.*

WILSON, A. E.

Edwardian Theatre.

The Lyceum, London, 1952.

Penny Plain and Twopence Coloured, London, 1932.

WINSTEN, S., *Days with Bernard Shaw*, London, n.d.

WINTER, WILLIAM

Other Days.

Henry Irving.

PLAYS

ALBERY, JAMES, Dramatic Works of (2 vols), London, 1939.

COLEMAN, GEORGE (the Younger), *The Iron Chest*, 1821.

COWLEY, MRS, Works of (2 vols), London, 1813.

English Nineteenth Century Plays, Ed. George Rowell, Oxford, 1972.

English Plays of the Nineteenth Century (4 vols), Ed. M. R. Booth, Oxford, 1969–73.

Golden Age of Melodrama, Ed. M. Kilgarriff, London, 1974.

KNOWLES, SHERIDAN, Dramatic Works of, London, 1873.

LYTTON, THE RT HON. LORD, Dramatic Works of (2 vols), London, 1883.

Nineteenth Century Drama, Ed. R. W. Corrigan, New York, 1967.

SHAKESPEARE: 8 volumes of the Complete Works, edited by Henry Irving and Frank Marshall, London, n.d.

STEVENSON, R. L., and HENLEY, W. E., Plays.

TAYLOR, TOM

Plot and Passion, London, n.d.

New Men and Old Acres, London, n.d.

Our American Cousin, printed in the USA, 1869.

TCHEKOV, ANTON, Plays of, Trans. C. Garnett, London, 1935.

TENNYSON, ALFRED LORD

Becket.

The Cup.

Harold.

Queen Mary.

WILLS, W. G., *Charles I.*

Index